I Hate You—
Don't Leave Me

I Hate You— Don't Leave Me

UNDERSTANDING THE BORDERLINE PERSONALITY

THIRD EDITION

Jerold J. Kreisman, MD, and Hal Straus

A TarcherPerigee Book

tarcherperigee

TarcherPerigee
an imprint of Penguin Random House LLC
penguinrandomhouse.com

Originally published by HPBooks in 1989
Copyright © 2021 Jerold J. Kreisman, MD, and Hal Straus
Penguin supports copyright. Copyright fuels creativity, encourages diverse voices, promotes free speech, and creates a vibrant culture. Thank you for buying an authorized edition of this book and for complying with copyright laws by not reproducing, scanning, or distributing any part of it in any form without permission. You are supporting writers and allowing Penguin to continue to publish books for every reader.

TarcherPerigee with tp colophon is a registered trademark of Penguin Random House LLC.

Most TarcherPerigee books are available at special quantity discounts for bulk purchase for sales promotions, premiums, fund-raising, and educational needs. Special books or book excerpts also can be created to fit specific needs. For details, write: SpecialMarkets@penguinrandomhouse.com.

Library of Congress Cataloging-in-Publication Data

Names: Kreisman, Jerold J. (Jerold Jay), author. | Straus, Hal, author.
Title: I hate you—don't leave me: understanding the borderline personality /
Jerold J. Kreisman, MD, and Hal Straus.
Description: Third edition. | New York: TarcherPerigee, Penguin Random House LLC, 2021.
Identifiers: LCCN 2020055883 | ISBN 9780593418499 (trade paperback)
Subjects: LCSH: Borderline personality disorder.
Classification: LCC RC569.5.B67 K74 2021 | DDC 616.85/852—dc23
LC record available at https://lccn.loc.gov/2020055883

Printed in the United States of America
13th Printing

As all things,
even still,
for Doody

CONTENTS

Acknowledgments   ix

Preface   xi

A Note to the Reader   xiii

1. The World of Borderline Personality Disorder   1

2. Chaos and Emptiness   23

3. Roots of the Borderline Syndrome   57

4. The Borderline Society   77

5. The SET-UP System of Communication   112

6. Family and Friends: How to Cope   145

7. Seeking, Finding, and Engaging in Therapy   176

8. Specific Psychotherapeutic Approaches   210

9. Medications: The Science and the Promise   227

10. Understanding and Healing   240

Appendix A. Alternative Models for Diagnosing BPD   259

Appendix B. Evolution of the Borderline Syndrome   267

Resources   279

Notes   283

Index   307

ACKNOWLEDGMENTS

Dr. Kreisman is eternally grateful to his wife, Judy, whose support and forbearance have made all he does possible. We wish to thank our agent, Danielle Egan-Miller, at Browne & Miller Literary Associates, and Lauren Appleton at Penguin Random House for their encouragement and support for this project.

PREFACE

It is a most gratifying task to develop this third edition of *I Hate You—Don't Leave Me: Understanding the Borderline Personality*. We are humbled that our book, after more than thirty years and translation into ten languages, remains an important resource across the globe for both general and professional audiences and solicits this major revision.

In the ten years since our last revision, there have been significant advances in the neurobiological, physiological, and genetic fields. Refinements in developmental theories and treatment approaches have emerged. For the professional audience, we have preserved the classical reference materials, supplementing them with the most up-to-date references and resources, right up to the point of our writing deadline. For the general audience, we have again attempted to describe complex scientific and theoretical constructs in reader-friendly terms; toward that end, we have inserted many more case studies and patient examples to better illustrate concepts.

I Hate You—Don't Leave Me first emerged out of the primary author's frustration, as a clinician, over the lack of organized information for the general public and for many professionals about a disorder that was either mostly unknown or terribly misunderstood. We would like to think that, as the first popular book on the subject of BPD, it helped bring the disorder out of the shadows. Our second edition twenty years later emphasized the increasing research and treatment approaches and the recognition that borderline personality disorder was not a hopeless disease, but one with a favorable prognosis. Since then, the professional literature on BPD has burgeoned. Awareness in the general public has also greatly increased. Those experiencing the disorder have been more forthcoming about their experiences, including several in the public spotlight. Even the title of this book was used as the title of a Demi Lovato song that many of her fans interpreted as a song about a person struggling with BPD.

Unfortunately, the stigma associated with mental illness in general and with borderline personality disorder in particular remains strong. Media portrayals of BPD are mostly of disturbed, reckless people, usually women. The optimistic prognosis of the disorder is largely unrecognized. And research in this area remains inadequate compared to that dedicated to other less common illnesses. It is our hope that this iteration of our book will contribute to less aversion to and a greater understanding of all mental illness.

Jerold J. Kreisman, MD

Hal Straus

A NOTE TO THE READER

In previous editions of this book we have begged readers' indulgence in referring to individuals with BPD using the term "the borderline," as a less burdensome, reader-friendly reference than the more accurate designation of "an individual who exhibits signs and symptoms consistent with the formal diagnosis of Borderline Personality Disorder."

We have been concerned that this shorthand reference reduces a person to a stigmatizing label. In this revision, we have attempted to avoid this unsatisfying term by converting the noun to an adjective, by using less agile designations, such as "borderline individual" or "person with BPD," though the latter phrase implies company with an uninvited guest. We considered using "an individual who *has* borderline personality," but even this term implies the gripping custody of an unwelcome possession. We are content with none of these designations, but have been unable to conjure suitable replacements. Despite our failure to develop more satisfying nomenclature, we wish to emphasize our respect for those suffering with BPD, our sensitivity for those who care about them, and the need for greater understanding of all who struggle for mental wellness.

I Hate You—
Don't Leave Me

Chapter One

The World of Borderline Personality Disorder

Everything looked and sounded unreal. Nothing was what it is.
That's what I wanted—to be alone with myself in another world
where truth is untrue and life can hide from itself.

—From *Long Day's Journey into Night*, by Eugene O'Neill

Dr. White thought it would all be relatively straightforward. Over the five years he had been treating Jennifer, she'd had few medical problems. Her stomach complaints were probably due to gastritis, he thought, so he treated her with antacids. But when her stomach pains became more intense despite treatment and routine testing proved normal, Dr. White admitted Jennifer to the hospital.

After a thorough medical workup, Dr. White inquired about stresses Jennifer might be experiencing at work and home. She readily acknowledged that her job as a personnel manager for a major corporation was very pressured, but as she put it, "Many people have pressure jobs." She also revealed that her home life was more hectic recently. She was trying to cope with her husband's busy legal practice while tending to the responsibilities of being a mother. But she doubted the connection of these factors to her stomach pains.

When Dr. White recommended that Jennifer seek psychiatric consultation, she initially resisted. It was only after her discomfort turned into stabs of pain that she reluctantly agreed to see the psychiatrist Dr. Gray.

They met a few days later. Appearing childlike and younger than her twenty-eight years, Jennifer lay in bed in a hospital room that had been transformed from an anonymous cubicle into a personalized lair. A stuffed animal sat next to her in bed, and another lay on the nightstand beside several pictures of her husband and son. Get-well cards were meticulously displayed in a line along the windowsill, flanked by flower arrangements.

At first Jennifer was very formal, answering all of Dr. Gray's questions with great seriousness. Then she joked about how her job was "driving me to see a shrink." The longer she talked, the sadder she looked. Her voice became less domineering and more childlike.

She told him how a job promotion was exacting more demands— new responsibilities that were making her feel insecure. Her five-year-old son was starting school, which was proving to be a difficult separation for both of them. Conflicts with Allan, her husband, were increasing. She described rapid mood swings and trouble sleeping. Her appetite had steadily decreased and she was losing weight. Her concentration, energy, and sex drive had all diminished.

Dr. Gray recommended a trial of antidepressant medications, which improved her gastric symptoms and seemed to normalize her sleeping patterns. In a few days she was ready for discharge and agreed to continue outpatient therapy.

Over the following weeks, Jennifer talked more about her upbringing. Reared in a small town, she was the daughter of a prominent businessman and his socialite wife. Her father, an elder in the local church, demanded perfection from his daughter and her two older brothers, constantly reminding the children that the community was scrutinizing their behavior. Jennifer's grades, her behavior, even her thoughts were never quite good enough. She feared her father, yet constantly—and unsuccessfully—sought his approval. Her mother remained passive and detached. Her parents evaluated her friends, often deeming them unacceptable. As a result, she had few friends and even fewer dates.

Jennifer described her roller-coaster emotions, which seemed to have worsened when she started college. She began drinking for the first time, sometimes to excess. Without warning, she would feel lonely and depressed and then high with happiness and love. On occasion, she would burst out in rage against her friends—fits of anger that she had somehow managed to suppress as a child.

It was at about this time that she also began to appreciate the attention of men, something she had previously always avoided. Though she enjoyed being desired, she always felt she was "fooling" or tricking them somehow. After she began dating a man, she would sabotage the relationship by stirring up conflict.

She met Allan as he was completing his law studies. He pursued her relentlessly and refused to be driven away when she tried to back off. He liked to choose her clothes and advise her on how to walk, how to talk, and how to eat nutritiously. He insisted she accompany him to the gym where he frequently worked out.

"Allan gave me an identity," she explained. He advised her on how to interact with his society partners and clients, when to be aggressive, when to be demure. She developed a cast of "repertoire players"—characters or roles whom she could call to the stage on cue.

They married, at Allan's insistence, before the end of her junior year. She quit school and began working as a receptionist, but her employer recognized her intelligence and promoted her to more responsible jobs.

At home, however, things began to sour. Allan's career and his interest in bodybuilding caused him to spend more time away from home, which Jennifer hated. Sometimes she would start fights just to keep him home a little longer. Frequently, she would provoke him into hitting her. Afterward she would invite him to make love to her.

Jennifer had few friends. She devalued women as gossipy and uninteresting. She hoped that her son Scott's birth, coming two years after her marriage, would provide the comfort she lacked. She felt her son would always love her and always be there for her. But the demands of an infant were overwhelming, and after a while, Jennifer decided to return to work.

Despite frequent praise and successes at work, Jennifer continued to feel insecure, that she was "faking it." She became sexually involved with a coworker who was almost forty years her senior.

"Usually I'm okay," she told Dr. Gray. "But there's another side that takes over and controls me. I'm a good mother. But my other side makes me a whore; it makes me act crazy!"

Jennifer continued to deride herself, particularly when alone; during times of solitude, she would feel abandoned, which she attributed to her own unworthiness. Anxiety would threaten to overwhelm her unless she found some kind of release. Sometimes she'd indulge in eating binges, once consuming an entire bowl of cookie batter. She would spend long hours gazing at pictures of her son and husband, trying to "keep them alive in my brain."

Jennifer's physical appearance at her therapy sessions fluctuated dramatically. When coming directly from work, she would dress in a business suit that exuded maturity and sophistication. But on her days off, she showed up in short pants and knee socks, with her hair in braids; at these appointments she acted like a little girl with a high-pitched voice and used a more limited vocabulary.

Sometimes she would transform right before Dr. Gray's eyes. She could be insightful and intelligent, working collaboratively toward greater self-understanding, and then become a child, coquettish and seductive, pronouncing herself incapable of functioning in the adult world. She could be charming and ingratiating or manipulative and hostile. She could storm out of one session, vowing never to return, and at the next session cower with the fear that Dr. Gray would refuse to see her again.

Jennifer felt like a child clad in the armor of an adult. She was perplexed at the respect she received from other adults; she expected them to see through her disguise at any moment, revealing her to be an empress with no clothes. She needed someone to love and protect her from the world. She desperately sought closeness, but when someone came too close, she ran.

Jennifer is afflicted with Borderline Personality Disorder (BPD). She is not alone. Studies estimate that as many as 19 million or more Americans (3 to 6 percent of the population) exhibit primary symptoms of BPD, and many studies suggest this figure is an underesti-mation.[1,2] Approximately 10 percent of psychiatric outpatients and 20 percent of inpatients, and between 15 and 25 percent of *all* patients seeking psychiatric care, are diagnosed with the disorder. It is one of the most common of all of the personality disorders.[3,4]

Yet, despite its prevalence, BPD remains relatively unknown to the general public. Ask the man on the street about anxiety, depres-sion, or alcoholism, and he would probably be able to provide a sketchy, if not technically accurate, description of the illness. Ask him to define Borderline Personality Disorder, and he would prob-ably give you a blank stare. Ask an experienced mental health clini-cian about the disorder, on the other hand, and you will get a much different response. She will sigh deeply and exclaim that of all her psychiatric patients, borderline patients are the most difficult, the most dreaded, and the most to be avoided—more than those with schizophrenia, more than those suffering from alcoholism or sub-stance abuse, more than any other patient. For decades BPD has been lurking as a kind of "Third World" of mental illness—indistinct, massive, and vaguely threatening.

BPD has been underrecognized partly because the diagnosis is still relatively new. For years, "borderline" was used as a catchall category for patients who did not fit more established diagnoses. Peo-ple described as borderline seemed more ill than neurotic patients (who experience severe anxiety secondary to emotional conflict), yet less ill than psychotic patients (whose detachment from reality makes normal functioning impossible).

The disorder also coexists with, and borders on, other mental ill-nesses: depression, anxiety, bipolar (manic-depressive) disorder, schizophrenia, somatization disorder (hypochondriasis), dissociative identity disorder (multiple personality), attention deficit hyperactivity disorder (ADHD), post-traumatic stress disorder (PTSD), alcohol-ism, drug abuse (including nicotine dependence), eating disorders, phobias, obsessive-compulsive disorder, hysteria, sociopathy, and other personality disorders.

Though the term *borderline* was first coined in the 1930s, the condition was not clearly defined until the 1970s. For years, psychiatrists could not seem to agree on the separate existence of the syndrome, much less on the specific symptoms necessary for diagnosis. But as more and more people began to seek therapy for a unique set of life problems, the parameters of the disorder crystallized. In 1980, the diagnosis of Borderline Personality Disorder was first defined in the American Psychiatric Association's third edition of the *Diagnostic and Statistical Manual of Mental Disorders* (DSM-III), the diagnostic "bible" of the psychiatric profession. Since then, several revisions of the DSM have been produced, the most recent being DSM-5, published in 2013. Though various schools within psychiatry still quarrel over the exact nature, causes, and treatment of BPD, the disorder is officially recognized as a major mental health problem in America today. Indeed, BPD patients consume a greater percentage of mental health services than those with just about any other diagnosis.[5,6] Additionally, studies corroborate that about 90 percent of patients with the BPD diagnosis also share at least one other major psychiatric diagnosis.[7,8] BPD is also often connected to significant medical diseases, especially in women. These include chronic headaches and other pain, arthritis, and diseases of the cardiovascular, gastrointestinal, urinary, pulmonary, hepatic, immune, and oncological systems.[9,10,11,12,13,14,15] In 2008, the U.S. House of Representatives designated May as Borderline Personality Disorder Awareness Month. And yet, unfortunately, current government-sponsored research on BPD represents only a fraction of the work directed to less common disorders, such as schizophrenia or bipolar disorder.

In many ways, the borderline syndrome has been to psychiatry what a virus is to general medicine: an inexact term for a vague but pernicious illness that is frustrating to treat, difficult to define, and impossible for the doctor to explain adequately to his patient.

Demographic Borders

Who are the borderline people one meets in everyday life?

She is Carlotta, a friend since grade school. Over a minor slight, she accuses you of stabbing her in the back and tells you that you were really never her friend at all. Weeks or months later, Carlotta calls back, congenial and blasé, as if nothing had happened between you.

He is Bob, a boss in your office. One day Bob bestows glowing praise for your efforts in a routine assignment; another day, he berates you for an insignificant error. At times he is reserved and distant; other times he is suddenly and uproariously "one of the boys."

She is Arlene, your son's girlfriend. One week, she is the picture of preppy; the next, she is the epitome of punk. She breaks up with your son one night, only to return hours later, pledging endless devotion.

He is Brett, your next-door neighbor. Unable to come to grips with his collapsing marriage, he denies his wife's obvious unfaithfulness in one breath, and then takes complete blame for it in the next. He clings desperately to his family, caroming from guilt and self-loathing to raging attacks on his wife and children who have so "unfairly" accused him.

If the people in these short profiles seem inconsistent, it should not be surprising—inconsistency is the hallmark of BPD. Unable to tolerate paradox, those with borderline personality are walking paradoxes, human catch-22s. Their inconstancy is a major reason why the mental health profession has had such difficulty defining a uniform set of criteria for the illness.

If these people seem all too familiar, this also should not be surprising. The chances are good that you have a spouse, relative, close friend, or coworker who has borderline personality. Perhaps you know a little bit about BPD or recognize borderline characteristics within yourself.

Though it is difficult to get a firm grasp on the figures, mental health professionals generally agree that the number of borderline individuals in the general population is growing—and at a rapid pace—though some observers claim that it is the therapists' awareness of the disorder that is growing rather than the number of borderline patients.

Is borderline personality really a modern-day "plague," or is merely the diagnostic label *borderline* new? In any event, the disorder has provided new insight into the psychological framework of several related conditions. Numerous studies have linked BPD with anorexia, bulimia, ADHD, drug addiction, and teenage suicide—all of which have increased alarmingly over the last decade. Some studies have uncovered BPD in almost 50 percent of all patients admitted to a facility for an eating disorder.[16] Other studies have found that over 50 percent of substance abusers also fulfill criteria for BPD.

Self-destructive tendencies or suicidal gestures are very common among borderline patients—indeed, they are one of the syndrome's defining criteria. As many as 70 percent of BPD patients attempt suicide. The incidence of documented death by suicide is about 8 to 10 percent and even higher for borderline adolescents. A history of previous suicide attempts, a chaotic family life, and a lack of support systems increase the likelihood. The risk multiplies even more among borderline patients who also suffer from depressive or manic-depressive (bipolar) disorders, or from alcoholism or drug abuse.[17,18]

How Doctors Diagnose Psychiatric Disease

Before 1980, DSM-I and II described psychiatric illnesses in descriptive terms. However, starting with DSM-III, psychiatric disorders have been defined along structured, *categorical* paradigms; that is, several symptoms have been proposed to be suggestive of a particular diagnosis, and when a certain number of these criteria are met, the individual is considered to fulfill the categorical requirements for diagnosis. Interestingly, in the four revisions of DSM since 1980, only minor adjustments have been made to the definitional criteria for BPD. As we shall see shortly, nine criteria are associated with BPD, and an individual qualifies for the diagnosis if he exhibits five or more of the nine.

The categorical paradigm has stimulated controversy among psychiatrists, especially regarding the diagnosis of personality disorders. Unlike most other psychiatric illnesses, personality disorders are generally considered to develop in early adulthood and to persist for extended periods. These personality traits tend to be enduring and change only gradually over time. However, the categorical system of definitions may result in an unrealistically abrupt diagnostic change. In relation to BPD, a borderline patient who exhibits five symptoms of BPD theoretically ceases to be considered borderline if just one symptom changes. Such a precipitous "cure" seems inconsistent with the concept of personality.

For this reason and others, some researchers and clinicians have suggested adjusting the DSM to a *dimensional* approach to diagnosis. Such a model would attempt to determine what could be called "degrees of BPD," since clearly some borderline individuals function at a higher level than others. These authors suggest that, rather than concluding that an individual is—or is not—borderline, the disorder should be recognized along a spectrum. This approach would put different weights on some of the defining criteria, depending upon which symptoms are shown by research to be more prevalent and enduring. Such a method could develop a representative, "pure" borderline prototype, which could standardize measures based on how closely a patient "matches" the description. A dimensional approach might be used to measure functional impairment. In this way, a higher or lower functioning borderline patient would be identified by her ability to manage her usual tasks of living. Another methodology would gauge particular traits, such as impulsivity, novelty-seeking, reward dependence, harm avoidance, neuroticism (capturing such characteristics as vulnerability to stress, poor impulse control, anxiety, mood lability, etc.) that have been associated with BPD.[19,20,21]

Such adaptations may more accurately measure changes and degrees of improvement, rather than merely determining the presence or absence of the disorder.

To understand the difference between these two definitional approaches, consider the way we perceive "gender." The determination that one is male or female is a *categorical* definition, based on objective physical, genetic, and hormonal factors. Designations of masculinity or femininity, however, are *dimensional* concepts, influenced by personal, cultural, and other less objective criteria. Three-dimensional models that have already been proposed and are being refined are described in Appendix A. These include the American Psychiatric Association's Alternative DSM-5 Model for Personality Disorders (AMPD), the World Health Organization's International Classification of Diseases (ICD-11), and the National Institute of Mental Health's Research Domain Criteria (RDoC). It is likely that future iterations of the DSM will incorporate dimensional features of diagnosis.

Diagnosis of BPD

DSM-5 lists nine categorical criteria for BPD, five of which must be present for diagnosis.[22] With few modifications, these formal defining characteristics of BPD have remained unchanged for over forty years. At first glance, these criteria may seem unconnected or only peripherally related. When explored in depth, however, the nine symptoms are seen to be intricately connected, interacting with one another so that one symptom sparks the rise of another like the pistons of a combustion engine.

The nine criteria may be summarized as follows (each is described in depth in chapter 2):

1. Frantic efforts to avoid real or imagined abandonment.
2. Unstable and intense interpersonal relationships.
3. Lack of clear sense of identity.

4. Impulsiveness in potentially self-damaging behaviors, such as substance abuse, sex, shoplifting, reckless driving, binge eating.
5. Recurrent suicidal threats or gestures, or self-mutilating behaviors.
6. Severe mood shifts and extreme reactivity to situational stresses.
7. Chronic feelings of emptiness.
8. Frequent and inappropriate displays of anger.
9. Transient, stress-related feelings of unreality or paranoia.

This constellation of nine symptoms can be grouped into four primary areas toward which treatment is frequently directed:

1. Mood instability (criteria 1, 6, 7, and 8).
2. Impulsivity and dangerous uncontrolled behavior (criteria 4 and 5).
3. Interpersonal psychopathology (criteria 2 and 3).
4. Distortions of thought and perception (criterion 9).

Emotional Hemophilia

Beneath the clinical nomenclature lies the anguish experienced by borderline individuals and their loved ones. For someone with BPD, much of life is a relentless emotional roller coaster. For those living with, loving, or treating someone with BPD, the trip can seem just as wild, hopeless, and frustrating.

Jennifer and millions of other BPD patients are provoked to rage uncontrollably against the people they love most. They feel helpless and empty, with an identity splintered by severe emotional contradictions.

Mood changes come swiftly, explosively, carrying the borderline individual from the heights of joy to the depths of depression. Filled with anger one hour, calm the next, he often has little inkling about why he was driven to such wrath. Afterward, the inability to understand the origins of the episode brings on more self-hate and depression.

A borderline individual suffers a kind of "emotional hemophilia"; she lacks the clotting mechanism needed to moderate her spurts of feeling. Prick a passion, stab a sentiment in the delicate "skin" of a borderline personality, and she will emotionally bleed to death. Sustained periods of contentment are foreign to the BPD sufferer. Chronic emptiness depletes him until he is desperate to do anything to escape. In the grip of these lows, he is prone to a myriad of impulsive, self-destructive acts—drug and alcohol binges, eating marathons, anorexic fasts, bulimic purges, gambling forays, shopping sprees, sexual promiscuity, and self-mutilation. He may attempt suicide, often not with the intent to die but to feel *something*, to confirm he is alive.

"I hate the way I feel," confesses one borderline patient. "When I think about suicide, it seems so tempting, so inviting. Sometimes it's the only thing I relate to. It is difficult not to want to hurt myself. It's like, if I hurt myself, the fear and pain will go away."

Central to the borderline syndrome is the lack of a core sense of identity. When describing themselves, BPD people typically paint a confused or contradictory self-portrait, in contrast to other patients who generally have a much clearer sense of who they are. To overcome their indistinct and mostly negative self-image, borderline individuals, like actors, are constantly searching for "good roles," complete "characters" they can inhabit to fill their identity void. So they often adapt like chameleons to the environment, situation, or companions of the moment, much like the title character in Woody Allen's film *Zelig*, who literally assumes the personality, identity, and appearance of people around him.

The lure of ecstatic experiences, whether attained through sex, drugs, or other means, is sometimes overwhelming for the BPD sufferer. In ecstasy, he can return to a primal world where the self and the external world merge—a form of second infancy. During periods of intense loneliness and emptiness, he will go on drug binges, bouts with alcohol, or sexual escapades (with one or several partners), sometimes lasting days at a time. It is as if when the struggle to find an identity becomes intolerable, the solution is either to lose one's identity altogether or to achieve a semblance of self through pain or numbness.

The family background of someone with BPD is often marked by alcoholism, depression, and emotional disturbances. A borderline childhood is frequently a desolate battlefield, scarred with the debris of indifferent, rejecting, or absent parents, emotional deprivation, and chronic abuse. Most studies have found a history of severe psychological, physical, or sexual abuse in many borderline patients. Indeed, a history of mistreatment, witness to violence, neglect, or invalidation of experience by parents or primary caregivers distinguishes borderline patients from other psychiatric patients.[23,24] Such patients are more vulnerable to other medical illnesses and are more likely to exhibit alterations in hormonal, inflammatory, genetic, and other neurobiological processes.[25] One study of pregnant women with a history of childhood adversity examined chromosomal patterns in their offspring. There was direct correlation between the severity of the mother's past childhood abuse and the degree of shortening of the infant's telomere length (telomeres are the protective caps at the ends of chromosomes), which was also associated with increased behavioral problems at eighteen months.[26]

These unstable relationships carry over into adolescence and adulthood, where romantic attachments are highly charged and usually short-lived. The borderline individual will frantically pursue a partner one day and send him packing the next. Longer romances—usually measured in weeks or months rather than years—are usually filled with turbulence and rage, wonder, and excitement. This may be related to research indicating hypersensitivity to physical touching and preference for interpersonal distance among individuals with a past history of childhood maltreatment.[27]

Splitting: The Black-and-White World of the Borderline

The world of a borderline adult, like that of a child, is split into heroes and villains. A child emotionally, the individual with BPD cannot tolerate human inconsistencies and ambiguities; he cannot reconcile another's good and bad qualities into a constant, coherent understanding of that person. At any particular moment, one is either "good" or "evil"; there is no in-between, no gray area. Nuances and shadings are grasped with great difficulty, if at all. Lovers and mates, mothers and fathers, siblings, friends, and psychotherapists may be idolized one day, totally devalued and dismissed the next.

When the idealized person finally disappoints (as we all do, sooner or later), the borderline person must drastically restructure her strict, inflexible conceptualization. Either the idol is banished to the dungeon or she banishes *herself* in order to preserve the "all-good" image of the other person.

This type of behavior, referred to as "splitting," is the primary defense mechanism employed in BPD. Technically defined, splitting is the rigid separation of positive and negative thoughts and feelings about oneself and others; that is, the inability to synthesize these feelings. Most individuals can experience ambivalence and perceive two contradictory feeling states at one time; those with BPD characteristically shift back and forth, entirely unaware of one emotional state while immersed in another.

Splitting creates an escape hatch from anxiety: the borderline person typically experiences a close friend or relation (call him "Joe") as two separate people at different times. One day, she can admire "Good Joe" without reservation, perceiving him as completely good; his negative qualities do not exist; they have been purged and attributed to "Bad Joe." Other days, she can guiltlessly and totally despise "Bad Joe" and rage at his evil without self-reproach—for now his positive traits do not exist; he fully deserves the rage.

Intended to shield BPD experience from a barrage of contradictory feelings and images—and from the anxiety of trying to reconcile those images—the splitting mechanism often and ironically achieves the opposite effect: the frays in the personality fabric become full-fledged rips; the sense of her own identity and the identities of others shift even more dramatically and frequently.

Stormy Relationships

Despite feeling continually victimized by others, a borderline individual desperately seeks out new relationships; for solitude, even temporary aloneness, is more intolerable than mistreatment. To escape the loneliness, the person with BPD will flee to singles bars, hookup websites, the arms of recent pickups, somewhere—anywhere—to meet someone who might save her from the torment of her own thoughts. She is constantly searching for Mr. Goodbar or Ms. Tinder.

In the relentless search for a structured role in life, she is typically attracted to—and attracts to her—others with complementary personality traits. Jennifer's husband, for example, with his domineering, narcissistic personality, cast her in a well-defined role with little effort. He was able to give her an identity even if the identity involved submissiveness and mistreatment.

Yet in BPD, relationships often disintegrate quickly. Maintaining closeness with her requires an understanding of the syndrome and a willingness to walk a long, perilous tightrope. Too much closeness threatens her with suffocation. Keeping one's distance or leaving her alone—even for brief periods—recalls the sense of abandonment she felt as a child. In either case, the borderline individual reacts intensely.

In a sense, someone with BPD is like an emotional explorer who carries only a sketchy map of interpersonal relations; he finds it extremely difficult to gauge the optimal psychic distance from others, particularly significant others. To compensate, he caroms back and forth from clinging dependency to angry manipulation, from gushes of gratitude to fits of irrational anger. He fears abandonment, so he clings; he fears engulfment, so he pushes away. He craves intimacy and is terrified of it at the same time. He winds up repelling those with whom he most wants to connect.

Job and Workplace Problems

Though people with BPD may have extreme difficulties managing their personal lives, many are able to function productively in a work situation—particularly if the job is well structured, clearly defined, and supportive. Some perform well for long periods, but then suddenly—because of a change in the job structure, or a drastic shift in their personal life, or just plain boredom and a craving for change—they abruptly leave or sabotage their position and go on to the next opportunity. Many complain of frequent or chronic minor medical illnesses, leading to recurrent doctor visits and sick days.[28]

The work world can provide sanctuary from the anarchy of their social relationships. For this reason, borderline individuals frequently function best in highly structured work environments. The helping professions—medicine, nursing, clergy, counseling—also attract many with BPD, who strive to achieve the power or control that elude them in social relationships. Perhaps more important, in these roles they can provide the care for others—and receive the recognition from others—that they yearn for in their own lives. Borderline individuals are often very intelligent and display striking artistic abilities; fueled by easy access to powerful emotions, they can be creative and successful professionally.

But a highly competitive or unstructured job or a highly critical supervisor can trigger the intense, uncontrolled anger and the hypersensitivity to rejection to which she is susceptible. The rage can permeate the workplace and literally destroy a career.

A "Woman's Illness"?

Until recently, studies suggested that women borderlines outnumbered men by as much as three or four to one. However, more recent epidemiological research confirms that the prevalence is similar in both genders, although women enter treatment more frequently. Moreover, the severity of symptoms and disability are greater among women. These factors may help explain why females have been overrepresented in clinical trials. But there may be other factors that contribute to the impression that BPD is a "woman's disease."

Some critics feel that a kind of clinician bias operates with borderline diagnoses. Psychotherapists may perceive problems with identity and impulsivity as more "normal" in men; as a result, they may underdiagnose BPD among males. Where destructive behavior in women may be seen as a result of mood dysfunction, similar behavior in men may be perceived as antisocial. Where women in such predicaments may be directed toward treatment, men may instead be channeled through the criminal justice system, where they may elude correct diagnosis forever.

BPD in Different Age Groups

Many of the features of the borderline syndrome—impulsivity, tumultuous relationships, identity confusion, mood instability—are major developmental hurdles for any adolescent. Indeed, establishing a core identity is the primary quest for both the teenager and the borderline. It follows, then, that BPD is diagnosed more commonly among adolescents and young adults than other age groups.[29]

BPD appears to be rare in the elderly. Recent studies demonstrate that the greatest decline in diagnosis of BPD occurs after the mid-forties. From this data, some researchers hypothesize that many older borderline adults "mature out" and are able to achieve stabilization over time. However, elderly adults must contend with a progressive decline in physical and mental functioning, which can be a perilous adaptive process for some aging adults. For a fragile identity, the task of altering expectations and adjusting self-image can exacerbate symptoms. The older borderline individual with persistent psychopathology may deny deteriorating functions, project the blame for deficiencies onto others, and become increasingly paranoid; at other times, he may exaggerate handicaps and become more dependent.

Socioeconomic Factors

Borderline pathology has been identified in all cultures and economic classes in the United States. However, rates of BPD were significantly higher among those separated, divorced, widowed, or living alone, and among those with lower income and education. The consequences of poverty on infants and children—higher stress levels, less education, and lack of good childcare, psychiatric care, and pregnancy care (perhaps resulting in brain insults or malnutrition)—might lead to higher incidence of BPD among the poor.

The societal costs of BPD are considerable. Borderline patients not only often have higher costs for psychiatric and other medical disorders but also have higher costs for lost work productivity related to these illnesses, compared to the general population. An extensive fifteen-year Danish study involving thousands of patients compared healthcare costs for BPD patients with those for the general population. Data confirmed that other medical costs were higher even five years before the BPD diagnosis was made. Spouses of patients with BPD also show increased healthcare costs and costs of lost productivity.[30]

Geographic Borders

Although most of the theoretical formulations and empirical studies of the borderline syndrome have been conducted in the United States, other countries—Canada, Mexico, Germany, Israel, Sweden, Denmark, other Western European nations, and Russia, China, Korea, Japan, and other Eastern countries—have recognized borderline pathologies within their populations.

Comparative studies are scant and contradictory at this point. For example, some studies indicate higher rates of BPD among Hispanics, while others do not confirm this finding. Some studies have found greater rates of BPD among Native American men. Consistent studies are meager but could provide great insight into the child-rearing, cultural, and social threads that compose the causal fabric of the syndrome.

Borderline Behavior in Celebrities and Fictional Characters

Whether the borderline personality is a new phenomenon or simply a new label for a long-standing interrelated cluster of internal feelings and external behaviors is a topic of some interest in the mental health community. Most psychiatrists believe that the borderline syndrome has been around for quite some time; that its increasing prominence results not so much from its spreading (like an infectious disease or a chronic debilitating condition) in the minds of patients but from the awareness of clinicians. Indeed, many psychiatrists believe that some of Sigmund Freud's most interesting cases of "neurosis" at the turn of the century would today be clearly diagnosed as borderline.[31]

Perceived in this way, the borderline syndrome becomes an interesting new perspective from which to understand some of our most complex personalities—both past and present, real and fictional. Conversely, well-known figures and characters can be understood to illustrate different aspects of the syndrome. Along these lines, biographers and others have speculated that the term might apply to such wide-ranging figures as Princess Diana, Marilyn Monroe, Zelda Fitzgerald, Thomas Wolfe, T. E. Lawrence, Adolf Hitler, and Muammar al-Gaddafi. Cultural critics can observe borderline features in fictional characters like Blanche DuBois in *A Streetcar Named Desire*, Martha in *Who's Afraid of Virginia Woolf?*, Sally Bowles in *Cabaret*, Travis Bickle in *Taxi Driver*, Howard Beale in *Network*, Rebecca Bunch in the TV show *Crazy Ex-Girlfriend,* and Carmen in Bizet's opera. Although borderline symptoms or behaviors may be spotted in these characters, BPD should not be assumed to necessarily cause or propel the radical actions or destinies of these real people or the fictional characters or the works in which they appear. Hitler, for example, was probably driven by mental malfunctions and societal forces much more prominent in his psyche than BPD; the root causes of Marilyn Monroe's (alleged) suicide were probably more complex than to say simply it was caused by BPD. There is little evidence that the filmmakers of *Taxi Driver* or *Network* were consciously trying to create a borderline protagonist. What the borderline syndrome does furnish is another perspective from which to interpret and analyze these fascinating personalities.

Over the last decade, there have been rumors circulating that many celebrities, including well-known actors and musicians, exhibit borderline personality symptoms, though many do not discuss it publicly. Others, such as *Saturday Night Live* cast member Pete Davidson and former NFL star Brandon Marshall, have been outspoken about their BPD diagnosis, the pain of the affliction, and the stigma of mental illness. Dr. Marsha Linehan, the well-known researcher and founder of dialectical behavioral therapy (DBT), a major treatment approach for BPD, has revealed that she also has struggled with the disorder, having received extensive hospitalization during adolescence for self-mutilation and other symptoms.

Advances in Research and Treatment

Since publication of the first edition of this book, significant strides have been made in research into the root causes of BPD and its treatment. Our understanding of the biological, physiological, and genetic underpinnings of psychiatric diseases is growing exponentially. Interactions between different parts of the brain and intersections between emotions and executive reasoning are being illuminated. The roles of neurotransmitters, hormones, immunological systems, and chemical reactions in the brain are better understood. Genetic vulnerability, the switching on and off of genes, and the collision with life events to determine personality functioning are being studied. New psychotherapeutic techniques have evolved.

Long-term studies confirm that many patients recover over time and even more improve significantly. After sixteen years of follow-up, 99 percent of borderline patients achieved at least two years of remission and 78 percent experienced an eight-year remission (defined as no longer fulfilling five of the nine defining criteria). However, despite diminution of some of the more acute defining symptoms, such as destructive impulsivity, self-mutilation, suicide attempts, and quasi-psychotic thinking, many of these patients continue to struggle in social and work or school environments. Although recurrence rates are as high as 34 percent, after ten years, full and complete recovery with good social and vocational functioning is achieved in 50 percent of patients.[32,33,34,35] Many borderline patients improve without consistent treatment, although continued therapy hastens improvement.[36]

The Question of Borderline "Pathology"

To one degree or another, we all struggle with the same issues as the borderline patient—the threat of separation, the fear of rejection, confusion about identity, feelings of emptiness and boredom. How many of us have not had a few intense unstable relationships? Or flown into a rage now and then? Or felt the allure of ecstatic states? Or dreaded being alone, or gone through mood swings, or acted in a self-destructive manner in some way?

If nothing else, BPD serves to remind us that the line between "normal" and "pathological" may sometimes be a very thin one. Many of the descriptions in this book illustrate the extremes of this disorder. Do we all display, to one degree or another, some symptoms of borderline personality? The answer is probably yes. Indeed, many of you reading this first chapter might be thinking that this sounds like you or someone you know. The discriminating factor, however, is that not all of us are controlled by the syndrome to the degree that it disrupts—or rules—our lives. With its extremes of emotion, thought, and behavior, BPD represents some of the best and worst of human character—and of our society—in the first twenty years of the twenty-first century. By exploring its depths and boundaries, we may be facing up to our ugliest instincts and our highest potentials—and the hard road we must travel to get from one point to the other.

Chapter Two

Chaos and Emptiness

All is caprice. They love without measure those whom they will
soon hate without reason.

—Thomas Sydenham, seventeenth-century English physician, on
"hystericks," the equivalent of today's borderline personality

"I sometimes wonder if I'm possessed by the devil," says Carrie,
a social worker in the psychiatric unit of a large hospital. "I don't
understand myself. All I know is, this borderline personality of mine
has forced me into a life where I've cut everyone out. So it's very,
very lonely."

Carrie was diagnosed with the borderline syndrome after twenty-
two years of therapy, medication, and hospitalizations for a variety
of mental and physical illnesses. By then, her medical file resembled
a well-worn passport, the pages stamped with the numerous psychiatric "territories" through which she had traveled.

"For years I was in and out of hospitals, but I never found a therapist who understood me and knew what I was going through."

Carrie's parents were divorced when she was an infant, and she
was raised by her alcoholic mother until she was nine. A boarding
school took care of her for four years after that.

When she was twenty-one, overwhelming depression forced her
to seek therapy; she was diagnosed and treated for depression at that
time. A few years later, her moods began to fluctuate wildly, and she
was treated for bipolar disorder (manic depression). Throughout

this period, she repeatedly overdosed on medications and cut her wrists many times.

"I was cutting myself and overdosing on tranquilizers, antidepressants, or whatever drug I happened to be on," she recalls. "It had become almost a way of life."

In her mid-twenties, she began to have auditory hallucinations and became severely paranoid. At this time she was hospitalized for the first time and diagnosed as schizophrenic.

And still later in life, Carrie was hospitalized in a cardiac-care unit numerous times for severe chest pains, subsequently recognized to be anxiety-related. She went through periods of binge eating and starvation fasting; over a period of several weeks, her weight would vary by as much as seventy pounds.

When she was thirty-two, she was brutally raped by a physician on the staff of the hospital in which she worked. Soon after, she returned to school and was drawn into a sexual relationship with one of her female professors. By the time she was forty-two, her collection of medical files was filled with almost every diagnosis imaginable, including schizophrenia, depression, bipolar disorder, hypochondriasis, anxiety, anorexia nervosa, sexual dysfunction, and post-traumatic stress disorder.

Despite her mental and physical problems, Carrie was able to perform her work fairly well. Though she changed jobs frequently, she managed to complete a doctorate in social work. She was even able to teach for a while at a small women's college.

Her personal relationships, however, were severely limited. "The only relationships I've had with men were ones in which I was sexually abused. A few men have wanted to marry me, but I have a big problem with getting close or being touched. I can't tolerate it. It makes me want to run. I was engaged a couple of times, but had to break the engagements off. It's unrealistic of me to think I could be anybody's wife."

As for friends, she says, "I'm very self-absorbed. I say everything I think, feel, know, or don't know. It's so hard for me to get interested in other people."

After more than twenty years of treatment, Carrie's symptoms were finally recognized and diagnosed as BPD. Her dysfunction evolved from ingrained, enduring personality traits, more indicative of a personality or "trait" disorder than her previously diagnosed, transient "state" illnesses.

"The most difficult part of being a borderline personality has been the emptiness, the loneliness, and the intensity of feelings," she says today. "The extreme behaviors keep me so confused. At times I don't know what I'm feeling or who I am."

A better understanding of Carrie's illness has led to more consistent treatment. Medications have been useful for treating acute symptoms and providing the glue for maintaining a more coherent sense of self; at the same time, she has acknowledged the limitations of the medications.

Her psychiatrist, working with her other physicians, has helped her to understand the connection between her physical complaints and her anxiety and to avoid unnecessary medical tests, drugs, and surgeries. Psychotherapy has been geared for the "long haul," focusing on her dependency and stabilization of her identity and relationships, rather than on an endless succession of acute emergencies.

Carrie, at forty-six, has had to learn that an entire set of previous behaviors are no longer acceptable. "I don't have the option of cutting myself or overdosing or being hospitalized anymore. I vowed I would live in and deal with the real world, but I'll tell you, it's a frightening place. I'm not sure yet whether I can do it or whether I *want* to do it."

Borderline: A Personality Disorder

Carrie's journey through this maze of psychiatric and medical symptoms and diagnoses exemplifies the confusion and desperation experienced by individuals afflicted with mental illness and by those who minister to them. Though the specifics of Carrie's case might be considered extreme by some, millions of women—and men—suffer similar problems with relationships, intimacy, depression, and drug abuse. Perhaps if she had been diagnosed earlier and more accurately, she would have been spared some of the pain and loneliness.

Though patients with borderline personality suffer a tangle of painful symptoms that severely disrupt their lives, only recently have psychiatrists begun to more fully understand the disorder and treat it effectively. What is a "personality disorder"? What exactly does borderline border? How is borderline personality similar to and different from other disorders? How does the borderline syndrome fit into the overall schema of psychiatric medicine? These are difficult questions even for the professional, particularly in light of the elusive, paradoxical nature of the illness and its curious evolution in psychiatry.

One widely accepted model suggests that individual personality is actually a combination of *temperament* (inherited personal characteristics, such as impatience, vulnerability to addiction, etc.) and *character* (developmental values emerging from environment and life experiences)—in other words, a "nature-nurture" mix. *Temperament* characteristics may be correlated with genetic and biological markers, develop early in life, and are perceived as instincts or habits. *Character* emerges more slowly into adulthood, shaped by encounters in the world. Through the lens of this model, BPD may be viewed as the collage resulting from the collision of genes and environment.[1,2]

BPD is one of ten personality disorders noted in DSM-5. These disorders are distinguished by a cluster of developing *traits* that become prominent in an individual's behavior. These traits are relatively inflexible and result in maladaptive patterns of perceiving, behaving, and relating to others.

In contrast, *state* disorders (such as depression, schizophrenia, anorexia nervosa, chemical dependency) are usually not as enduring as *trait* disorders. These illnesses are more often time- or episode-limited. Symptoms may emerge suddenly and then be resolved as the patient returns to "normal." Many times these illnesses are directly correlated with imbalances in the body's biochemistry and can often be treated with medications, which virtually eliminate the symptoms.

Symptoms of a personality disorder, on the other hand, tend to be more durable traits and change more gradually; medications are in general less effective. Indeed, though several pharmaceutical companies have tested medicines, there remains no current medication specifically indicated for the treatment of BPD. Psychotherapy is primarily recommended, though other treatments, including medication, may alleviate many symptoms, especially severe agitation or depression (see chapter 9). In most cases, borderline and other personality disorders are a secondary diagnosis, describing the underlying characterological functioning of a patient who exhibits more acute and prominent symptoms of a state disorder.

Comparisons to Other Disorders

Because the borderline syndrome often masquerades as a different illness and is often associated with other illnesses, clinicians often fail to recognize that BPD may be an important component in evaluating a patient. As a result, the borderline patient often becomes, like Carrie, a well-traveled patient, evaluated by multiple hospitals and doctors and accompanied throughout life by an assortment of diagnostic labels.

BPD can interact with other disorders in several ways (see Figure 2-1). First, BPD can coexist with state disorders in such a way that borderline pathology is camouflaged. For example, BPD may be submerged in the wake of a more prominent and severe depression. After resolution of the depression with antidepressant medications, borderline characteristics may surface and only then be recognized as the underlying character structure requiring further treatment.

Second, BPD may be closely linked and perhaps even contribute to the development of another disorder. For example, the impulsivity, self-destructiveness, interpersonal difficulties, deflated self-image, and moodiness often exhibited by patients with substance abuse or eating disorders may be more reflective of BPD than the primary

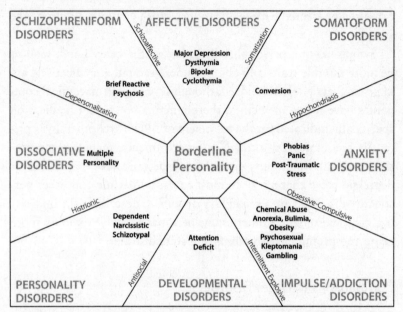

FIGURE 2-1. Schematic of position of BPD in relation to other mental disorders.

disorder. Although it could be argued that chronic abuse of alcohol could eventually alter personality characteristics in such a way that a borderline pattern could evolve secondarily, it seems just as likely that underlying character pathology would develop first and contribute to the development of alcoholism.

The question of which is the chicken and which is the egg may be difficult to resolve, but the development of illnesses associated with BPD may represent a kind of psychological vulnerability to stress. Just as certain individuals have genetic and biological dispositions to physical diseases—heart attacks, cancers, gastrointestinal disorders, etc.—many also have biologically determined propensities to psychiatric illnesses, particularly when stress is added to an underlying vulnerability to BPD. Thus, under stress, one borderline patient turns to drugs, another develops an eating disorder, and still another becomes severely depressed.

Third, BPD may so completely mimic another disorder that the patient may be erroneously diagnosed with schizophrenia, anxiety, bipolar disease, attention deficit hyperactivity disorder (ADHD), or other illnesses.

Comparison to Schizophrenia and Psychosis

Schizophrenic patients are usually much more severely impaired than borderline patients and less capable of manipulating and relating to others. Both kinds of patients may experience agitated psychotic episodes. The estimated prevalence of psychosis in BPD (including auditory and visual hallucinations, paranoid delusions, and dissociative experiences) is 20 to 50 percent.[3] In contrast to schizophrenia, psychotic symptoms in BPD are usually less consistent and less pervasive over time and are usually stress-related. Schizophrenic patients are much more likely to grow accustomed to their hallucinations and delusions and are often less disturbed by them. Although both groups may be destructive and self-mutilating, the borderline patient usually can function more appropriately; the schizophrenic patient is typically emotionally blunted, withdrawn, and much more severely impaired socially.[4]

Comparison to Affective Disorders (Depressive and Bipolar Disorders)

About 96 percent of BPD patients have a mood disorder during their life. Anxiety disorders frequently accompany affective illnesses. Major depression is estimated to affect 71 to 83 percent of borderline patients.

"Mood swings" and "racing thoughts" are common patient complaints, to which the knee-jerk diagnostic response from the clinician is to diagnose depression or bipolar disorder (manic depression). However, such symptoms are consistent with BPD, and even ADHD, both of which are significantly more prevalent than bipolar disorder. Though some have argued that BPD is a form of bipolar disorder, clinical, genetic, and imaging studies distinguish the illnesses, and the clinical differences between these syndromes are dramatic. For those afflicted with bipolar disorder, episodes of depression or mania represent radical departures in functioning. Mood changes last from days to weeks. Between mood swings, these individuals maintain relatively normal lives and can usually be treated effectively with medications. Borderline patients, in contrast, typically have difficulties in functioning (at least internally) even when not displaying prominent mood swings. When exhibiting hyperactive, self-destructive, or suicidal behaviors, or experiencing wide and rapid mood swings, the borderline individual may appear bipolar. However, BPD mood variations are more transient (lasting hours rather than days or weeks), more unstable, and more often reactive to environmental stimuli.[5,6] The criteria that most effectively distinguish BPD from bipolar disorder are abandonment fears and identity disturbance.[7] Nevertheless, both disorders have a 20 percent overlap in diagnostic frequency—that is to say, 20 percent of patients with bipolar disorder evidence co-occurring BPD, and 20 percent of patients with BPD also have bipolar disorder. Those patients with both diagnoses have decidedly more severe symptoms and complicated outcomes.[8,9]

BPD and ADHD

Individuals with ADHD are subjected to a constant scramble of flashing cognitions. Like borderline patients, they often experience wild mood changes, racing thoughts, impulsivity, anger outbursts, impatience, and low frustration tolerance; have a history of drug or alcohol abuse (self-medicating) and torturous relationships; and are easily bored. Indeed, many borderline personality characteristics correspond to the "typical ADHD temperament," such as frequent novelty-seeking (searching for excitement) coupled with low reward dependence (lack of concern for immediate consequences).[10] Not surprisingly, several studies have noted correlations between these diagnoses. Some prospective studies have noted that children diagnosed with ADHD frequently develop a personality disorder, especially BPD, as they get older. A Swedish study indicated that individuals with a diagnosis of ADHD were almost twenty times more likely to also have a BPD diagnosis than those not diagnosed with ADHD.[11] Retrospective researchers have determined that adults with the diagnosis of BPD often fit a childhood diagnosis of ADHD.[12,13,14] Whether one illness causes the other, whether they frequently travel together, or, possibly, whether they are merely related manifestations of the same disorder remains for intriguing further investigation. Interestingly, one study demonstrated that treatment of ADHD symptoms also ameliorated BPD symptoms in patients diagnosed with both disorders.[15]

BPD and Pain

Borderline individuals exhibit paradoxical reactions to pain. Many studies have shown a significantly decreased sensitivity to *acute* pain, particularly when self-inflicted[16] (see "Self-Destruction" later in this chapter). However, borderline patients exhibit greater sensitivity to *chronic* pain. About 30 percent of patients with chronic pain (such as fibromyalgia, arthritis, back pain) also appear to suffer from BPD.[17] This "pain paradox" appears unique in BPD and has not been satisfactorily explained. Some posit that acute pain, especially when self-inflicted, satisfies certain psychological needs for the patient and is associated with changes in electrical brain activity and perhaps quick release of endogenous opioids, the body's own narcotics. However, ongoing pain, experienced outside the borderline person's control, may result in less internal analgesic protection and cause more anxiety. It may also be enlisted to gain more attention and caring responses from others. A study on pain tolerance following knee surgery in borderline patients demonstrated a poorer response and was related to borderline coping mechanisms with ongoing pain.[18] As BPD patients age, they appear to become more sensitive to pain.[19]

BPD and Somatization Disorder

The borderline individual may focus on his physical ills, complaining loudly and dramatically to medical personnel and acquaintances, in order to maintain dependency relationships with them. He may be considered merely a hypochondriac, while the underlying understanding of his problems is completely ignored. Somatization disorder is a condition defined by the patient's multiple physical complaints (including pain, gastric, neurological, and sexual symptoms), unexplained by any known medical condition. In hypochondriasis, the patient is convinced he has a terrible disease despite a medical evaluation that reveals no evidence of one.[20]

BPD and Dissociative Disorders

Dissociative disorders include such phenomena as amnesia or feelings of unreality about oneself (*depersonalization*) or about the environment (*derealization*). The most extreme form of dissociation is dissociative identity disorder (DID), previously referred to as "multiple personality." Almost 75 percent of individuals with BPD experience some dissociative phenomena.[21] The prevalence of BPD in those suffering from the most severe form of dissociation, DID, as a primary diagnosis is even greater.[22] Both disorders share common symptoms—impulsivity, anger outbursts, disturbed relationships, severe mood changes, and a propensity for self-mutilation. There is frequently a childhood history of mistreatment, abuse, or neglect.

BPD and Post-Traumatic Stress Disorder

Post-traumatic stress disorder (PTSD) is a complex of symptoms that follows an extraordinarily severe traumatic event, such as a natural disaster or combat. It is characterized by intense fear, an emotional re-experiencing of the event, nightmares, irritability, an exaggerated startle response, avoidance of associated places or activities, and a sense of helplessness. Since both BPD and PTSD have frequently been associated with a history of extreme abuse in childhood and reflect similar symptoms—such as extreme emotional reactions and impulsivity—some have posited that they are the same illness. Although some studies indicate that they may occur together as much as 50 percent or more of the time, they are distinctly different disorders with different defining criteria.[23] When BPD patients also suffer from PTSD, symptoms are more severe. Female patients, particularly, are more likely to nonlethally self-injure, especially seeking attention. They are also more likely to suffer from anxiety illnesses, such as panic disorder, obsessive-compulsive disorder (OCD), and agoraphobia. PTSD patients with co-occurring different personality disorders do not experience as severe complications.[24,25]

BPD and Associated Personality Disorders

Many characteristics of BPD overlap with those of other personality disorders. For example, dependent personality disorder shares with BPD the features of dependency, avoidance of being alone, and strained relationships. But the dependent personality lacks the self-destructiveness, anger, and mood swings of a borderline patient. Similarly, those with schizotypal personality disorder exhibit poor relations with others and difficulty in trusting, but are more eccentric and less self-destructive. Often a patient exhibits enough characteristics of two or more personality disorders to warrant diagnoses for each. For example, a patient may demonstrate characteristics that lead to diagnoses of both borderline personality disorder and obsessive-compulsive personality disorder.

In previous editions of the DSM, BPD was grouped in a cluster of personality disorders that generally reflect dramatic, emotional, or erratic features. The others in this group are narcissistic, antisocial, and histrionic personality disorders. All of these are more closely related to BPD.

Both those with BPD and narcissistic personality disorder display hypersensitivity to criticism; failures or rejections can precipitate severe depression. Both can exploit others; both demand almost constant attention. The person with narcissistic personality disorder, however, usually functions at a higher level. He exhibits an inflated sense of self-importance (often camouflaging desperate insecurity), displays disdain for others, and lacks even a semblance of empathy. In contrast, the borderline person has a lower self-esteem and is highly dependent on others' reassurance. She desperately clings to others and is usually more sensitive to their reactions.

Like the borderline individual, the person with antisocial personality disorder exhibits impulsivity, poor tolerance of frustration, and manipulative relationships. Someone with antisocial personality disorder, however, lacks a sense of guilt or conscience; he is more detached and is not purposefully self-destructive.

The person with histrionic personality disorder shares with the borderline personality tendencies of attention-seeking, manipulativeness, and shifting emotions. The histrionic personality, however, usually develops more stable roles and relationships. He is usually more flamboyant in speech and manner, and his emotional reactions are exaggerated. Physical attractiveness is a primary concern. One study compared psychological and social functioning in patients with BPD, schizotypal, obsessive-compulsive, or avoidant personality disorders and patients with major depression. Patients with borderline and schizotypal personality disorders were significantly more functionally impaired than those with the other personality disorders and those with major depression.[26]

BPD and Substance Abuse

BPD and chemical abuse are frequently associated. Nearly a third of those with a lifetime diagnosis of substance abuse also fulfill criteria for BPD. And over a lifetime 50 to 72 percent of BPD patients also abuse alcohol or other substances.[27,28,29] Alcohol or drugs might reflect self-punishing, angry, or impulsive behaviors, a craving for excitement, or a mechanism of coping with loneliness. Drug dependency may be a substitute for nurturing social relationships, a familiar, comforting way to stabilize or self-medicate fluctuating moods, or a way to establish some sense of belonging or self-identification. These possible explanations for the appeal of chemical abuse are also some of the defining criteria for BPD.

Anorexia/Bulimia and BPD

Anorexia nervosa and bulimia nervosa have become major health problems in this country, especially among young women. Eating disorders are fueled by a fundamental distaste for one's own body and a general disapproval of one's identity. The anorexic patient sees herself in absolute black-or-white extremes—as either obese (which she always feels) or thin (which she feels she never completely achieves). Since she constantly feels out of control, she impulsively utilizes starvation or binging and purging to maintain an illusion of self-control. Patients with anorexia or bulimia are obviously engaged in self-damaging behavior. They usually have a distorted sense of identity and experience feelings of emptiness. The similarity of this pattern to the borderline pattern has led many mental health professionals to infer a strong connection between the two.[30] In one study[31] patients with either anorexia or bulimia endorsed feelings of unstable relationships, emptiness, suicidal behavior, and dissociative experiences. BPD symptoms of mood instability, impulsivity, and anger were more closely related to patients with bulimia than to patients with anorexia. Anorexic patients were comparatively more affected by a disturbed sense of identity. The prevalence of BPD in the binge eating/purging form of anorexia nervosa is 25 percent. BPD is present in 28 percent of those suffering with bulimia nervosa.[32]

BPD and Compulsive Behaviors

Certain compulsive or destructive behaviors may reflect borderline patterns. For example, a compulsive gambler will continue to gamble despite a shortage of funds. He may be seeking a thrill from a world that habitually leaves him bored, restless, and numb. Or the gambling may be an expression of impulsive self-punishment. Shoplifters often steal items they do not need. Fifty percent of bulimic patients exhibit kleptomania, drug use, or promiscuity.[33] When these behaviors are governed by compulsion, they may represent a need to feel or a need to self-inflict pain.

Promiscuity often reflects a need for constant love and attention from others, in order to hold on to positive feelings about oneself. The borderline individual typically lacks consistent positive self-regard and requires continuous reassurance. A borderline woman, lacking in self-esteem, may perceive her physical attractiveness as her only asset and may require confirmation of her worth by engaging in frequent sexual encounters. Such involvements avoid the pain of being alone and create artificial relationships she can totally control. Feeling desired can instill a sense of identity. When self-punishment becomes a prominent part of the psychodynamics, humiliation and masochistic perversions may enter the relationships. From this perspective, it is logical to speculate that many prostitutes and pornographic actors and models may harbor borderline pathology.

Difficulties with relationships may result in private ritualistic thinking and behaviors, often expressed as obsessions or compulsion. A borderline patient may develop specific phobias as he employs magical thinking to deal with fears; sexual perversions may evolve as a mechanism to approach intimacy.

BPD and Autism Spectrum Disorder (ASD)

Individuals with ASD experience impairment in forming relationships. Behavior may be unpredictable, including sudden anger outbursts and impulsive self-harming actions. There may be difficulty tolerating separations or other changes. In contrast, BPD patients are more mood reactive to situational stimuli and more expressive; communication is more directed. BPD individuals are more able to respond (although often inappropriately) to environmental sources. ASD patients are more locked into internal stimuli.

Appeal of Cults

Because a person with BPD yearns for direction and acceptance, he may be attracted to strong leaders of disciplined groups. The cult can be very enticing, since it provides instant and unconditional acceptance, automatic intimacy, and a paternalistic leader who will be readily idealized. The borderline individual can be very vulnerable to such a black-and-white world view in which "evil" is personified by the outside world and "good" is encompassed within the cult group.

BPD and Suicide

As many as 70 percent of BPD patients attempt suicide, and the rate of completed suicide approaches 10 percent, almost a thousand times the rate seen in the general population. In the high-risk group of adolescents and young adults (ages fifteen to twenty-nine), BPD was diagnosed in a third of suicide cases. Hopelessness, impulsive aggressiveness, major depression, concurrent drug use, and a history of childhood abuse increase the risk. Among the defining borderline criteria in BPD patients, symptoms of identity disturbance, feelings of emptiness, and fears of abandonment are most closely associated with suicide attempts.[34] Although anxiety symptoms are often associated with suicide in other illnesses, borderline patients who exhibit significant anxiousness are actually *less* likely to commit suicide. A large California study examined subsequent suicide mortality following presentation to an emergency department with deliberate self-harm or suicidal ideation. Within one year, compared to other patients who consulted the ED, suicide was over fifty times higher in patients who initially presented with self-harm and over thirty times higher in those who had appeared with suicidal thoughts.[35]

Premature death not due to suicide is more than two and a half times more common in borderline patients than in comparison groups. The most common causes of these premature deaths include cardiovascular disease (especially heart attacks), substance-related complications (such as liver disease), cancer, and accidents.[36,37,38,39,40]

Clinical Definition of Borderline Personality Disorder

The current official definition of borderline pathology is contained in the DSM-5 diagnostic criteria of Borderline Personality Disorder.[41] This designation emphasizes descriptive, observable behavior. (An alternative model for diagnosis of personality disorders is described in a separate Section III of DSM-5. See Appendix A for a summary of this and other diagnostic proposals.)

The diagnosis of BPD is confirmed when at least five of the following nine criteria are present.

"Others Act Upon Me, Therefore I Am"

Criterion 1. Frantic efforts to avoid real or imagined abandonment.

Just as an infant cannot distinguish between the temporary absence of her mother and her "extinction," the borderline individual often experiences temporary aloneness as perpetual isolation. As a result, she becomes severely depressed over the real or perceived abandonment by significant others and then enraged at the world (or whoever is handy) for depriving her of this basic fulfillment.

Fears of abandonment in someone with BPD can even be measured in the brain. One study utilized positron emission tomography (PET) scanning to demonstrate that women with BPD experienced alterations of blood flow in certain areas of the brain when exposed to memories of abandonment.[42] Particularly when they are alone, borderline patients may lose the sensation of existing, of feeling real. Rather than embracing Descartes's "I think, therefore I am" principle of existence, they live by a philosophy closer to "Others act upon me, therefore I am."

The theologian and philosopher Paul Tillich wrote that "loneliness can be conquered only by those who can bear solitude." Because the borderline person finds solitude so difficult to tolerate, she is trapped in a relentless metaphysical loneliness from which the only relief comes in the form of the physical presence of others. So she will often rush to singles bars or other crowded haunts, often with disappointing—or even violent—results. As the twentieth century wound to a close, thousands of singles bars closed down, to be replaced briefly by lavish nightclubs geared toward younger clienteles, but both milieus were doomed to extinction by online dating services. In the grips of the Great Recession and saddled by enormous student loan debt, Gen Xers and millennials could "meet" hundreds of potential Mr. or Ms. Rights for the same price as a nightclub bar tab, though the price may turn out to be just as high in terms of disappointment and loneliness. (For further discussion, see chapter 4.)

In *Marilyn: An Untold Story*, Norman Rosten recalled Marilyn Monroe's hatred of being alone. Without people constantly around her, she would fall into a void, "endless and terrifying."[43]

For most of us, solitude is longed for, cherished, a rare opportunity to reflect on memories and matters important to our well-being—a chance to get back in touch with ourselves, to rediscover who we are: "The walls of an empty room are mirrors that double and redouble our sense of ourselves," the late John Updike wrote in *The Centaur*.

But the borderline character, with only the weakest sense of self, looks back at only vacant reflections. Solitude recapitulates the panic that he experienced as a child when faced with the prospect of abandonment by parents: Who will take care of me? The pain of loneliness can be relieved only by the rescue of a fantasized lover, as expressed in the lyrics of countless love songs.

The Relentless Search for Mr./Ms. Right

> **Criterion 2. Unstable and intense interpersonal relationships, with marked shifts in attitudes toward others (from idealization to devaluation or from clinging dependency to isolation and avoidance).**

The borderline adult's unstable relationships are directly related to his intolerance of separation and fear of intimacy. He is typically dependent, clinging, and idealizing until the lover, spouse, or friend repels or frustrates these needs with some sort of rejection or indifference; then he caroms to the other extreme—devaluation, resistance to intimacy, and outright avoidance. A continual tug-of-war develops between the wish to merge and be taken care of, on the one hand, and the fear of engulfment, on the other. In BPD, engulfment means the obliteration of separate identity, the loss of autonomy, and a feeling of nonexistence. He vacillates between a desire for closeness, to relieve the emptiness and boredom, and a fear of intimacy, which is perceived as the thief of self-confidence and independence.

In relationships, these internal feelings are dramatically translated into intense, shifting, manipulative couplings. Someone with BPD often makes unrealistic demands of others, appearing to observers as spoiled. Manipulativeness is manifested through physical complaints and hypochondriasis, expressions of weakness and helplessness, provocative actions, and masochistic behaviors. Suicidal threats or gestures are often used to obtain attention and rescue. She may use seduction as a manipulative strategy, even with someone known to be inappropriate and inaccessible, such as a therapist or a minister.

Though very sensitive to others, the borderline person sometimes lacks true empathy, especially for those closest to him. He may be dismayed to encounter an acquaintance, such as teacher, coworker, or therapist, outside of his usual place of business because it is difficult to conceive of that person as having a separate life. Furthermore, he may not understand or be extremely jealous of his therapist's separate life, or even of other patients he may encounter. This "borderline empathy paradox" reflects the theory that patients with BPD experience heightened sensitivity for social cues but are impaired in integrating this interpersonal information.[44] It has also been observed that borderline patients empathize more with people in distressful or negative situations than with people in positive social situations. This may reflect their greater familiarity with negative emotions and situations. One study examined the effect of intranasal oxytocin on empathy in borderline women. Oxytocin is a hormone that promotes social sensitivity and trust. In the study, borderline women showed an increased positive effect in emotional empathy (feeling another's pain) but not in cognitive empathy (understanding the ramifications of another's pain).[45]

The borderline identity lacks *object constancy,* the ability to understand others as complex human beings who nonetheless can relate in consistent ways. She experiences another on the basis of the current encounter, rather than on a broader-based, consistent series of interactions. Therefore, a constant, predictable perception of another person never emerges—as if afflicted with a kind of targeted amnesia, she continues to respond to that person as someone new on each occasion.

Because of the borderline individual's inability to see the big picture, to learn from previous mistakes, and to observe patterns in his own behavior, he often repeats destructive relationships. A female with BPD, for example, will typically return to her abusive ex-husband, who proceeds to abuse her again; a BPD male frequently couples with similar inappropriate men or women with whom he repeats sadomasochistic affiliations. Since the borderline character's dependency is often disguised as passion, she remains in the destructive relationship "because I love him." Later, when the relationship disintegrates, one partner can blame the other's pathology. Thus, as is often heard in the therapist's office, "My first wife/husband was a borderline!"

The borderline condition's endless quest is to find a perfect caregiver who will be all-giving and omnipresent. The search often leads to partners with complementary pathology: both lack insight into their mutual destructiveness. For example, Michelle desperately craves protection and comfort from a man. Amin displays bravura self-assurance; even though the self-assurance covers his deep insecurity, it fits the bill for Michelle. Just as Michelle needs Amin to be her protective white knight, so Amin needs Michelle to remain helpless and dependent on his beneficence. After a while, both fail to live up to their assigned stereotypes. Amin cannot bear the narcissistic wounds of challenge or failure and begins to cover his frustrations by drinking too much and by physically abusing Michelle. Michelle bristles under his controlling yoke yet becomes frightened when she sees his weaknesses. The dissatisfactions lead to more provocation and more conflict.

Afflicted with self-loathing, the borderline person distrusts others' expressions of caring. Like Groucho Marx, he would never belong to a club that would have him as a member. Sam, for example, was a twenty-one-year-old college student whose chief complaint in therapy was "I need a date." An attractive man with serious interpersonal problems, Sam characteristically approached women he deemed inaccessible. However, whenever his overtures were accepted, he immediately devalued the woman as no longer desirable.

All of these characteristics make it difficult to achieve meaningful intimacy. As Carrie relates, "A few men have wanted to marry me, but I have a big problem with getting close or being touched. I can't tolerate it." The borderline self cannot seem to gain enough independence to be dependent in healthy, rather than desperate, ways. True sharing is sacrificed to a demanding dependency and a desperate need to merge with another person in order to complete one's own identity, as kind of Siamese twins of the soul. And when the relationship is threatened, the borderline person may feel like a piece of herself is ripped away. "You complete me," the famous line from the film *Jerry Maguire*, turns into an elusive goal that is always just out of reach.

Who Am I?

Criterion 3. Marked and persistent identity disturbance manifested by an unstable self-image or sense of self.

In BPD, there is a lack of a constant core sense of identity, just as there is a lack of a constant core conceptualization of others. The borderline individual does not accept her own intelligence, attractiveness, or sensitivity as constant traits, but rather as comparative qualities to be continually re-earned and judged against others'. She may view herself as intelligent, for example, based solely on the results of a just-administered IQ test. Later that day when she makes a "dumb mistake," she will revert to seeing herself as "stupid." She considers herself attractive until she spies a woman whom she feels is prettier; then she feels ugly. Surely she envies the self-acceptance of Popeye, who maintains "I yam what I yam." As in her close relationships, the borderline identity becomes mired in a kind of amnesia—about herself. The past becomes obfuscated; she is much like the demanding boss who continually asks herself and others, "Yeah, so? What have you done for me lately?"

In BPD her worthiness is graded on the curve, compared to others, but identity is evaluated in isolation. Who she is (and what she does) today determines her status, with little regard to what has come before. She allows herself no laurels on which to rest. Like Sisyphus, she is doomed to roll the boulder repeatedly up the hill, needing to prove herself over and over again. Self-esteem is attained only through impressing others, so pleasing others becomes critical to loving herself.

In his book *Marilyn*, Norman Mailer describes how Marilyn Monroe's search for identity became her driving force, absorbing all aspects of her life:

> What an obsession is identity! We search for it, because the private sensation when we are in our own identity is that we feel sincere as we speak, we feel *real*, and this little phenomenon of good feeling conceals an existential mystery as important to psychology as the *cogito ergo sum*—it is nothing less than that the emotional condition of feeling real is, for whatever reason, so far superior to the feeling of a void in oneself that it can become for protagonists like Marilyn a motivation more powerful than the instinct of sex, or the hunger for position or money. Some will give up love or security before they dare to lose the comfort of identity.[46]

Later, Marilyn found sustenance in acting, particularly using the Method:

> Actors in the Method will *act out*; their technique is designed like psychoanalysis itself, to release emotional lava, and thereby enable the actor to become acquainted with his depths, then possess them enough to become possessed by his role. A magical transaction. We can think of Marlon Brando in *A Streetcar*

Named Desire. To be possessed by a role is *satori* (or intuitive illumination) for an actor because one's identity can feel whole so long as one is living in the role.[47]

The borderline struggle in establishing a consistent identity is related to a prevailing sense of inauthenticity—a constant sense of "faking it." Most of us experience this sensation at various times in our lives. When one starts a new job, for example, one tries to exude an air of knowledge and confidence. After one gains experience, the confidence becomes increasingly genuine because one has learned the system and no longer needs to fake it. As Kurt Vonnegut wrote in *Mother Night,* "We are what we pretend to be, so we must be careful about what we pretend to be." Or as some phrase it, "Fake it till you make it."

The borderline adult never reaches that point of confidence. He continues to feel like he is faking it and is terrified that he will sooner or later be "found out." This is particularly true when he achieves some kind of success—it feels misplaced, undeserved.

This chronic sense of being a fake or sham probably originates in childhood. As explored in chapter 3, the pre-borderline child often grows up feeling inauthentic due to various environmental circumstances—suffering physical or sexual abuse or being forced to adopt an adult's role while still a child or to parent his own sick parent. At the other extreme, he may be discouraged from maturing and separating, and may be trapped in a dependent child's role, well past an appropriate time for separation. In all of these situations, the emerging borderline identity never develops a separate sense of self but continues to "fake" a role that is prescribed by someone else. ("He never chooses an opinion," was how Leo Tolstoy described one of his characters, "he just wears whatever happens to be in style.") If he fails in the role, he fears he will be punished; if he succeeds, he is sure he will soon be uncovered as a fraud and be humiliated.

Unrealistic attempts at achieving a state of perfection are often part of the borderline pattern. For example, a borderline patient with anorexia might try to maintain a constant low weight and become horrified if it varies as little as one pound, unaware that this expectation is unrealistic. Perceiving themselves as static, rather than in a dynamic state of change, individuals with BPD may view any variation from this inflexible self-image as shattering.

Conversely, the borderline adult may search for satisfaction in the opposite direction—by frequently changing jobs, careers, goals, friends, and sometimes even gender. By altering external situations and making drastic changes in lifestyle, he hopes to achieve inner contentment. Some instances of so-called midlife crisis or male menopause represent an extreme attempt to ward off fears of mortality or deal with disappointments in life choices. A borderline adolescent may constantly change his clique of friends—from "jocks" to "burnouts" to "brains" to "geeks"—hoping to achieve a sense of belonging and acceptance. Even sexual identity can be a source of confusion in the borderline experience.

Cult groups that promise unconditional acceptance, a structured social framework, and a circumscribed identity are powerful attractions for the borderline personality. When the individual's identity and value system merge with the accepting group's, the faction's leader assumes extraordinary power. Keith Raniere, who founded the cult Nxivm, maintained a harem of sex slaves who submitted to branding, until his conviction for sex trafficking and other crimes in 2019. The leader's influence may extend to the point where he can induce followers to emulate his actions, even if fatal, as witnessed by the Jonestown Massacre in 1978, the fatal conflict with Branch Davidians in 1993, and the mass suicides of the Heaven's Gate cult in 1997. Aaron, after dropping out of college, attempted to assuage his feelings of aimlessness by joining the "Moonies." He left the cult after two years, only to return after two more years of directionless wandering among different cities and jobs. Ten months later he left the group again, but this time, lacking a stable set of goals or a comfortable sense of who he was or what he wanted, he attempted suicide.

The phenomenon of "cluster suicides," especially among teenagers, may reflect weaknesses in identity formation. The national suicide rate rises dramatically after the suicide of a famous person, such as Marilyn Monroe, Kurt Cobain, or Robin Williams. The same dynamics may operate among adolescents with fragile identity structures: they are susceptible to the suicidal tendencies of the peer group leader or of another suicidal teenage group in the same region.

The Impulsive Character

> Criterion 4. Impulsiveness in at least two areas that are potentially self-destructive, e.g., substance abuse, sexual promiscuity, gambling, reckless driving, shoplifting, excessive spending, or overeating.

Borderline behaviors may be sudden and contradictory, since they result from strong momentary feelings—perceptions that represent isolated, unconnected snapshots of experience. The immediacy of the present exists in isolation, without the benefit of the experience of the past or the hopefulness of the future. Because historical patterns, consistency, and predictability are unavailable to the borderline experience, similar impulsive mistakes are repeated again and again. Christopher Nolan's 2000 film *Memento* presents metaphorically what the borderline individual faces on a regular basis. Afflicted with short-term memory loss, insurance investigator Leonard Selby must hang Polaroids and Post-it Notes all over his room—and even tattoo messages on his own body—to remind himself what has happened only hours or minutes before. (In one car-chase scene, trying to avenge his wife's murder, he cannot remember if he is chasing someone or being chased!) The film dramatically illustrates the loneliness of a man who constantly feels "like I just woke up." Limited patience and need for immediate gratification may be connected to behaviors that define other BPD criteria: Impulsive conflict and rage may emerge from the frustrations of a stormy relationship (criterion 2); precipitous mood changes (criterion 6) may result in impulsive outbursts; inappropriate outbursts of anger (criterion 8) may develop from a failure to control impulses; self-destructive or self-mutilating behaviors (criterion 5) may result from the borderline individual's severe frustrations. Often, impulsive actions such as drug and alcohol abuse serve as defenses against feelings of loneliness and abandonment. MRI studies have demonstrated alterations in blood flow in specific areas of the cortex in borderline patients with high impulsivity scores compared to circulation in those areas in control subjects.[48]

Joyce was a thirty-one-year-old divorced woman who increasingly turned to alcohol after her divorce and her husband's subsequent remarriage. Though attractive and talented, she let her work deteriorate and spent more time at bars. "I made a career out of avoiding," she later said. When the pain of being alone and feeling abandoned became too great, she would use alcohol as anesthesia. She would sometimes pick up men and take them home with her. Characteristically, after such alcohol or sexual binges, she would berate herself with guilt and feel deserving of her husband's abandonment. Then the cycle would start again, as she required more punishment for her worthlessness. Thus, impulsive self-destructive behaviors became both a means of avoiding pain and a mechanism for inflicting it as expiation for her sins.

Self-Destruction

> **Criterion 5. Recurrent suicidal threats, gestures, or behavior, or self-mutilating behaviors.**

Suicidal threats and gestures—reflecting both the propensity for overwhelming depression and hopelessness and the knack for manipulating others—are prominent features of BPD. Self-harming behavior is both a cry for help and a self-imposed punishment for being "bad."

As many as 75 percent of BPD patients have a history of self-mutilation, and the vast majority of those have made at least one suicide attempt.[49] The most common type of self-harm is cutting, but burning, overdosing, reckless risk-taking, self-beating, and other types of self-harm also occur.[50] Often, the frequent threats or half-hearted suicide attempts are not a wish to die but rather a way to communicate pain and a plea for others to intervene. Unfortunately, when habitually repeated, these suicidal gestures often lead to just the opposite scenario—others get fed up and stop responding, which may result in progressively more serious attempts. Suicidal behavior is one of the most difficult BPD symptoms for family and therapists to cope with: addressing it can result in endless unproductive confrontations; ignoring it can result in death (see chapter 6). Although many of the defining criteria for BPD diminish over time, including self-harming threats, the risk of suicide persists throughout the life cycle.[51,52] Borderline patients with a childhood history of sexual abuse are ten times more likely to attempt suicide.[53]

BPD is the only medical diagnosis partially defined by self-injuring behavior. Self-mutilation—except when clearly associated with psychosis—is a hallmark of BPD. This behavior may take the form of self-inflicted wounds to the genitals, limbs, or torso. For these borderline patients, the body becomes a road map highlighted with a lifetime tour of self-inflicted scars. Razors, scissors, fingernails, and lit cigarettes are some of the more common instruments used; excessive use of drugs, alcohol, or food can also inflict the damage. Suicide is not the intent of self-mutilation, although death can come accidentally if the cut is too deep, the burn too intense, the self-injury too extreme.

Often, self-mutilation begins as an impulsive self-punishing action, but over time it may become a studied, ritualistic procedure. In such instances the borderline patient may carefully scar body areas that are covered by clothing—which illustrates his intense ambivalence: he feels compelled to flamboyantly self-punish, yet he carefully conceals the evidence of his tribulation. Though many people get tattoos for decorative reasons, on a societal level the increasing fascination with tattoos and piercings over the past three decades may be less a fashion trend than a reflection of borderline tendencies in society (see chapter 4). Sometimes the desperate need to fit in may stimulate a person with BPD (usually an adolescent) to "copycat" cutting or to carve words or names in her skin.

Jennifer (see chapter 1) would fulfill her need to self-inflict pain by scratching her wrists, abdomen, and waist, leaving deep finger-nail marks that could easily be covered.

Sometimes the self-punishment is more indirect. The borderline person may claim to be the victim of a string of "accidents" or may provoke frequent fights in which he feels less directly responsible; circumstances or others provide the violence for him.

When Carlos, for example, broke up with his girlfriend, he blamed his parents. They had not been supportive enough or friendly enough, he thought, and when she ended the affair after six years, he was forlorn. At twenty-eight he continued to live in an apartment paid for by his parents and worked sporadically in his father's office. Earlier in his life he had attempted suicide but decided he wouldn't give his parents "the satisfaction" of killing himself. Instead, he engaged in increasingly dangerous behaviors. He had numerous automobile accidents, some while intoxicated, and continued to drive despite the revocation of his driver's license. He frequented bars where he sometimes picked fights with much bigger men. Carlos recognized the destructiveness of his behavior and sometimes wished that "one of these times I would just die."

These dramatic self-destructive behaviors and threats may be explained in several ways. The self-inflicted pain may reflect the need to feel, to escape an encapsulating numbness. Those with BPD may form a kind of insulating bubble that not only protects them from emotional hurt but also serves as a barrier from the sensations of reality. The experience of pain, then, becomes an important link to existence. Often, however, the inflicted pain is not strong enough to transcend this barrier (though the blood and scars may be fascinating to observe), in which case the frustration may compel him to increase the number of attempts to induce pain or the amount of pain self-inflicted.

Self-induced pain can also function as a distraction from other forms of suffering. One patient, when feeling lonely or afraid, would cut different parts of her body as a way "to take my mind off" the loneliness. Another would bang her head in the throes of stress-related migraine headaches. Relief of inner tension may be the most common reason for self-harming.[54]

Self-damaging behavior can also serve as an expiation for sin. One man, guilt-ridden after the breakup of his marriage, for which he totally blamed himself, would repeatedly drink gin—a taste he abhorred—until reaching the point of retching. Only after enduring this discomfort and humiliation would he feel redeemed and able to return to his usual routine.

Painful, self-destructive behavior may be employed in an attempt to constrict actions that are felt to be dangerously out of control. One adolescent boy cut his hands and penis to dissuade himself from masturbation, an act he considered loathsome. He hoped that the memory of the pain would prevent him from further indulging in this repugnant behavior.

Impulsive self-destructive acts (or threats) may result from a wish to punish another person, often a close relation. One woman persistently described in great detail her promiscuous behavior (often involving degrading masochistic rituals) to her boyfriend. These affairs invariably occurred when she was angry and wanted to punish him.

Finally, self-destructive behavior can evolve from a manipulative need for sympathy or rescue. One woman, after arguments with her boyfriend, repeatedly slashed her wrists in his presence, forcing him to secure medical assistance for her.

Many with BPD deny feeling pain during self-mutilation and even report a calm euphoria after it. Before hurting themselves, they may experience great tension, anger, or overwhelming sadness; afterward there is a sensation of discharge and relief from anxiety, like the release that occurs when one is building a higher and higher tower of blocks that eventually teeters and collapses.

This relief may result from psychological or physiological factors, or a combination of both. Physicians have long recognized that following severe physical trauma, such as battle wounds, the patient may experience an unexpected calm and a kind of natural anesthesia despite the lack of medical attention. Some have noted that during such times, the body releases biological substances, called endorphins, the body's internal opiate drugs (like morphine or heroin), which serve as the organism's self-treatment of pain. When exposed to controlled pain experiences, BPD patients exhibit differences in brain circuit connectivity as measured by an MRI. These affected brain regions are associated with cognitive and emotional perceptions of pain.[55]

Radical Mood Shifts

Criterion 6. Affective instability due to marked reactivity of mood, with severe episodic shifts to depression, irritability, or anxiety, usually lasting a few hours and only rarely more than a few days.

The borderline individual undergoes abrupt and extreme mood shifts, lasting for short periods—usually hours. His base mood is not usually calm and controlled, but more often either hyperactive and irrepressible or pessimistic, cynical, and depressed. These mood shifts are usually responses to the immediate situation and may be way out of proportion to the circumstances.

Audrey was giddy with excitement as she flooded Owen with kisses after he surprised her with flowers he bought on the way home from work. As he washed up for dinner, Audrey took a call from her mother, who again berated her for not calling to ask about her constant body aches. By the time Owen returned from the bathroom, Audrey had mutated into a raging shrew, screaming at him for not helping with dinner. He could only sit there, stunned and perplexed at the transformation.

Justin was rushed to the emergency room by his girlfriend after increasing expressions of desperation and intention to overdose. On admission to the psychiatric unit, he tearfully expressed his hopelessness and persistent wishes to die to the nurse, sobbing uncontrollably. Yet literally minutes later he was spied laughing and joking with his new roommate.

Always Half Empty

Criterion 7. Chronic feelings of emptiness.

Lacking a core sense of identity, individuals with BPD commonly experience a painful loneliness that motivates them to search for ways to fill up the "holes." At other times they may simply withdraw and resist seeking help.

The painful, almost physical sensation is lamented by Shakespeare's Hamlet: "I have of late,—but wherefore I know not,—lost all my mirth, forgone all custom of exercises; and indeed it goes so heavily with my disposition, that this goodly frame, the earth, seems to me a sterile promontory."

Tolstoy defined boredom as "the desire for desires"; in this context it can be seen that the borderline search for a way to relieve the boredom often results in impulsive ventures into destructive acts and disappointing relationships. In many ways the borderline character seeks out a new relationship or experience not for its positive aspects but as an escape from the feeling of emptiness, acting out the existential destinies of characters described by Sartre, Camus, and other philosophers.

The borderline person frequently endures a kind of existential angst, which can be a major obstacle in treatment, for it saps the motivational energy to get well. From this feeling state radiate many of the other features of BPD. Suicide may appear to be the only rational response to a perpetual state of emptiness. The need to fill the void or relieve the boredom can lead to outbursts of anger and self-damaging impulsiveness—especially drug abuse. Abandonment may be more acutely felt. Relationships may be impaired. A stable sense of self cannot be established in an empty shell. And mood instability may result from the feelings of loneliness. Indeed, depression and feelings of emptiness often reinforce each other.

Raging Bull

Criterion 8. Inappropriate, intense anger, or lack of control of anger, e.g., frequent displays of temper, constant anger, recurrent physical fights.

Along with affective instability, anger is a persistent symptom of BPD over time.[56]

Outbursts of rage are as unpredictable as they are frightening. Violent scenes are disproportionate to the frustrations that trigger them. Domestic fracases that may involve chases with butcher knives and thrown dishes are typical of borderline rage. The anger may be sparked by a particular (and often trivial) offense, but underneath the spark lies an arsenal of fear from the threat of disappointment and abandonment. After a disagreement over a trivial remark about their contrasting painting styles, Vincent van Gogh picked up a butcher knife and chased his good friend Paul Gauguin around his house and out the door. He then turned his rage on himself, using the same knife to slice off a section of his ear.

The rage, so intense and so near the surface, is often directed at those close to the BPD person—spouse, children, parents. Borderline anger may represent a cry for help, a testing of devotion, or a fear of intimacy—whatever the underlying factors, it pushes away those whom he needs most. The spouse, friend, lover, or family member who sticks around despite these assaults may be very patient and understanding, or, sometimes, very disturbed himself. In the face of these eruptions, empathy is difficult, and the relation must draw on every resource at hand in order to cope (see chapter 5).

The rage often carries over to the therapeutic setting, where psychiatrists and other mental health professionals become the target. Carrie, for example, often raged against her therapist, constantly looking for ways to test his commitment to staying with her in therapy. At times she would storm out of her therapist's office and command the secretary to cancel her future appointments. Then she would call back the next day and ask to reschedule. The secretary soon learned to postpone adjusting Carrie's appointments! Treatment becomes precarious in this situation (see chapter 7), and therapists may drop (or "fire") borderline patients for this reason. Many therapists will try to limit the number of borderline patients they treat.

Sometimes I Act Crazy—Lies, Damned Lies, and Delusions

Criterion 9. Transient, stress-related paranoid thoughts or symptoms of severe dissociation.

The most common psychotic experiences for BPD patients involve feelings of unreality and paranoid delusions. Unreality feelings involve dissociation from usual perceptions. The individual or those around her feel unreal. Some experience a kind of internal splitting, in which they feel different aspects of their personality emerge in different situations. Distorted perceptions can involve any of the five senses.

The borderline adult may become transiently psychotic when confronted with stressful situations (such as feeling abandoned) or placed in very unstructured surroundings. For example, therapists have observed episodes of psychosis during classical psychoanalysis, which relies heavily on free association and uncovering past trauma in an unstructured setting. Psychosis may also be stimulated by illicit drug use. Unlike patients with psychotic illnesses, such as schizophrenia, mania, psychotic depression, or organic/drug illnesses, borderline psychosis is usually of shorter duration and perceived as more acutely frightening to the patient and extremely different from his ordinary experience. And yet, to the outside world, the presentation of psychosis in BPD may be indistinguishable, in the acute form, from the psychotic experiences of these other illnesses. The main difference is duration. Within hours or days, the breaks with reality may disappear, as the borderline patient recalibrates to usual functioning, unlike other forms of psychosis.

Dr. Jill Sanchez, the on-call psychiatric resident, was summoned to evaluate Lorenzo, a disheveled twenty-three-year-old graduate student brought to the emergency department by his roommate. The roommate described increasing paranoid and bizarre behavior over the last twenty-four hours. Lorenzo had been under increasing pressure completing his graduate dissertation while confronting family issues since the recent death of his father. He was unable to sleep and was eating little. Lorenzo had begun mumbling to himself, then suddenly yelling at his dissertation adviser as if he were in their apartment. He voiced fears that the university was against him and wanted him to fail. He accused his roommate of being part of the conspiracy. He said he had to leap into a different dimension, since he was now no longer existing in this world.

In her assessment Dr. Sanchez uncovered no previous documented psychiatric history or family history of mental illness. A drug screen ruled out drug use. The roommate confirmed no previous unusual behavior, although he did describe Lorenzo as "volatile," with occasional extreme mood swings and infrequent disproportionate anger outbursts. Dr. Sanchez admitted Lorenzo to the psychiatric unit with a tentative diagnosis of incipient schizophrenia. She administered a low dose of a sedating antipsychotic, hoping to ease his anxiety and promote sleep.

The next morning Lorenzo appeared to be a different person. Freshly showered and cleaned up, he was calm and responsive to the doctor. His memory of the past two days was spotty, but he confirmed that he had been feeling overwhelmed with school and family stressors. He conveyed embarrassment as he vaguely recalled his agitated and suspicious behavior. He felt the good night's sleep had been a great relief, and since he was feeling better, requested discharge so he could return to school. At the doctor's insistence Lorenzo agreed to stay in the hospital one more day, during which he spent his time helping the nurses with other agitated patients. At discharge, Lorenzo acknowledged his need to better handle school pressure. He also conceded that the death of his father had stirred up much anxiety over past family conflicts. Lorenzo agreed to follow up with a psychiatrist.

The Borderline Mosaic

BPD is clearly becoming acknowledged by mental health profession-als as one of the more common psychiatric maladies in the USA. The professional must be able to recognize the features of BPD to effec-tively treat large numbers of patients. The layperson must be able to recognize them to better understand those with whom he shares his life.

While digesting this chapter, the astute reader will observe that these symptoms typically interact; they are less like isolated lakes than streams that feed into one another and eventually merge into rivers and then into bays or oceans. They are also interdependent. The deep furrows etched by these floods of emotions inform not only the borderline character but also parts of the culture in which he lives. How these markings are formed in the individual and reflected in our society is explored in the next chapters.

Chapter Three

Roots of the Borderline Syndrome

All happy families resemble one another; every unhappy family is unhappy in its own fashion.

—From *Anna Karenina*, by Leo Tolstoy

Growing up was not easy for Dixie Anderson. Her father was rarely at home, and when he was, he didn't say much. For years, she didn't even know what he did for a living, just that he was gone all the time. Margaret, Dixie's mother, called him a workaholic. Throughout her childhood, Dixie sensed that her mother was hiding something, though Dixie was never quite sure what it was.

But when Dixie turned eleven, things changed. She was an "early developer," as her mother put it, though Dixie really wasn't sure what that meant. All she knew was that her father was suddenly home more than he had ever been, and he was also more attentive. Dixie enjoyed the new attention and the new feeling of power she had over him when he was finished touching her. After he was done, he would do whatever she asked of him.

About this same time, Dixie suddenly became more popular in the family's affluent suburban Chicago neighborhood. The kids began to offer her their secret stashes of pot and, a few years later, mushrooms and ecstasy.

Middle school was a drag. Halfway through a school day, she'd wind up fighting with some of the other kids, which did not rattle her at all: she was tough; she had friends and drugs; she was cool. Once she even punched her science teacher, whom she felt was a real jerk. He didn't take it well at all and went to the principal, who expelled her.

At age thirteen she saw her first psychiatrist, who diagnosed her as hyperactive and treated her with several medications that didn't make her feel anywhere near as good as weed. She decided to run away. She packed an overnight bag, took a bus to the interstate, stuck out her thumb, and in a few minutes was on her way to Las Vegas.

The way Margaret saw it, no matter what she did, it always seemed to turn out the same with Dixie: her older daughter could not be pleased. Dixie had obviously inherited her dad's genes, always criticizing the way Margaret looked and the way she kept the house. Margaret had tried everything to lose weight—amphetamines, booze, even gastric stapling—yet nothing seemed to work. She'd always been fat, always would be.

She often wondered why Roger had married her. He was a handsome man; from the beginning she could not understand why he wanted her. After a while it was obvious he didn't want her: he simply stopped coming home at night.

Dixie was the one bright spot in Margaret's life. Her younger daughter, Julie, was already obese at age five and seemed a lost cause. But Margaret would do anything for Dixie. She clung to her daughter like a lifeline. But the more Margaret clung, the more Dixie resented it. She became more demanding, throwing tantrums and screaming about her mother's weight. The doctors could do nothing to help Margaret; they said she was manic-depressive and addicted to alcohol and amphetamines. The last time Margaret was in the hospital they gave her electroshock treatment. And now with Roger gone and Dixie always running away, the world was closing in.

After a few frantic months in Vegas, Dixie took off for Los Angeles, which was the same story as Vegas: she was promised cars and money and good times. Well, she had ridden in a lot of cars, but the good times were few and far between. Her friends were losers and sometimes she had to sleep with a guy to "borrow" a few bucks.

Finally, with nothing but a few dollars in her jeans, she went back home.

Dixie arrived to find Roger gone and her mother in a thick fog of depression and drug-induced numbness. With all this bleakness at home, Dixie soon fell back into her alcohol and drug habits. At fifteen she had been hospitalized twice for chemical abuse and was treated by a number of therapists. At sixteen, she became pregnant by a man she had met only a few weeks before. She married him soon after the pregnancy test.

Seven months later, when Kim was born, the marriage began to fall apart. Dixie's husband was a weak and passive oaf who could not get his own life together, much less provide a solid home environment for their child.

By the time the baby was six months old, the marriage was over, and Dixie and Kim moved in with Margaret. It was then that Dixie became obsessed with her weight. She would go entire days without eating, and then eat frantically and voluminously only to vomit it all up in the toilet. What she couldn't get rid of by vomiting she eliminated in other ways: she ate squares of Ex-Lax as if they were candy. She exercised until sweat drenched her clothes and she was too exhausted to move. The pounds dropped off—but her health suffered and her mood worsened. Her periods stopped; her energy waned; her capacity to concentrate weakened. She became very depressed about her life, and for the first time, suicide seemed like a real alternative.

Initially she felt safe and comfortable when she was readmitted to the hospital, but soon her old self returned. By the fourth day, she was trying to seduce her doctor; when he didn't respond, she threatened him with all sorts of retaliation. She demanded extra privileges and special attention from the nurses and refused to participate in unit activities.

As abruptly as she had gone into the hospital, she pronounced herself cured and demanded discharge, just days after admission. Over the next year, she would be readmitted to the hospital several times. She would also see several psychotherapists, none of whom seemed to understand or know how to treat her dramatic mood shifts, her depression, her loneliness, her impulsiveness with men and drugs. She began to doubt that she could ever be happy.

It wasn't long before Margaret and Dixie were again fighting and screaming at each other. For Margaret it was like seeing herself growing up all over again and making the same mistakes. She couldn't bear to watch it any longer.

Margaret's father had been just like Roger, a lonely, unhappy man who had little to do with his family. Her mother ran the family much like Margaret ran hers. And just as Margaret clung to Dixie, so had her mother clung to Margaret, trying desperately to mold her every step of the way. Margaret was fed her mother's ideas and feelings—and enough food for a battalion. By the age of sixteen, she was grossly obese and taking large amounts of amphetamines prescribed by the family doctor to suppress her appetite. By the age of twenty, she was drinking alcohol and taking Fiorinal to bring her down from the amphetamines.

Margaret was never able to please her mother even as the constant struggle for control between them raged on. Nor could Margaret please her own daughter or husband. She had never been able to make anyone happy, she realized, not even herself. Yet she persisted in trying to please people who would not be pleased.

Now, with Roger gone and Dixie so sick, Margaret's life seemed to be falling apart. Dixie finally told her mother how Roger had sexually abused her. And before Roger left, he had bragged all about his women. Despite everything, Margaret still missed him. He was alone, she knew, just like she was.

It was time, Dixie recognized, to do something about the plight of this self-destructive family. Or at least herself anyway. A job would be the first priority, something to combat the relentless boredom. But she was nineteen years old with a two-year-old child and no husband, and she still hadn't graduated from high school.

With characteristic compulsiveness, she flung herself into a high school equivalency program and received her diploma in a matter of months. Within days of obtaining her diploma, she was applying for loans and grants to attend college.

Margaret had begun to take care of Kim, and in many ways the arrangement looked like it might work: raising Kim gave Margaret some meaning in her life, Kim had built-in childcare, and Dixie had time for her new mission in life. But soon the system showed cracks: Margaret sometimes got too drunk or depressed to be of any help. When this happened, Dixie had a simple solution: she would threaten to take Kim away from Margaret. But the grandmother and the granddaughter obviously needed each other desperately, so Dixie was able to totally control the household.

Through it all, Dixie still managed to find time for men, though her frequent liaisons were usually of short duration. She seemed to follow a pattern: whenever a man started to care for her, she became bored. Distant, older men—unavailable doctors, married acquaintances, professors—were her usual type, but she would drop them the instant they responded to her flirtations. The young men she did date were all members of a church that was strictly opposed to premarital sex.

Dixie avoided women and had no female friends. She thought women were weak and uninteresting. Men, at least, had some substance. They were fools if they responded to her flirtations and hypocrites if they did not.

As time went on, the more Dixie succeeded in her studies, the more frightened she became. She could pursue a particular interest—school, a certain man—relentlessly, almost obsessively, but each success spurred ever higher, and more unrealistic, demands. Despite good grades, she would explode in rage and threaten to kill herself when she performed below her expectations on an exam.

At times like these, her mother would try to console her, but Margaret was also becoming preoccupied with suicide, and the roles were often reversed. Mother and daughter were again shuffling in and out of the hospital trying to overcome depression and chemical abuse.

Like her mother and her grandmother, Kim didn't know her father very well. Sometimes he came to visit; sometimes she went to the house that he shared with his mother. He always seemed awkward around her.

With her mother detached and her grandmother ineffectual or preoccupied with her own problems, Kim had taken control of the household by the time she was four. She ignored Dixie, who responded by ignoring her. If Kim threw a tantrum, Margaret would cave in to her wishes.

The household was in an almost constant state of chaos. Sometimes both Margaret and Dixie would be in the hospital at the same time—Margaret for her drinking, Dixie for her bulimia. Kim would then go to her father's house, although he was unable to care for her and would have his own mother tend to her.

On the surface, Kim seemed oddly mature for a six-year-old, despite the chaos around her. To her, other kids were "just kids," without her experience. She didn't think her particular type of maturity was unusual at all: she had seen old photographs of her mother and her grandmother when they were her age, and in the snapshots they all had the same look.

Across Generations

In many respects, the Andersons' saga is typical of borderline cases: the factors contributing to the borderline syndrome often transcend generations. The genealogy of BPD is often rife with deep and long-lasting problems, including suicide, incest, drug abuse, violence, losses, and loneliness.

It has been observed that borderline people often have borderline mothers, who in turn have borderline mothers. This hereditary predisposition to BPD prompts a number of questions, such as: How do borderline traits develop? How are they passed down through families? Are they, indeed, passed down at all?

In examining the roots of this illness, these questions resurrect the traditional "nature versus nurture" (or *temperament* versus *character*) quandary. The two major theories on the causes of BPD—one emphasizing developmental (psychological) roots, the other constitutional (biological and genetic) origins—reflect the dilemma. Studies indicate that approximately 42 to 55 percent of BPD features are thought to be attributable to genetic influences, the rest derived from environmental experiences.[1,2,3]

In addition to interpersonal stressors and ordeals, environmental influences include sociocultural factors, such as our fast-paced, fragmented societal structure, destruction of the nuclear family, increased divorce rates, increased reliance on nonparental day care, greater geographical mobility, and changing patterns of gender roles (see chapter 4). Though empirical research on these environmental elements is limited, some professionals speculate that these factors would tend to increase the prevalence of BPD.

The available evidence points to no one definitive cause—or even type of cause—of BPD. Rather, genetic, developmental, neurobiological, and social factors all contribute to the development of the illness.

Genetic and Neurobiological Roots: The "Nature" Aspects

Family studies suggest that first-degree relatives of borderline patients are several times more likely to show signs of a personality disorder, especially BPD, than the general public. These close family members are also significantly more likely to exhibit mood, impulse, and substance abuse disorders. In family studies focusing on components of the four major sectors that define BPD (mood, interpersonal, behavioral, cognitive), a single genetic pathway accounted for convergence of these symptoms in family members. One study found that a family member of someone with BPD is almost four times more likely to develop BPD than a nonrelative.[4] Another study of twins examining all nine BPD criteria also concluded that most genetic effects on BPD criteria derive from one heritable general BPD factor. In this research, impulsivity levels in BPD patients appeared to be more highly heritable. In contrast, interpersonal and self-image features were less connected among family members, suggesting these symptoms were more likely influenced by life experiences and were less genetically determined.[5] Some have suggested that a sector on chromosome 9, which encompasses many genes, may be associated with BPD.[6]

It is unlikely that one single gene completely determines BPD; instead, like most medical disorders, many chromosomal loci are involved, some activated or subdued—probably influenced by environmental factors—in the development of what we label BPD. Genes that are determined at birth can also be altered through a process known as epigenetics. Stress or trauma, such as PTSD, can result in DNA methylation, a process that is far beyond the scope of this book; suffice to say here that it is a mechanism that turns a gene on or off.[7] Biological and anatomical correlations with BPD have been demonstrated. In our book *Sometimes I Act Crazy*, we discuss in more detail how specific genes affect neurotransmitters (brain hormones, which relay messages between brain cells).[8] Dysfunction in some of these neurotransmitters, such as serotonin, norepinephrine, dopamine, glutamate, and others, are associated with impulsivity, mood disorders, dissociation, and other characteristics of BPD. These neurotransmitters also affect the balance of glucose, adrenaline, and steroid production in the body. Oxytocin, sometimes dubbed the "love hormone," for its association with maternal bonding, increased socialization, and decreased anxiety, may be dysregulated by BPD. Studies have demonstrated paradoxical reactions to this neuropeptide in the BPD population.[9,10] Disrupted secretion of cortisol, a key substance related to stress response through the endocrine system, is observed in BPD patients.[11] Some of the genes affecting these neurobiological substances have been associated with several psychiatric illnesses. However, studies with variable results demonstrate that *multiple* genes (intersecting with environmental stressors) contribute to the expression of most medical and psychiatric disorders.

In BPD, frequent abuse of food, alcohol, and other drugs—typically interpreted as self-destructive behavior—may also be seen as an attempt to self-medicate inner emotional turmoil. Borderline patients frequently report the calming effects of self-mutilation; rather than feeling pain, they experience soothing relief or distraction from internal psychological pain. Self-mutilation, like any other physical trauma or stress, may result in the release of endorphins—the body's natural narcotic-like substances that provide relief during childbirth, physical traumas, long-distance running, and other physically stressful activities. BPD patients exhibit alterations in the body's endogenous opioid system that affects not only pain perception but also soothing, pleasurable feelings.[12,13]

Changes in brain metabolism and morphology (or structure) are also associated with BPD. Borderline patients express hyperactivity in the part of the brain associated with anger, fear, emotionality, and impulsivity (limbic areas, especially the amygdala), and decreased activity in the section that controls rational thought and regulation of emotions (the prefrontal cortex). In perhaps an oversimplified way, this suggests that in BPD, the evolutionarily more developed, reasoning, "rational" part of the brain is overwhelmed and unable to control the more primitive, instinctual, "impulsive" portion of the mental system. (Similar imbalances are observed in patients suffering from depression and anxiety.) Additionally, volume changes in these parts of the brain are also associated with BPD and are correlated with these physiological changes.[14,15]

In response to external injury or internal stress, the immune system stimulates a cascade of biological interactions resulting in inflammation. This stimulates pro- and anti-inflammatory factors that can be measured in the blood. Inflammatory processes have been associated with several major psychiatric disorders, including major depression, bipolar disorder, schizophrenia, PTSD, obsessive-compulsive disorder, and others.[16] It would not be surprising if some of the features of BPD (anger, impulsivity, etc.) were associated with this kind of autoimmune dysfunction.

These alterations in the brain may be related to brain injury or disease. A significant percentage of borderline patients have a history of brain trauma, encephalitis, epilepsy, learning disabilities, ADHD, and maternal pregnancy complications.[17] These abnormalities are reflected in brain wave (EEG, or electroencephalogram) irregularities, metabolic dysfunction, and reductions in white and gray matter volume.

Since failure to achieve healthy parent-child attachment may result in later character pathology, cognitive impairment on the part of the child and/or the parent may hinder the relationship. As the latest research strongly suggests that BPD is partly inherited, parent and child may both experience dysfunction in cognitive and/or emotional connection. A poor communication fit may perpetuate the insecurities and impulse and affective defects that result in BPD.

Developmental Roots: The Nurture Aspects

Developmental theories on the causes of BPD focus on the delicate interactions between child and caregivers, especially during the first few years of life. The ages between eighteen and thirty months, when the child begins the struggle to gain autonomy, are particularly crucial. Some parents actively resist the child's progression toward separation and insist instead on a controlled, exclusive, often suffocating symbiosis. At the other extreme, other parents offer only erratic parenting or are absent during much of the child-raising period and so fail to provide sufficient attention to, and validation for, the child's feelings and experiences. Either extreme of parental behavior— behavioral over-control and/or emotional under-involvement—can result in the child's failure to develop a positive, stable sense of self and may lead to a constant intense need for attachment and chronic fears of abandonment.

In many cases the broken parent-child relationship takes the more severe form of early parental loss or prolonged traumatic separation, or both. As with Dixie, many borderline children have an absent or psychologically disturbed father. Primary mother figures (who may sometimes be the father) tend to be erratic and depressed and have significant psychopathology themselves, often BPD. The borderline family background is frequently marked by incest, violence, and/or alcoholism. Many cases show an ongoing hostile or combative relationship between mother and pre-borderline child.

Object Relations Theory and Separation-Individuation in Infancy and Childhood

Object relations theory, a model of infant development, emphasizes the significance of the child's interactions with his environment, as opposed to internal psychic instincts and biological drives unconnected to sensations outside himself. According to this theory, the child's relationships with "objects" (people and things) in his environment determine his later functioning. A major result is the child's failure to feel connected, or "attached."

The primary object relations model for the early phases of infant development was created by Margaret Mahler and colleagues.[18] They postulated that the infant's first one to two months of life were characterized by an obliviousness to everything except himself (the *autistic phase*). During the next four or five months, designated the *symbiotic phase*, he begins to recognize others in his universe, not as separate beings, but as extensions of himself.

In the following *separation-individuation period*, extending through ages two to three years, the child begins to separate and disengage from the primary caregiver and begins to establish a separate sense of self. Mahler and others consider the child's ability to navigate through this phase of development successfully to be crucial for later mental health.

During the entire separation-individuation period, the developing child begins to sketch out boundaries between self and others, a task complicated by two central conflicts—the desire for autonomy versus closeness and dependency needs, and fear of engulfment versus fear of abandonment.

A further complicating factor during this time is that the developing infant tends to perceive each individual in the environment as two separate personae. For example, when mother is comforting and sensitive, she is seen as "all-good." When she is unavailable or unable to comfort and soothe, she is perceived as a separate "all-bad" mother. When she leaves his sight, the infant perceives her as annihilated, gone forever, and cries for her return to relieve the despair and panic. As the child develops, this normal "splitting" is replaced by a healthier integration of mother's good and bad traits, and separation anxiety is replaced by the knowledge that mother exists even when she is not physically present and will in time return—a phenomenon commonly known as *object constancy* (see below). Prevailing over these developmental milestones is the child's developing brain, which can sabotage normal adaptation.

Mahler divides separation-individuation into four overlapping subphases.

DIFFERENTIATION PHASE (5–8 MONTHS). In this phase of development, the infant becomes aware of a world separate from mother. Social smiling begins—a reaction to the environment, but directed mostly at mother. Near the end of this phase, the infant displays the opposite side of this same response—stranger anxiety, the recognition of unfamiliar people in the environment.

If the relationship with mother is supportive and comforting, reactions to strangers are mainly characterized by curious wonder. If the relationship is unsupportive, anxiety is more prominent; the child begins to divide positive and negative emotions toward other individuals, relying on splitting to cope with these conflicting emotions.

(It remains unknown what effect the prolonged social distancing imposed by the Covid-19 pandemic may have on infants later in life. Where social interactions are limited, the development of differentiating reactions to mother figures and strangers is compromised.)

PRACTICING PHASE (8–16 MONTHS). The practicing phase is marked by the infant's increasing ability to move away from mother, first by crawling, then by walking. These short separations are punctuated by frequent reunions to check in and refuel, behavior that demonstrates the child's first ambivalence toward his developing autonomy.

RAPPROCHEMENT PHASE (16–25 MONTHS). In the rapprochement phase, the child's expanding world sparks the recognition that he possesses an identity separate from those around him. Reunions with mother and the need for her approval shape the deepening realization that she and others are separate real people. It is in the rapprochement phase, however, that both child and mother confront conflicts that will determine future vulnerability to the borderline syndrome.

The parent's role during this time is to encourage the child's experiments with individuation, yet simultaneously provide a constant supportive refueling reservoir. The normal two-year-old not only develops a strong bond with parents but also learns to separate temporarily from them with sadness rather than with rage or tantrum. The so-called terrible twos represent some of the conflict during this transition. When reunited with the parent, the child is likely to feel happy as well as angry over the separation. The nurturing mother empathizes with the child and accepts the anger without retaliation. After many separations and reunions, the child develops an enduring sense of self, love and trust for parents (attachment), and a healthy ambivalence toward others.

In theory, the mother of a pre-borderline child, however, tends to respond to her child in a different way—either by pushing her child away prematurely and discouraging reunion (perhaps due to her own fear of closeness) or by insisting on a clinging symbiosis (perhaps due to her own fear of abandonment and need for intimacy). In either case, the child becomes burdened by intense fears of abandonment and/or engulfment that are mirrored back to him by the mother's own fears.

As a result, the child never grows into an emotionally separate human being. Later in life, the borderline adult's inability to achieve intimacy in personal relationships reflects this infant stage. When an adult with BPD confronts closeness, she may resurrect from childhood either the devastating feelings of abandonment that always followed her futile attempts at intimacy or the feeling of suffocation from mother's constant smothering. Defying such controls risks losing mother's love; satisfying her attempts at intimacy risks losing oneself.

This fear of engulfment is well illustrated by T. E. Lawrence (*Lawrence of Arabia*), who at age thirty-eight writes about his fear of closeness to his overbearing mother: "I have a terror of her knowing anything about my feelings, or convictions, or way of life. If she knew, they would be damaged; violated; no longer mine."[19]

OBJECT CONSTANCY PHASE (25–36 MONTHS). By the end of the second year of life, assuming the previous levels of development have progressed satisfactorily, the child enters the object constancy phase, wherein the child recognizes that the absence of mother (and other primary caregivers) does not automatically mean her annihilation. The child learns to tolerate ambivalence and frustration. The temporary nature of mother's anger is recognized. The child also begins to understand that his own rage will not destroy his mother. He begins to appreciate the concept of unconditional love and acceptance and develops the capacity to share and to empathize. The child becomes more responsive to father and others in the environment. Self-image becomes more positive, despite the self-critical aspects of an emerging conscience.

Aiding the child in all these tasks are transitional objects—the familiar comforts (teddy bears, dolls, blankets) that represent the mother and are carried everywhere by the child to help ease separations. The object's form, smell, and texture are physical representations of the comforting mother. Transitional objects are one of the first compromises made by the developing child in negotiating the conflict between the need to establish autonomy and the need for dependency. This conflict of opposites is the first "dialectic" that a child learns to negotiate. (Such dialectical oppositions are confronted in dialectical behavioral therapy [DBT], one of the treatment approaches to BPD, discussed in more detail in chapter 8.) Eventually, in normal development, the transitional object is abandoned when the child is able to internalize a permanent image of a soothing, protective mother figure.

Developmental theories propose that the individual with BPD is never able to progress to this object constancy stage. Instead, she is fixated at an earlier developmental phase, in which splitting and other defense mechanisms remain prominent.

Because they are locked into a continual struggle to achieve object constancy, trust, and a separate identity, borderline adults continue to rely on transitional objects for soothing. One woman, for example, always carried in her purse a newspaper article that contained quotes from her psychiatrist. When she was under stress, she would pull out the article, calling it her "security blanket." Seeing her doctor's name in print reinforced his existence and his continued interest and concern for her.

Princess Diana also took comfort in transitional objects, keeping a menagerie of stuffed animals—"my family," she called them—at the foot of her bed. As her lover James Hewitt observed, they "lay in a line, about thirty cuddly animals—animals that had been with her in her childhood, which she had tucked up in her bed at Park House and which had comforted her and represented a certain security." When she went on trips, Diana took a favorite teddy bear with her.[20] Hospitalized borderline patients, similarly, often bring teddy bears or other bedtime objects from home to comfort them while in treatment. Ritualized superstitious acts, when carried out to the extreme, may represent borderline utilization of transitional objects. The ballplayer who wears the same socks or refuses to shave while in the midst of a hitting streak, for example, may simply be prone to the superstitions that prevail in sports; only when such behaviors are repeated compulsively and inflexibly and interfere with routine functioning does the person cross the border into the borderline syndrome.

Childhood Conflicts

The child's evolving sense of object constancy is consistently challenged as he progresses through developmental milestones. The toddler, entranced by fairy tales filled with all-good and all-bad characters, encounters numerous situations in which he uses splitting as a primary coping strategy. (Snow White, for example, can be conceptualized only as all good and the evil queen as all bad; the fairy tale does not elicit sympathy for a queen who was perhaps the product of a chaotic upbringing or allow criticism of the heroine's cohabitation with the seven short guys!) Though now trusting in mother's permanent presence, the growing child must still contend with the fear of losing her love. The four-year-old who is scolded for being "bad" may still feel threatened with the withdrawal of his mother's love; he may not yet conceive of the possibility that his mother may be expressing her own frustrations quite apart from his own behavior, nor has he learned that his mother can be angry and yet love him just as much at the same time.

Eventually, children are confronted with the separation anxiety of starting school. "School phobia" is neither a real phobia nor related exclusively to school itself, but instead represents the subtle interplay between the child's anxiety and the reactions of parents who may reinforce the child's clinging with their own ambivalence about the separation.

Adolescent Conflicts

Separation-individuation issues are repeated during adolescence, when questions of identity and closeness to others once again become vital concerns. During both the rapprochement phase of infancy and adolescence, the child's primary mode of relating is less acting than *re*acting to others, especially parents. While the two-year-old tries to elicit approval and admiration from parents by molding his identity to emulate caregivers, the adolescent tries to imitate peers or adopts behaviors that are consciously different—even opposite— from those of the parents. In both stages, the child's behavior is based less on independently determined internal needs than on *re*acting to the significant people in the immediate environment. Behavior then becomes a quest to *discover* identity rather than to reinforce an established one.

An insecure teenager may ruminate endlessly about her boyfriend in a "he loves me, he loves me not" fashion. Failure to integrate these positive and negative emotions and to establish a firm, consistent perception of others leads to continued splitting as a defense mechanism. The borderline adolescent's failure to maintain object constancy results in later problems with sustaining consistent, trusting relationships, establishing a core sense of identity, and tolerating anxiety and frustration.

Often, entire families adopt a borderline system of interaction, with the family members' undifferentiated identities alternately merging with and separating from one another. Melanie, the adolescent daughter in one such family, closely identified with her chronically depressed mother, who felt abandoned by her philandering husband. With her husband often away from home and her other children much younger, the mother latched on to her teenage daughter, relating intimate details of the unhappy marriage and invading the teenager's privacy with intrusive questions about her friends and activities. Melanie's feelings of responsibility for her mother's happiness interfered to the point where she could not attend to her own needs. She even selected a college nearby so she could continue to live at home. Eventually, Melanie developed anorexia nervosa, which became her primary mechanism for feeling in control, independent, and comforted.

Similarly, Melanie's mother felt responsible and guilty for her daughter's illness. The mother sought relief in extravagant spending sprees (which she concealed from her husband) and then covered the bills by stealing money from her daughter's bank account. Mother, father, and daughter were trapped in a dysfunctional family swamp, which they were unwilling to confront and from which they were unable to escape. In such cases, others involved with the borderline individual often suffer and struggle in the stressful home environment.[21] Treatment of the identified borderline patient may require treatment of the entire family (see chapter 7). Family therapy interventions may be focused on education about BPD and skills training for family and others who care deeply. There are three primary family scenarios that can be addressed in helping the BPD person and loved ones: (1) caring for the BPD person and family of origin; (2) caring for the BPD person and his or her new, adult family; (3) helping the BPD person be an effective parent.[22] In some cases an individual therapy for the borderline patient is best directed toward distancing or separating from an unremittingly pathological family system.

Traumas

Major traumas—parental loss, neglect, rejection, physical or sexual abuse—during the early years of development can increase the probability of BPD in adolescence and adulthood. Indeed, case histories of borderline patients are typically desolate battlefields, scarred by broken homes, chronic abuse, and emotional deprivation.

Norman Mailer described the effect of an absent parent on Marilyn Monroe, who never knew her father. Though his absence would contribute to her emotional instability in later life, it would also ironically be one of the motivating forces in her career:

> Great actors usually discover they have a talent by first searching in desperation for an identity. It is no ordinary identity that will suit them, and no ordinary desperation can drive them. The force that propels a great actor in his youth is insane ambition. Illegitimacy and insanity are the godparents of the great actor. A child who is missing either parent is a study in the search for identity and quickly becomes a candidate for actor (since the most creative way to discover a new and possible identity is through the close fit of a role).[23]

Similarly, Princess Diana, rejected by her mother and reared by a cold, withdrawn father, exhibited similar characteristics. "I always used to think that Diana would make a very good actress because she would play out any role she chose," said her former nanny, Mary Clarke.[24]

Raised in an orphanage during many years of her early childhood, Marilyn had to learn to survive with a minimum of love and attention. It was her self-image that suffered the most and led to her manipulative behavior with lovers later in life. For Diana, her "deep feelings of unworthiness" (in the eulogizing words of her brother,

Charles) hindered her relationships with men. "I'd always kept [boy-friends] away, thought they were all trouble—and I couldn't handle it emotionally. I was very screwed up, I thought."[25]

Not all children who are traumatized or abused become border-line adults, of course; nor do all borderline adults have a history of trauma or abuse. Further, most studies on the effects of childhood trauma are based on inferences from adult reports and not on longi-tudinal studies that follow young children through to adulthood. Finally, other studies have demonstrated less extreme forms of abuse in the histories of borderline patients, particularly neglect (some-times from the father) and a rigid, tight marital bond that excludes adequate protection and support for the child.[26,27,28] Nevertheless, the large amount of anecdotal and statistical evidence demonstrates a link between various forms of abuse, neglect, and BPD.

Nature Versus Nurture

The "nature-nurture" question is, of course, a long-standing and controversial one that applies to many aspects of human behavior. Is one afflicted with BPD because of a biological destiny inherited from one's parents or because of the way parents handled—or mishandled—one's upbringing? Do the biochemical and neurologi-cal signs of the disorder cause the illness—or are they caused *by* the illness? Why do some people develop BPD in spite of an apparently healthy upbringing? Why do others burdened with a background filled with trauma and abuse not develop it?

These "chicken or egg" dilemmas can lead to false assumptions. For example, one might conclude, based on developmental theories, that the causal direction is strictly downward; that is, an aloof, detached mother would produce an insecure borderline child. But the relationship might be more complex, more interactive than that: a colicky, unresponsive, unattractive infant may generate disappoint-ment and detachment in the mother. Regardless of which comes first, both continue to interact and perpetuate interpersonal patterns, which may endure over many years and extend to other relationships. The mitigating effects of other factors—a supportive father, an accepting family and friends, a superior education, physical and mental abilities—will help determine the ultimate emotional health of the individual.

Though no evidence supports a specific BPD gene, humans may inherit chromosomal vulnerabilities that are later expressed as a particular illness, depending on a variety of contributing factors— childhood frustrations and traumas, specific stress events in life, healthy nutrition, exposure to environmental changes or toxins, access to health care, and so on. Just as some have postulated that heritable biological defects in the body's metabolism of alcohol may be associated with an individual's propensity to develop alcoholism, so there may exist a genetic predisposition for BPD, involving a biological weakness in stabilizing mood and impulses.

As many persons with BPD learn that they must reject the either-or, black-or-white ways of thinking, researchers are beginning to appreciate that the most likely model for BPD (and for most medical and psychiatric illnesses) recognizes multiple contributing factors—nature *and* nurture—working and interacting simultaneously. Borderline personality disorder is a complex tapestry, richly embroidered with innumerable intersecting threads.

Chapter Four

The Borderline Society

Where there is no vision, the people perish.

—Proverbs 29:18

States are as the men are; they grow out of human characters.

—From Plato's *Republic*

From the beginning Lisa Barlow couldn't do anything right. Her older brother was the golden boy: good grades, polite, athletic, perfect. Her younger sister, who had asthma, was also lavished with constant attention. Lisa was never good enough, especially in the eyes of her father. She remembered how he constantly reminded all three children that he had started with nothing; that his parents had no money, didn't care about him, and drank too much. But he had prevailed. He had worked his way through high school, college, and through several promotions at a national investment bank. In 1999, he made a fortune in the dot-com stock boom, only to lose it all a year later after some professional missteps.

Lisa's earliest memories of her mother were of her lying on the couch either sick or in pain, ordering Lisa to do one chore or another around the house. Lisa tried hard to care for her mother and to persuade her to stop taking the pain pills and tranquilizers that seemed to make her so foggy and distant.

Lisa felt that if she was just good enough, she could not only make her mother better but also please her father. Though her grades were always excellent (even better than her brother's), her father always maligned her achievements: the course was too easy or she could have done even better than a B+ or an A-. At one point, she thought she might want to become a doctor, but her father convinced her she would never make it.

During Lisa's childhood and adolescence, the Barlows moved constantly—from Omaha to St. Louis to Chicago and finally to New York—following whatever job or promotion her father chased after. Lisa hated these moves and realized later that she resented her mother for never objecting to them. Every couple of years Lisa would be packed up and shipped like baggage to a strange new city, where she would attend a new school filled with strange new students. (Years later she would recount these experiences to her therapist as "feeling like a kidnap victim or a slave.") By the time the family arrived in New York, Lisa was in high school. She vowed never to make another friend so she would never have to say goodbye again.

The family moved into a posh home in a posh New York suburb. Sure, the house was bigger and the lawn more manicured, but that didn't come close to compensating for the friendships she left behind. Her father rarely came home in the evenings, and when he did, it was late and he would start drinking and railing against Lisa and her mother for doing nothing all day. When her father drank too much, he became violent, sometimes hitting the kids harder than he intended. The most frightening time of all was when he was drunk and their mother was spaced out on pain pills; then there was no one to take care of the family—except Lisa, and she hated it.

In 2000, everything started coming apart. Somehow her father's firm (or her father himself, she was never sure which) lost everything when the stock market crashed. Her father was suddenly in danger of losing his job, and if he did, the Barlows would have to move again, to a smaller house in a less desirable neighborhood. He seemed to blame his family and especially Lisa. And then, on a clear, bright morning in September 2001, Lisa came downstairs to find her father lying on the sofa, tears streaming down his cheeks. Had it not been for a hangover from a drinking bout the night before, he would have been killed in his office in the World Trade Center.

For months afterward her father was helpless and so was her mother. They eventually divorced six months later. During this period, Lisa felt lost and isolated. It was similar to the way she felt in biology class when she'd look around the room and observe the other kids squinting into their microscopes, taking notes, apparently knowing exactly what to do, while she became queasy, not quite understanding what was expected of her and feeling too scared to ask for help.

After a while she just stopped trying. In high school she began to hang out with the "wrong kids." She made sure her parents saw them and their freaky outfits. The bodies of many of her friends were covered—almost literally—with tattoos and body piercings, and the local tattoo parlor became a second home for Lisa as well.

Because her father insisted she couldn't make it as a doctor, Lisa went into nursing. At her first hospital job, she met a "free spirit" who wanted to bring his nursing expertise to underprivileged areas. Lisa was enthralled by him, and they married soon after meeting. His habitual "social" drinking became more pronounced as the months went by, and he began hitting her. Bruised and battered, Lisa still felt it was her fault—she just wasn't good enough, couldn't make him happy. She had no friends, she said, because he wouldn't let her have any, but deep down she knew it was due more to her own fears of closeness.

She was relieved when he finally left her. She had wanted the split but couldn't cut the cord herself. But after the relief came fear: "Now what do I do?"

Between the divorce settlement and her salary Lisa had enough money to return to school. This time she was determined to be a doctor and, much to her father's shock, was accepted into medical school. She was starting to feel good again, valued and respected. But then while she was in medical school the self-doubts returned. Her supervisors said she was too slow, clumsy with simple procedures, disorganized. They criticized her for not ordering the right tests or getting lab results back in time. Only with the patients did she feel comfortable. With them, she could be whoever she needed to be: kind and compassionate when that was needed, confrontational and demanding when that was called for.

Lisa also experienced a great deal of prejudice in medical school. She was older than most of the other students; she had a much different background; and she was a woman. Many of the patients called her "nurse," and some of the male patients didn't want "no lady doctor." She was hurt and angry because, like her parents, society and its institutions had also robbed her of her dignity.

The Disintegrating Culture

Psychological theories take on a different dimension when looked upon in light of the culture and time period from which they emanate. At the turn of the century, for instance, when Freud was formulating the system that would become the foundation of modern psychiatric thought, the cultural context was a formally structured Victorian society. His theory that the primary origins of neuroses were the repression of unacceptable thoughts and feelings—aggressive and especially sexual—was entirely logical in this strict social context.

Now, over a century later, aggressive and sexual instincts are expressed more openly, and the social milieu is much more confused. What it means to be a man or a woman is much more ambiguous in modern Western civilization than in early twentieth-century Europe. Social, economic, and political structures are less fixed. The family unit and cultural roles are less defined, and the very concept of "traditional" is unclear.

Though social factors may not be direct causes of BPD (or other forms of mental illness), they are at the very least important indirect influences. Social factors interact with BPD in several ways and cannot be overlooked. First, if borderline pathology originates early in life—and much of the evidence points in this direction—an increase in the pathology is likely tied to the changing social patterns of family structure and parent-child interaction. In this regard, it is worthwhile to examine social changes in the area of child-raising patterns, stability of home life, and child abuse and neglect.

Second, social changes of a more general nature have an exacerbative effect on people already suffering from the borderline syndrome. The lack of structure in American society, for example, is especially difficult for borderline individuals to handle, since they typically have immense problems creating structure for themselves. Women's shifting role patterns (career versus homemaker, for example) tend to aggravate identity problems. Indeed, some researchers partly attribute the prominence of BPD diagnosed more frequently in women to this social role conflict, now so widespread in our society. The increased severity of BPD in these cases may in turn be transmitted to future generations through parent-child interactions, multiplying the effects over time.

Third, the growing recognition of personality disorders in general, and borderline personality more specifically, may be seen as a natural and inevitable response to—or an expression of—our contemporary culture. As Christopher Lasch noted in *The Culture of Narcissism*,

> Every society reproduces its culture—its norms, its underlying assumptions, its modes of organizing experience—in the individual, in the form of personality. As Durkheim said, personality is the individual socialized.[1]

For many, American culture has lost contact with the past and remains unconnected to the future. The flood of technological advancement and information that swept over the late twentieth and early twenty-first centuries, much of it involving personal computers, cell phones, the internet, and so on, often requires greater individual commitment to solitary study and practice, thus sacrificing opportunities for real social interaction. Indeed, the preoccupation—some would say obsession—with computers and other digital gadgetry, especially among the young on social media (Facebook, Twitter,

Instagram, YouTube, Snapchat, TikTok, etc.), may be resulting iron-ically in more self-absorption and less physical interaction; texting, blogging, posting, and tweeting all avoid eye contact, or indeed any real-time face-to-face contact of any kind. Solitary reflection is sac-rificed upon the altar of FOMO (fear of missing out).

Increasing divorce rates and greater geographical mobility have all contributed to a society that lacks constancy and reliability. Baby boomers were the last generation to grow up who typically attended the same schools and churches their parents (and maybe grand-parents) attended. They are the last generation surrounded by rela-tives and long-term neighbors. In today's world of frequent moves, intimate lasting personal relationships become difficult or even impossible to achieve, and deep-seated loneliness, self-absorption, emptiness, anxiety, depression, and loss of self-esteem ensue.

The borderline syndrome represents a pathological response to these stresses. Without outside sources of stability and validation of worthiness, borderline symptoms of black-and-white thinking, self-destructiveness, extreme mood changes, impulsivity, tumultu-ous relationships, an impaired sense of identity, and anger become understandable reactions to our culture's tensions. Borderline traits, which may be present to some extent in many people, are being elicited—perhaps even bred—on a wide scale by the prevailing social conditions. *New York Times* writer Louis Sass put it this way:

> Each culture probably needs its own scapegoats as expressions
> of society's ills. Just as the hysterics of Freud's day exemplified
> the sexual repression of that era, the borderline, whose identity
> is split into many pieces, represents the fracturing of stable
> units in our society.[2]

Though conventional wisdom presumes that borderline pathol-ogy has increased over the last few decades, some psychiatrists believe that the symptoms were just as common early in the twentieth cen-tury. They claim that the change is not in the prevalence of the dis-order, but in the fact that it is now officially identified and defined, and therefore simply diagnosed more frequently. Even some of Freud's early cases, scrutinized in the light of current criteria, might be diagnosed today as borderline personalities.

This possibility, however, by no means diminishes the importance of the growing number of borderline patients who are ending up in psychiatrists' offices and of the growing recognition of borderline characteristics in the general population. In fact, the major reason that it has been identified and covered so widely in the clinical and popular literature is its prevalence in both therapeutic settings and the general culture.

The Breakdown of Structure: A Fragmented Society

Few would dispute the notion that American society has become more fragmented since the end of World War II. Family structures in place for decades—the nuclear family, the extended family, one-wage-earner households, geographical stability—have been replaced by a wide assortment of patterns, movements, and trends. Divorce rates have soared. Alcohol and drug abuse, as evidenced by the methamphetamine and opioid epidemics in the 2010s, and reports of child neglect and abuse have skyrocketed. Crime, terrorism, and political violence have become widespread; mass/school shootings, previously rare aberrations, have sadly become in some schools as common as fire drills. Periods of economic uncertainty, exemplified in roller-coaster boom-and-bust scenarios, have become the rule, not the exception.

Some of these changes may be related to society's failure to achieve a kind of social rapprochement. As noted in chapter 3, during the separation-individuation phase, the infant ventures cautiously away from mother but returns to her reassuring warmth, familiarity, and acceptance. Disruption of this rapprochement cycle often results in a lack of trust, disturbed relationships, emptiness, anxiety, and an uncertain self-image—characteristics that comprise the borderline syndrome. Similarly, it may be seen that contemporary culture interferes with a healthy social rapprochement by obstructing access to comforting anchors. At no time has this disruption been more evident than in the first decades of the twenty-first century, racked by economic collapse, recession, loss of jobs, foreclosures, pandemic-required isolation, and so on. In most areas of the country, the need for two incomes to maintain an acceptable standard of living forces many parents to relinquish parenting duties to others; paid parental leave or on-site day care for new parents is still relatively rare and almost always limited. Jobs, as well as economic and social pressures, encourage frequent moves, and this geographical mobility in turn removes us from our stabilizing roots, as it did in Lisa's family. We are losing (or have already lost) the comforts of supportive nearby family and consistent social roles.

When the accoutrements of custom disappear, they may be replaced by a sense of abandonment, of being adrift in unchartered waters. Our children lack a sense of history and belonging—of an anchored presence in the world. To establish a sense of control and comforting familiarity in an alienating society, the individual may resort to a wide range of pathological behavior—substance addiction, eating disorders, criminal behaviors, and so on.

Society's failure to provide rapprochement with reassuring, stabilizing bonds is reflected in the relentless series of sweeping societal movements over the past fifty years. We pinballed from the explosive other-directed fight-for-social-justice "We Decade" of the 1960s, to the narcissistic "Me Decade" of the 1970s, to the materialistic look-out-for-number-one "Whee Decade" of the 1980s. The relatively prosperous and stable 1990s was followed by two turbulent decades, 2000 through 2020: periods of financial boom-and-bust (dot-com in 2000, Great Recession in 2008); natural catastrophes (Katrina and other hurricanes, major tsunamis, earthquakes, wildfires, and the looming planetary threat of global warming); viral pandemics (SARS, MERS, Ebola, H1N1, coronavirus); prolonged wars in Iraq and Afghanistan; and sociopolitical movements (antiwar, LGBTQ rights, Black Lives Matter, the Me Too movement, etc.)—bringing us almost full circle back to the 1960s.

One of the big losers in these tectonic shifts has been group loyalties—devotion to family, neighborhood, church, occupation, and country. As society continues to foster detachment from people and institutions that provide reassuring rapprochement, individuals are responding in ways that virtually define the borderline syndrome: a decreased sense of validated identity, worsening interpersonal relationships, isolation and loneliness, boredom, and (without the stabilizing force of group pressures) impulsivity.

Like the world of those with borderline personality, ours in many ways is a world of massive contradictions. We presume we believe in peace, yet our streets, schools, movies, television, video games, and sports are filled with aggression and violence. We are a nation virtually founded on the principle of "Help thy neighbor," yet we have become one of the most politically conservative, self-absorbed, and materialistic societies in the history of humankind. Assertiveness and action are encouraged; reflection and introspection are equated with weakness and incompetency.

Contemporary social forces implore us to embrace a mythical polarity—black or white, right or wrong, good or bad, guilty or innocent—relying on our nostalgia for simpler times, for our own childhoods. The political system presents candidates who adopt polar stances: "I'm right, the other guy is wrong"; America is good, the Soviet Union is "the Evil Empire," and Iran, Iraq, and North Korea are the "Axis of Evil." Today, politics in the United States and Europe is more polarized than it has ever been (see Extreme Polarization later in this chapter). Religious factions exhort us to believe that theirs is the only route to salvation. The legal system, built on the premise that one is either guilty or not guilty with little or no room for gray areas, perpetuates the myth that life is intrinsically fair and justice can be attained—that is, when something bad does happen, it necessarily follows that it is someone else's fault and that person should pay.

The flood of information and leisure alternatives makes it difficult to establish priorities in living. Ideally, we—as individuals and as a society—attempt to achieve a balance between nurturing the body and the mind, between work and leisure, between altruism and self-interest. But in an increasingly materialistic society it is a small step from assertiveness to aggressiveness, from individualism to alienation and isolation, from self-preservation to self-absorption.

The ever-growing reverence for technology has led to an obsessive pursuit of precision. Calculators replaced memorized multiplication tables and slide rules, and then were replaced by computers, which have become omnipresent in almost every aspect of our lives—our cars, our appliances, our cell phones—running whatever machine or device they are a part of. The microwave relieves adults from the chore of cooking. Velcro absolves children from having to learn how to tie shoelaces. Creativity and intellectual diligence are sacrificed to convenience and precision.

All these attempts to impose order and fairness on a naturally random and unfair universe endorse the borderline individual's futile struggle to choose only black or white, right or wrong, good or bad. But the world is neither intrinsically fair nor exact; it is composed of subtleties that require less simplistic approaches. A healthy civilization can accept the uncomfortable ambiguities. Attempts to eradicate or ignore uncertainty tend only to encourage a borderline society, ripped apart by polarizations.

We would be naive to believe that the cumulative effect of all this change—the excruciating pull of opposing forces—has had no effect on our psyches. In a sense, we all live in a kind of "borderland"— between the prosperous, healthy high-technology America, on the one hand, and the underbelly of poverty, homelessness, drug abuse, and mental illness on the other; between the dream of a sane, safe, secure world and the insane nightmare of nuclear holocaust or a catastrophic climate event.

The price tag of social change has arrived in the form of stress and stress-related physical disorders, such as heart attacks, strokes, hypertension, and diabetes. We must now confront the possibility that mental illness has become part of the psychological price.

Dread of the Future

Over the past five decades, therapeutic settings have seen a basic change in defining psychopathology—from symptom neuroses to character disorders. As far back as 1975, psychiatrist Peter L. Giovachinni wrote: "Clinicians are constantly faced with the seemingly increasing number of patients who do not fit current diagnostic categories. [They suffer not from] definitive symptoms but from vague ill-defined complaints. . . . When I refer to this type of patient, practically everyone knows to whom I am referring."[3] Beginning in the 1980s, such reports have become commonplace, as personality disorders have replaced classical neurosis as a prominent pathology. Which social and cultural factors have influenced this change in pathology? Many, including Lasch, believe that one factor is our devaluation of the past:

> To live for the moment is the prevailing passion—to live for yourself, not for your predecessors or posterity. . . . We are fast losing the sense of historical continuity, the sense of belonging to a succession of generations originating in the past and stretching into the future.[4]

This loss of historical continuity reaches both backward and forward: devaluation of the past breaks the perceptual link to the future, which becomes a huge unknown, a source of dread as much as hope, a vast quicksand, from which it becomes incredibly difficult to extricate oneself. Time is perceived as isolated snapshot points instead of as a continuous logical string of events influenced by past achievement, present action, and hopeful anticipation of the future.

The looming possibility of a catastrophic event—the threat of nuclear annihilation, another massive terrorist attack like 9/11, environmental destruction due to global warming, global pandemics, and so on—contributes to our lack of faith in the past and our dread of the future. Empirical studies with adolescents and children consistently show "awareness of the danger, hopelessness about surviving, a shortened time perspective, and pessimism about being able to reach life goals. Suicide is mentioned again and again as a strategy for dealing with the threat."[5] Other studies have found that the threat of world catastrophe rushes children to a kind of "early adulthood," similar to the type witnessed in pre-borderline children (like Lisa) who are forced to take control of families that are out of control due to BPD, alcoholism, and other mental disorders.[6] Many U.S. youth ages fourteen to twenty-two expect to die before age thirty, according to a 2008 study published in the *Journal of Adolescent Health*. About one out of fifteen young people (6.7 percent) expressed such "unrealistic fatalism," the study concludes. The findings are based on four years of survey data totaling 4,201 adolescents conducted between 2002 and 2005 by the Health and Risk Communication Institute of the Annenberg Public Policy Center. With an increase in the suicide rate for ten- to twenty-four-year-olds, suicide is the second leading cause of death in this age group.[7,8,9]

Over half a century ago The Who sang, "I hope I die before I get old." That sentiment among the young may well endure. The prevalence of mass/school shootings in the first two decades of the twenty-first century has increased dread of the future—especially among adolescents and children.[10] (See Catastrophic Events: Mass/School Shootings and Global Pandemics later in this chapter.) The borderline individual, as we have seen, personifies this orientation to the now. With little interest in the past, he is almost a cultural amnesiac; his cupboard of warm memories (which sustain most of us in troubled times) is bare. As a result, he is doomed to suffer torment with no breathers, no cache of memories of happier times to get him through the tough periods. Unable to learn from his mistakes, he is doomed to repeat them.

Parents who fear the future are not likely to be engrossed by the needs of the next generation. A modern parent, emotionally detached and alienated—yet at the same time pampering and overindulgent—becomes a likely candidate to mold future borderline personalities.

The Jungle of Interpersonal Relationships

Perhaps the hallmark social changes over the last seventy years have come in the area of sexual mores, roles, and practices—from the suppressed sexuality of the 1950s, to the "free love" and "open marriage" trends of the 1960s sexual revolution, to the massive sexual reevaluation in the 1980s (resulting in large part from the fear of AIDS and other sexually transmitted diseases), to the gay and lesbian movements over the last two decades. The massive proliferation of dating and hookup sites on social media has made it so easy to establish personal contact that the old brick-and-mortar pickup bar has become increasingly irrelevant. Innocent—or illicit—romantic or sexual relationships can now be initiated with a few keyboard strokes or a text message. The jury is out on whether cyberspace has "civilized" the world of interpersonal relationships or turned it into more of a dangerous jungle than it ever was.

As a result of these and other societal forces, deep and lasting friendships, love affairs, and marriages have become increasingly difficult to achieve and maintain. Sixty percent of marriages for couples between the ages of twenty and twenty-five end in divorce; the number is 50 percent for those over twenty-five. (These rates decreased somewhat over the period from 2008 to 2016, though the decline can be attributed to fewer and delayed marriages among millennials.)[11,12] Even back in 1982, Lasch noted that "as social life becomes more and more warlike and barbaric, personal relations, which ostensibly provide relief from those conditions, take on the character of combat."[13]

Ironically, borderline individuals may be well suited for this kind of combat. The narcissistic man's need to dominate and be idolized fits well with the borderline woman's ambivalent need to be controlled and punished. Some borderline women, as we saw with Lisa at the start of this chapter, marry at a young age to escape the chaos of family life. They cling to dominating husbands with whom they re-create the miasma of home life. Both may enter a kind of "Slap! . . .

Thanks, I needed that!" sadomasochistic dyad. Less typical, but still common, is a reversal of these roles, with a borderline male linked with a narcissistic female partner.

Masochism is a prominent characteristic of borderline relationships. Dependency coupled with pain elicits the familiar refrain "Love hurts." In childhood, the borderline adult has often experienced pain and confusion in trying to establish a maturing relationship with his mother or primary caregiver. Later in life, other partners—spouse, friends, teacher, employer, minister, doctor—renew this early confusion. Criticism or abuse particularly reinforces his self-image of worthlessness. Lisa's later relationships with her husband and supervisors, for example, recapitulated the profound feelings of worthlessness ingrained by her father's constant criticisms.

Sometimes borderline masochistic suffering transforms into sadism. For example, Ann would sometimes encourage her husband Liam to drink, knowing about his drinking problem. Then she would instigate a fight, fully aware of Liam's violent propensities when drunk. Following a beating, Ann would wear her bruises like war medals, reminding Liam of his violence, and would insist they go out in public, where Ann would explain away her marks as "accidents," such as "running into doors." After each episode, Liam would feel profoundly regretful and humiliated, while Ann would present herself as a long-suffering martyr. In this way Ann used her beatings to exact punishment from Liam. The identification of the real victim in this relationship becomes increasingly vague.

Even when a relationship is apparently ruptured, the borderline sufferer comes crawling back for more punishment, feeling he deserves the denigration. The punishment is comfortably familiar, easier to cope with than the frightening prospect of solitude or a different partner.

A typical scenario for modern social relationships is a pattern of overlapping lovers, sometimes referred to as shingling—establishing a new romance before severing a current one. BPD exemplifies this constant need for partnership: As she climbs the jungle gym of relationships, she cannot let go of the lower bar until she has firmly grasped the next one. Typically, she will not leave her current abusive spouse until a new "white knight" is at least visible on the horizon.

Periods of relaxed sociosexual mores and less structured romantic relationships (such as in the late 1960s and 1970s) are more difficult for individuals with BPD to handle; increased freedom and lack of structure paradoxically imprison those who are severely handicapped in devising their own individual systems of values. Conversely, the sexual withdrawal period of the late 1980s (due in part to the AIDS epidemic) was often ironically therapeutic for those with BPD. Social fears enforce strict boundaries that can be crossed only at the risk of great physical harm; impulsivity and promiscuity now have severe penalties in the form of STDs, violent sexual deviants, and so on. This external structure can help protect him from his own self-destructiveness.

Shifting Gender-Role Patterns

Earlier in the last century, social roles were fewer, more well defined, and much more easily combined. Mother was domestic, working in the home, in charge of the children. Mother's outside interests, such as school involvement, hobbies, and charity work, flowed naturally from these duties. Father's work and community visibility also combined smoothly. And together their roles worked synchronously.

The complexities of modern society, however, dictate that the individual develop a plethora of social roles—many of which do not combine so easily. The working mother, for example, has two distinct roles and must struggle to perform both well. Most employers insist that the working mom keep the home and workplace separate; as a result, many mothers feel guilty or embarrassed when problems from one impact the other.

A working father also finds work and home roles compartmentalized. He is no longer the owner of the local grocery who lives above the store. More likely, he works miles from home and has much less time to be with his family. What's more, the modern dad plays an increasingly participatory role, with heavy familial responsibility. For both parents, the increasing preference (or need) to work from home, a skyrocketing trend in the era of Covid-19, has caused more strain on managing work and parenting obligations.

Shifting role patterns over the last several decades are central to theories on why BPD is identified more commonly in women. In the past, a woman had essentially one life course—getting married (usually in her late teens or early twenties), having children, staying in the home to raise those children, and repressing any career ambitions. Today, in contrast, a young woman is faced with a bewildering array of role models and expectations—from the single career woman, to the married career woman, to the traditional nurturing mother, to the supermom, who strives to combine marriage, career, and children successfully.

Men are also expected to take on new roles, of course, but not nearly so wide-ranging—nor conflicting—as those of women. In previous generations, a father who took time away from work to watch his daughter's volleyball game would have appeared to be shirking his commitment to provide for his family. Today men are expected to be more sensitive and open and to take a larger part in child-raising than in previous eras, yet these qualities and responsibilities usually fit within the overall role of provider or co-provider. It is the rare man who, for example, abandons career ambitions to take on the role of househusband, nor is this usually expected of him.

Men have fewer adjustments to make during the evolution of relationships and marriages. For example, relocations are usually dictated by the man's career needs, since he is most often the primary wage earner. Throughout pregnancy, birth, and child-rearing, few changes occur in the man's day-to-day reality. Not only does the woman have to endure the physical demands of pregnancy and childbirth and have to leave her job to give birth, but she also must make the transition back to work or give up her career. And yet in many dual-earner households, although it may not be openly stated, the woman simply assumes the primary responsibility for the maintenance of the home. She is the one who usually adjusts her plans to stay home with a sick child or wait for the repairman to come.

Though women have struggled successfully to achieve increased social and career options, they may be forced to pay an exacting price in the process. Even though it's widely accepted that women can both be excellent mothers and work (and may need to in many households), "traditional" expectations can still cause pressure in the form of excruciating life decisions about career, families, and children; strains on their relationships with their children and husband; the stress resulting from making and living with these decisions; and confusion about who they are and who they want to be. From this perspective, it is understandable that women should be more closely associated with BPD, a disorder in which identity and role confusion are such central components.

A major change in the very concept of marriage has added to the confusion. The traditional Judeo-Christian norm of marriage between a man and a woman has been significantly challenged over the last twenty years, not only in religious discussions but also in the political and social arenas. In 2004, Americans opposed same-sex marriage by a margin of 60 to 31 percent; based on polling in 2019, public opinion has flipped—a majority of Americans (61 percent) support same-sex marriage, while 31 percent oppose it.[14] Mirroring public opinion, bans on same-sex marriage in thirteen U.S. states were struck down as unconstitutional in 2015 by the Supreme Court ruling in *Obergefell v. Hodges*.

The recognition and legalization of same-sex marriage, however, has fueled public debate rather than defusing it. Over the past decade, homosexuality in general and same-sex marriage in specific have emerged as central issues in the extreme polarization of the country.

Sexual Orientation and BPD

Sexual orientation may also play a part in borderline role confusion. For centuries, homosexuality has been a controversial if not downright explosive issue, running the gamut from acceptance, to minor sin, to condemnation and illegality, to prohibition under penalty of death—depending on the society and the era. As recently as the 1980s, homosexuality was deemed to be a psychiatric disorder, until the *Diagnostic and Statistical Manual* removed all references to it in 1987 (DSM-III-R).

In parallel with the social turmoil, for gay, lesbian, or transgender people the personal decision to "come out of the closet" is usually ridden with anxiety and the potential of severe social and/or family repercussions. Yet the social context has changed. According to recent surveys, 7 percent of millennials self-identify as gay, as opposed to 3.5 percent in 2011.[15]

Transsexualism has added more ambiguity to the understanding of what defines maleness and femaleness. As one of the criteria of the BPD diagnosis, identity confusion is always a significant concern. Some have demanded changes in how pronouns describe them. Rejecting identification as "him" or "her," they prefer to be referred to as the gender-neutral "them." The increasing ambiguity about identity and sexuality—and indeed, about what constitutes "normality"—is especially impactful for borderline individuals. Increasingly intense debate between conservative evangelical and religious organizations and liberal, LGBTQ, and pro-choice supporters causes more anxiety for those borderline individuals still trying to establish a firm sense of identity and to develop stable relationships.

Family and Child-Rearing Patterns

Since the end of World War II, our society has experienced striking changes in family and child-rearing patterns:

- The institution of the nuclear family has been in steady decline. Largely due to divorce, half of all American children born in the 1990s spent part of their childhood in a single-parent home.[16] According to the U.S. Census Bureau, between 1960 and 2016, the percentage of children living with two parents dipped from 88 percent to 69 percent, and in 6 percent of those households the two parents were not married. During that interval, children living with only their mother almost tripled, from 8 percent to 23 percent. In 2016, 4 percent of children lived only with their father.[17] A more recent Pew Research study (2019) confirmed that 23 percent of children under eighteen years of age in the U.S. were living with a single parent, compared to 7 percent in the rest of the world.[18]

- Alternative family structures (such as blended families, in which a single parent with children combines with another one-parent household to form a new family unit) have led to situations in which many children are raised by persons other than their birth parents. Due to increased geographical mobility, among other factors, the traditional extended family, with grandparents, siblings, cousins, and other family relations living in close proximity, is almost extinct, leaving the nuclear family virtually unsupported.

- The number of women working outside the home has increased dramatically. Forty percent of workingwomen are mothers of children under age eighteen; 71 percent of all single mothers are employed.[19]

- As a result of women working outside the home, more children than ever before are being placed in various forms of day care—and at a much earlier age. The number of infants in day care increased 45 percent during the 1980s.[20]

- The evidence clearly suggests that the incidence of child neglect and physical and sexual abuse increased significantly over the last years of the twentieth century.[21]

What are the psychological effects of these child-rearing changes—on both children and parents? Psychiatrists and developmental experts generally agree that children growing up in settings marked by turmoil, instability, or abuse are at much greater risk for emotional and mental problems in adolescence and adulthood. Moreover, parents in such environments are much more likely to develop stress, guilt, depression, lower self-esteem—all characteristics associated with BPD.

Please do not misunderstand: We do not mean to say that single-parent homes or homes with two working parents are in any way inferior to traditional nuclear families, especially in the area of fostering mental illness—the evidence simply does not support that claim.[22] In fact, today only a minority of American households are traditional two-parent nuclear families, and only a third of American individuals live in this kind of family structure. Millions of parents in non-nuclear-family situations are able to cope with, or even thrive in, the emotional and financial stress of divorce, or the desire of both parents to pursue their jobs and careers, or out of simple economic necessity. Though there is no evidence that the increase in day care has led to an increase in mental illness or child abuse, affordable, quality day care to support working parents has lagged far behind the needs of working-parent households. The same goes for children growing up in these situations. Indeed, a single-parent home or a home with two working parents is often a vast improvement over the unhappy, turbulent situation it replaced. What we are suggesting is that parents and children in these family structures should anticipate the possible associated stress and develop coping skills to handle it, through reading, counseling/therapy, advice from family and friends, and so on.

Child Abuse and Neglect: Destroyer of Trust

Child abuse and neglect have become significant health problems. In 2007, about 5.8 million children were involved in an estimated 3.2 million child abuse reports and allegations in the United States.[23]

Some studies estimate that 25 percent of girls experience some form of sexual abuse (from parents or others) by the time they reach adulthood.[24]

Characteristics of physically abused preschool-age children include inhibition, depression, attachment difficulties, behavior problems (such as hyperactivity and severe tantrums), poor impulse control, aggressiveness, and peer-relation problems.

"Violence begets violence," said John Lennon, and this is particularly true in the case of battered children. Because those who are abused often become abusers themselves, this problem can self-perpetuate over many decades and generations. In fact, about 30 percent of abused and neglected children will later abuse their own children, continuing the vicious cycle.[25]

The incidence of abuse or neglect among borderline patients is high enough to be a factor that separates BPD from other personality disorders. Verbal or psychological abuse is the most common form, followed by physical and then sexual abuse. Physical and sexual abuse may be more dramatic in nature, but the emotionally abused child can suffer total loss of self-esteem.

Emotional child abuse can take several forms:

- *Degradation.* Constantly devaluing the child's achievements and magnifying misbehavior. After a while, the child becomes convinced that he really is bad or worthless.

- *Unavailability/Neglect.* Psychologically absent parents show little interest in the child's development and provide no affection in times of need.

- *Domination.* Use of extreme threats to control the child's behavior. Some child development experts have compared this form of abuse to the techniques used by terrorists to brainwash captives.[26]

Recall from Lisa's story that she probably suffered all of these forms of emotional abuse: her father hammered her constantly that she was "not good enough"; her mother rarely stood up for Lisa, almost always deferring to her husband in all important decisions; and Lisa perceived the family's numerous relocations as "kidnappings."

The pattern of the neglected child, as described by psychologist Hugh Missildine, mirrors the dilemmas of borderline patients in later life:

> If you suffered from neglect in childhood, it may cause you to go from one person to another, hoping that someone will supply whatever is missing. You may not be able to care much about yourself, and think marriage will end this, and then find yourself in the alarming situation of being married but emotionally unattached. . . . Moreover, the person who [has] neglect in his background is always restless and anxious because he cannot obtain emotional satisfaction. . . . These restless, impulsive moves help to create the illusion of living emotionally. . . . Such a person may, for example, be engaged to be married to one person and simultaneously be maintaining sexual relationships with two or three others. Anyone who offers admiration and respect has appeal to them—and because their need for affection is so great, their ability to discriminate is severely impaired.[27]

From what we understand of the roots of BPD (see chapter 3), abuse, neglect, or prolonged separations early in childhood can greatly disrupt the developing infant's establishment of trust. Self-esteem and autonomy are crippled. The abilities to cope with separation and to form identity do not proceed normally. As they become adults, abused children may recapitulate frustrating relationships with others. Pain and punishment may become associated with closeness—they come to believe that "love hurts." As the borderline child or adolescent matures, self-mutilation may become the proxy for the abusive parent.

Children of Divorce: The Disappearing Father

Due primarily to divorce, more children than ever before are being raised without the physical and/or emotional presence of their father. Because most courts award children to the mother in custody cases, the large majority of single-parent homes are headed by mothers. Even in cases of joint custody or liberal visitation rights, the father, who is more likely to remarry sooner after divorce and start a new family, often fades from the child's upbringing.

The recent trend in child-raising, toward a more equal sharing of parental responsibilities between mother and father, makes subsequent divorce even more upsetting for the child. Children clearly benefit from dual parenting, but they also lose more when the marriage dissolves, especially if the breakup occurs during the formative years when the child still has many crucial developmental stages to go through.

Studies on the effects of divorce typically report profound upset, neediness, regression, and acute separation anxiety related to fears of abandonment in children of preschool age.[28] A significant number are found to be depressed[29] or antisocial in later stages of childhood.[30] Indeed, teens living in single-parent families are not only more likely to commit suicide but also more likely to suffer from psychological disorders, when compared to teens living in intact families.[31]

During separation and divorce, the child's need for physical intimacy increases. For example, it is typical for a young child at the time of separation to ask a parent to sleep with him. If the practice continues and sleeping in the same bed becomes the parent's need as well, the child's own sense of autonomy and bodily integrity may be threatened. This, combined with the loneliness and severe narcissistic injury caused by the divorce, places some children at high risk for developmental arrest or, if the need for affection and reassurance becomes desperate, for sexual abuse. A father separated from the home may demand more time with the child in order to relieve his own feelings of loneliness and deprivation. If the child becomes a lightning rod for his father's resentment and bitterness, he may again be at higher risk for abuse.

In many situations of parental separation, the child becomes the pawn in a destructive battle between his parents. Han, a divorced father who usually ignored his visitation privileges, suddenly demanded that his daughter stay with him whenever he was angry at her mother. These visits were usually unpleasant for the child as well as for her father and his new family, yet were used as punishment for his ex-wife, who would feel guilty and powerless at his demands. Isabella became embroiled in conflicts between her divorced parents when her mother periodically took her father back to court to extract more money for child support. Bribes of material gifts or threats to cut off support for school or home maintenance are common weapons used between continuously skirmishing parents; the bribes and threats are usually more harmful to the children than they are to the parents.

Children may even be drawn into court battles and forced to testify about their parents. In these situations, neither the parents nor the courts nor the relevant social welfare organizations can protect the child, who is often left with a sense of overwhelming helplessness (conflicts continue despite his input) or of intoxicating power (his testimony controls the battle between his parents). He may feel enraged at his predicament and yet fearful that he could be abandoned by everyone. All of this becomes fertile ground for the development of borderline pathology.

In addition to divorce, other powerful societal forces have contributed to the absent father syndrome. The past half century has witnessed the maturing of children of thousands of war veterans— World War II, the Korean War, the Vietnam War, and conflicts in the Persian Gulf, Iraq, and Afghanistan—not to mention many survivors of concentration and prison camps. Not only were many of these fathers absent during significant portions of their children's development, but many were found to develop post-traumatic stress disorders and delayed mourning ("impacted grief") related to combat that also influenced child development.[32] By 1970, 40 percent of World War II and Korean War POWs had met violent death by suicide, homicide, or auto accident (mostly one-car single-occupant accidents).[33] The same trend has continued with vets of the Iraq War and later combat. According to U.S. Army figures, five soldiers per day tried to commit suicide in 2007, compared to less than one per day before the war.[34] Children of Holocaust survivors often have severe emotional difficulties, rooted in their parents' massive psychic trauma.[35]

The absent father syndrome can lead to pathological consequences. Often in families torn by divorce or death, the mother tries to compensate by becoming the ideal parent, arranging every aspect of her child's life; naturally, the child has limited opportunity to develop his own identity. Without the buffering of another parent, the mother-child link can be too close to allow for healthy separating.

Though the mother often seeks to replace the missing father, in many cases it is actually the child who tries to replace the absent father. In the absence of the father, the symbiotic intensity of the bond with the mother is greatly magnified. The child grows up with an idealized view of the mother and fantasies of forever trying to please her. And a parent's dependence on the child may persist, interfering with growth and individuation, planting the seeds of BPD.

Permissive Child-Rearing Practices

Modern permissive child-rearing practices, involving the transfer of traditional parental functions to outside agencies—the school, mass media, industry—have significantly altered the quality of parent-child relationships. Parental "instinct" has been supplanted by a reliance on books and child-rearing experts. Child-rearing, in many households, takes a back seat to the demands of dual careers. "Quality time" becomes a guilt-induced euphemism for "not enough time."

Many parents overcompensate by lavishing attention on the child's practical and recreational needs, yet providing little real warmth. Narcissistic parents perceive their children as extensions of themselves or as objects/possessions, rather than as separate human beings. As a result, the child suffocates in emotionally distant attention, leading to an exaggerated sense of his own importance, regressive defenses, and loss of a sense of self.

Geographical Mobility: Where Is Home?

We are moving more than ever before. Greater geographical mobility can bring rich educational benefits and cultural exchange for a child, but numerous relocations are often also accompanied by a feeling of rootlessness. Some investigators have found that children who move frequently and stay in one place for only short periods of time often have confused responses, or no response at all, to the simple question "Where is your home?"

Because hypermobility is typically correlated with career-oriented lifestyles and job demands, one or both parents in mobile families tend to work long hours and so are less available to their offspring. For children who have few constants in their environment to provide ballast for development, mobility adds another disruptive force—the world turns into a menagerie of changing places and faces. Such children may grow up bored and lonely, looking for constant stimulation. Continually forced to adapt to new situations and people, they may lose the stable sense of self encouraged by secure community anchors. Though socially graceful, like Lisa they typically feel they are gracefully faking it.

Increasing geographical mobility weakens the stability of the neighborhood, community school systems, church and civic institutions, and friendships. Traditional affiliations are lost. About 44 percent of Americans profess affinity to a different church from the one in which they were raised.[36] Generations are becoming separated by long distances, and the extended family is lost for emotional support and childcare. Children are raised without knowing their grandparents, aunts, uncles, and cousins, losing a strong connection to the past and a source of love and warmth to nurture healthy emotional growth.

The Rise of the Faux Family

As society fragments, marriages dissolve, and families break up, the "faux family," or virtual community, often replaces the real communities of the past. This yearning for tribal affiliation manifests in a variety of ways: football fans identify themselves as Raider Nation; hordes of people wait for hours each week to vote for their favorite American Idol, simply to be a part of a larger group with a "common" purpose; and millions of young people join Facebook, Instagram, YouTube, Snapchat, and Twitter to be a member of a vast electronic social network. Sixty years ago in his novel *Cat's Cradle*, Kurt Vonnegut playfully (but prophetically) called these "connections" a "granfalloon"—a group of people who choose or claim to have a shared identity or purpose, but whose mutual association is actually meaningless. The author offered two examples—the Daughters of the American Revolution and the General Electric Company; if Vonnegut wrote the novel today, the examples could just as easily be huge swaths of Facebook or Twitter users.

Since 2003, social networking sites have rocketed from a niche activity into a phenomenon that engages tens of millions of internet users. In 2007, more than half (55 percent) of all online American youths ages twelve to seventeen used online social networking sites.[37] In 2018, according to a recent study by the Pew Research Center, 90 percent of teens say they go online "almost constantly" or "several times a day."[38] The initial evidence suggests that teens use these sites primarily to communicate, to stay in touch with and make plans with friends, and to make new friends. However, the motivation might not be this benign. For example, a study by Microsoft found that ego is the largest driver of participation: people contribute to "increase their social, intellectual, and cultural capital."[39]

Twitter, among the most popular electronic rages to sweep the (faux) nation, is unabashed in its narcissistic bent. An instant text-messaging service, tweeting is intended to announce (in 140 characters or less, doubled to 280 for non-Asian languages in 2017) "what I'm doing" or "what I'm thinking" to a group of followers. There is little pretense that the communication is intended to be a two-way street.

Few would dispute the growing narcissism in American culture. Initially documented by Tom Wolfe's landmark article "The 'Me' Decade and the Third Great Awakening" in 1976 and Christopher Lasch's *Culture of Narcissism* in 1979, the narcissistic impulse has been evidenced since then by a wide assortment of cultural trends: reality TV turning its participants into instant famous-for-being-famous celebrities; plastic surgery's explosion into a growth industry; indulgent parenting, celebrity worship, lust for material wealth, and now social networking creating one's own group of faux friends. As Jean M. Twenge and W. Keith Campbell note in *The Narcissism Epidemic* (2009): "The Internet brought useful technology but also the possibility of instant fame and a 'Look at me!' mentality. . . . People strive to create a 'personal brand' (also called 'self-branding'), packaging themselves like a product to be sold."[40]

The Turbulent Tens: A Decade of Massive Changes

Imagine for a moment that you have traveled back in time to the year 2009. Barack Obama had just been elected president, and he, along with other world leaders and central banks, was trying to pull the world out of the worst economic crisis since the Great Depression. About 77 percent of the American population owned a cell phone, of which the vast majority were teenagers who had purchased one in the last five years.[41] Facebook, Twitter, and YouTube were in their infancies, and Instagram and Snapchat did not even exist. Same-sex marriage was illegal in forty-five states. Mass shootings were occurring at the rate of about five per year.[42] The terms *tribal politics, cyberbullying, selfie,* and *emoji* had not yet entered the everyday cultural lexicon.

Regardless of political ideology, few could argue a decade later that the world has not gone through significant social, cultural, political, and technological change. Cell phones have become the primary communication device of our time. Social media is thriving as a primary (albeit controversial) communication mode, especially among young people. Mass/school shootings have become common catastrophic events—there were 194 mass shootings in the 2010s, nearly triple the number from the previous decade.[43] Polarized conflicts between Democrats and Republicans have frequently led to gridlock in local governments and the U.S. Congress.

Most important to this discussion, these societal forces have combined to form, if not the "seeds" of mental illness, then at least a petri dish in which the "germs" of anxiety, stress, and mental illness can flourish. According to recent U.S. studies and surveys, the following have all increased dramatically in the 2010s, especially during the 2016–2019 period: anxiety and stress levels; visits to therapists; and the number of diagnoses and severity of mental disorders.[44,45]

Times have been confusing for everyone, of course, but it's been much more confusing for those afflicted with mental illness in general, and with BPD in particular. Several of the social changes described below strain borderline thoughts, feelings, and behaviors, which is to say the nine BPD criteria, perhaps more than any other mental disorder. The job of the psychotherapist treating BPD has also been made more difficult. Like everyone else, mental health professionals live in the real world, not in a bubble; they are vulnerable to the same societal forces as their patients, and they struggle to understand and navigate them while helping their patients do the same.

Extreme Polarization and Tribal Politics

Extreme polarization and tribal politics have ramifications far beyond the ballot box. Now more than ever before, posts on social media advocating, for example, gay rights or women's reproductive rights are almost as likely to invite threats of violence or even death as rational disagreement. Indeed, in many cases, the warning signs of mass shootings and high-profile hate crimes were on display in social media postings.[46] In general, legislative bodies, law enforcement agencies, or the platforms themselves have not been diligent about, or are incapable of, regulating or monitoring social media sites for this type of criminal behavior, citing free speech, content creation, cost, or other reasons.[47]

The underlying mantras of tribal politics—"We're always right and the other side is always wrong" and "We're all good, the other side is all evil"—form a societal validation of the borderline person's black-or-white misperception of himself and those in his immediate orbit—the BPD defense mechanism known as splitting (see chapter 1). When TV news and social media rant about tribal politics on a daily—even *hourly*—basis, it raises an enormous obstacle for the borderline individual struggling with black-or-white perceptions to hurdle. The same holds true for the therapist trying to help his borderline patient see the grays in the world. According to recent surveys, 87 percent of therapists report that they have spoken with their patients about politics,[48] illustrating the pervasiveness of societal polarization not only in the minds of individuals seeking psychological help, but also among therapists in a setting that traditionally focuses on personal issues.

Catastrophic Events: Mass/School Shootings and Global Pandemics

It should come as no surprise to anyone living in America that the number of mass/school shootings and the resultant casualties have soared over the last decade. What may be surprising is the relative dearth of scientific studies concerning the mental health consequences of mass shootings. However, the limited research suggests that mass shooting incidents can lead to an array of mental health problems in members of affected communities and in indirectly exposed populations.[49]

The existing research points to an increased prevalence of major depressive disorder (MDD), PTSD, and generalized anxiety disorder (GAD) in the shooting's immediate aftermath and over the long term, in younger societal populations.[50] Like the baby boomers who as schoolchildren were terrorized by drills that instructed them to hide under their desks in case of a nuclear attack, today's children undergo practice evacuations to prepare for armed attacks. For those vulnerable with BPD symptoms, emotions like anxiety and fear are significantly magnified.

Global pandemics, such as the coronavirus (Covid-19) scourge that, as of this writing, has infected and killed millions of people worldwide, may be an even greater source of anxiety for people of all ages than the school-shooting epidemic. To combat the pandemic, citizens of all countries were instructed to practice social distancing, and many regions of the world ordered outright lockdowns or shelter-in-place restrictions where social gatherings of any size were banned. Mental health professionals were quick to point out the psychological dangers of social distancing: "As people distance themselves socially, we will also be headed for a social recession [as well as an economic one]," said Dr. Vivek Murthy, former U.S. Surgeon General. "Loneliness and social isolation are huge problems in our country . . . [leading to] shorter lives, high risk of heart disease, diabetes, dementia, depression, anxiety." The U.S. Department of Health Resources and Services Administration was even more blunt: "Loneliness can be as damaging as fifteen cigarettes a day."[51]

Undoubtedly, large portions of the world population experience anxiety, stress, and loneliness during pandemics, but for those afflicted with BPD, isolation and solitude can be excruciatingly painful, a "plague" to be avoided as much or more than the virus itself. Isolation can trigger feelings of hopelessness, emptiness, fear of abandonment, and paranoia—all primary criteria of BPD. Adding to this snowball effect, social distancing and stay-at-home edicts over extended periods depress attendance at much-needed group and one-on-one therapy meetings. Also, if partners/spouses are forced into isolation, in many cases in cramped quarters with their children, it can exacerbate unstable and intense interpersonal relationships and anger, also BPD criteria. As the Covid-19 pandemic is so recent, the long-term effects of prolonged or even short periods of isolation on adults—*and* children—are unknown, but future studies are likely to find that the deleterious effects are going to be more lasting for people with BPD or other mental illnesses.

Technology: The Antisocial Social Media, Identity Theft, and Hookup Havens

History shows that technological innovation is always a double-edged sword. Automation in manufacturing processes leads to increased productivity but often results in a loss of jobs. Online shopping, banking, and stock investing are incredibly convenient but also have unhealthy side effects: the closing of local brick-and-mortar businesses, identity theft, criminal digital corruption (think Bernie Madoff). The sudden loss of a job or of one's life savings is horrendous for anyone, but for someone with BPD such a profound and abrupt life disruption is catastrophic.

The internet provides great convenience and accessibility to scholarly research in numerous fields, but also the significant challenge of data unreliability and factual inaccuracy. Social media and dating websites have forged instantaneous connections for millions of people, but have also produced cyberbullying and dangerous liaisons. In fact, much of recent American history can be framed as the inability of governmental, educational, and social institutions to keep up with, much less control, technological innovation in such areas as (nuclear) war weaponry, global warming, mass shootings and street crime, and negative social interaction.

Antisocial Media

School bullies have been around as long as schools have existed, of course, but *cyberbullying* is a relatively new phenomenon that has developed along with social media. According to recent studies, the percentage of youth who experience cyberbullying ranges from 10 to 40 percent, depending on the age group and how cyberbullying is defined.[52] One commonly used definition is "an aggressive, intentional act or behavior carried out by a group or individual, using electronic forms of contact, repeatedly and over time, against a victim who cannot easily defend him- or herself."

Harmful bullying behavior—especially prevalent among teenagers using social media platforms such as Twitter and Facebook, but also present on online gaming sites and in text messaging—can include posting rumors, threats, compromising photos, sexual comments, the victim's personal information, or pejorative labels (i.e., hate speech). Victims of cyberbullying typically experience lower self-esteem, increased suicidal ideation and suicide attempts, and a variety of negative feelings—fear, anger, frustration, and depression.[53]

It is not difficult to conclude that those with BPD, who are already exhibiting many of these symptoms (see chapter 2), are particularly vulnerable. What's more, considering the conflicting sadistic and masochistic tendencies of BPD, the borderline individual may sometimes adapt to the role of either the bully or the bullied.

Identity Theft

Though we are repeatedly assured that our personal data will be kept safe and confidential, large-scale data breaches in major corporations, banks, and institutions have happened nevertheless: Yahoo, JPMorgan Chase, Marriott, Target, eBay, and Facebook are just a few of many companies in which the personal data of 50 million or more customers were compromised. Whether through internal snafus, corruption, or the heinous acts of hackers, the cases of identity theft in the United States almost tripled in 2016 compared to 2005. More than a third of victims who spent six months or more resolving financial and credit problems experienced severe emotional distress.[54]

Apart from the financial, practical, and emotional distress these thefts cause, there's the psychological toll. For a mentally healthy person, identity theft is quite a blow; for someone with BPD, who is already burdened with a shaky sense of identity, the theft of her identity (see chapter 1)—or the widespread *threat* of theft—can be anxiety-provoking at best, devastating at worst.

Hookup Havens

Memberships in online dating websites, such as Match.com, eharmony, and others, have been increasing steadily for thirty years, spurring thousands of new relationships and marriages. Over the years, most members have come to recognize the efficiency benefits afforded by these sites and the hidden risks—namely, that the purported dashing forty-year-old millionaire may in real life turn out to be a homely sixty-year-old ex-convict living in his mother's basement. A standard protocol among prospective daters has developed over time—emails, then phone calls, and then meeting for the first time in a public place, such as a Starbucks. In short, most single people are aware of the risks, lower their expectations, and take precautions.

The emergence of sites often used to find a quick hookup in the 2010s, however, has changed the online dating landscape. To oversimplify, the intent of a hookup app is to quickly arrange a nearby one-night stand, by swiping left or right on a photo and brief profile. If things progress after that, so be it, but there are few expectations and even fewer precautions taken in terms of researching or getting to know one's date before meeting in person. Both Tinder and Grindr (the gay, bi, trans, and queer version of Tinder) have grown exponentially worldwide since their inception in 2012 and 2009, respectively; the vast majority of users are eighteen to thirty-five years old.[55] Proportionately, Tinder and Grindr hookups have been linked to violent and nonviolent crime far more often than the traditional dating sites, a trend first noted in the UK and confirmed by studies in the United States.[56]

According to several recent studies among college-age people, Tinder users—male and female—have lower self-esteem, more body dissatisfaction, and more mood swings.[57] It is not a huge leap to see the temptation—and potential danger—of hookup apps for the borderline person prone to impulsivity, promiscuity, chronic feelings of emptiness, and unstable and intense relationships. Indeed, for the borderline individual, consenting to sexual intimacy may in reality result in playful seduction, cruel manipulation, or destructive exploitation.

Microscopic "Mindfields"

From an early age we are conditioned by Hollywood to believe that mayhem comes in the form of mammoth monsters like Godzilla, King Kong, the runaway raptors of *Jurassic Park*, the huge hungry shark in *Jaws*, or the aliens in *War of the Worlds*. Or massive natural disasters—cyclones, earthquakes, hurricanes, tsunamis, or asteroids—like those shown in *Twister*, *Armageddon*, and *The Day After Tomorrow*. Or giant nuclear disasters, bombs, and missiles that hover over the apocalyptic genre in films such as *The Road*, *Dr. Strangelove*, or *Fail Safe*.

But movies are not the real world, and over the last two decades, we have learned that the infinitesimal and intangible can also wreak havoc. Invisible viruses and electronic bytes of code, imperceptible pollution agents, and hurtful miscommunication and disinformation mediated along microscopic brain synapses can wreak major psychological and physical damage. In tandem with individual action, a modern society must be prepared and willing to spend whatever it takes to protect, prepare, and deal with these invisible societal enemies for the sake of the physical—and mental—health of its people.

Chapter Five

The SET-UP System of Communication

All right . . . what do you want me to say? Do you want me to say it's funny, so you can contradict me and say it's sad? Or do you want me to say it's sad so you can turn around and say no, it's funny. You can play that damn little game any way you want to, you know!

—From *Who's Afraid of Virginia Woolf?* by Edward Albee

A person with BPD shifts her personality like a rotating kaleidoscope, rearranging the fragmented glass of her being into different formations—each collage different, yet each, her. Like a chameleon, she transforms herself into any shape that she imagines will please the viewer.

Dealing with borderline behavior can be frustrating for everyone in regular contact with BPD victims because, as we have seen, explosions of anger, rapid mood swings, suspiciousness, impulsive actions, unpredictable outbursts, self-destructive actions, and inconsistent communications are understandably upsetting to all those around them.

In this chapter we describe a consistent, structured method of communicating with those with BPD—the SET-UP system—that can be easily understood and adopted by family, friends, and therapists for use on a daily basis, and which may help in convincing an individual with BPD symptoms to consider treatment (see chapter 7).

The SET-UP system was originally developed in a hospital-affiliated system designed specifically for borderline patients. It evolved as a structured framework of communication with the borderline patient in crisis. Originally taught to hospital staff, it was adapted for the family members and loved ones of BPD patients. During stressful times, communication with a person with BPD is hindered by his impenetrable, chaotic internal force field, characterized by three major feeling states: terrifying aloneness, feeling misunderstood, and overwhelming helplessness.

As a result, concerned individuals are often unable to reason calmly with the borderline individual and instead are forced to confront outbursts of rage, impulsive destructiveness, self-harming threats or gestures, and unreasonable demands for caretaking. The SET-UP system will help you handle this onslaught of emotion with built-in SET-UP responses that can serve to address the underlying fears, dilute the borderline conflagration, and prevent a meltdown into greater conflict.

This communication system is not a formalized therapy. Unlike standard treatment programs directed at durable behavioral changes, SET-UP was designed to confront acute situational occurrences, to ease communication, and to avoid escalation during potential conflicts. Nevertheless, the goals of SET-UP, utilized by nonprofessionals, are consistent with those of formalized programs conducted by clinicians.

- Like CBT (cognitive behavioral therapy), SET-UP identifies negative thinking patterns and unproductive behavior and works with the borderline individual to make adjustments.

- Like DBT (dialectical behavioral therapy), SET-UP prioritizes destructive impulses and offers productive and logical responses to emotional distress.

- Like MBT (mentalization-based therapy), SET-UP emphasizes self-awareness and awareness of others, and confronts problems of trust and relationships.

- Like TFP (transference-focused psychotherapy), SET-UP attempts to alter distorted representations of the borderline self and others.

- Like SFT (schema-focused therapy), SET-UP deals with rejection hypersensitivity and abandonment concerns.

- Like exposure therapy used in treatment for phobias and PTSD (post-traumatic stress disorder), SET-UP confronts feared or traumatic situations.

For further discussion of these formalized programs, see chapter 8.

Like these and other standardized therapy programs, SET-UP encourages mentalization and mindfulness and the courage to confront painful reality dilemmas. (The concepts of mentalization and mindfulness involve focusing attention on the present moment and understanding the mental state of oneself and of others that underlies their behaviors. In the process, reflexive emotional responses are subdued.) Although the SET-UP program was originally developed specifically for the borderline patient in crisis, it can also be useful for others who require concise, consistent communication, even when not in crisis.

SET-UP Communication

SET—*Support, Empathy, Truth*—is a three-part system of communication (see Figure 5-1). During confrontations of destructive behavior, important decision-making sessions, or other crises, interactions with the borderline individual should invoke all three elements in balanced proportion. This SET portion is the primary ongoing strategy for maintaining a constructive interaction *in the moment*. UP stands for *Understanding* and *Perseverance*—the overarching attitudes that encourage continuing commitment to the relationship and the goals that all parties try to achieve and maintain *over the long term*.

The *S* stage of SET, *Support*, invokes a personal "I" statement of concern. "I am sincerely worried about how you are feeling," "I'm concerned about what you're dealing with," and "I want to help" are examples of *Support* statements. The emphasis is on the speaker's own feelings and is essentially a personal pledge to try to be of help.

With the *Empathy* segment, one attempts to acknowledge the sufferer's anguish and chaotic feelings with a "You" statement: "How awful you must be feeling." "This must be a difficult time for you." "You must have felt really desperate to do this." "It's impossible to imagine what you must be going through." It is important not to confuse empathy with sympathy ("I feel so sorry for you"; "you poor thing"), which may elicit rage over perceived condescension. Also, *Empathy* should be expressed in a neutral way with minimal personal reference to the speaker's own feelings. The emphasis here is on the borderline person's painful experience, not the speaker's. A statement like "I know just how bad you are feeling" invites a mocking rejoinder that indeed, you do not know, and only aggravates conflict.

The *T* statement, representing *Truth*, recognizes the reality of the

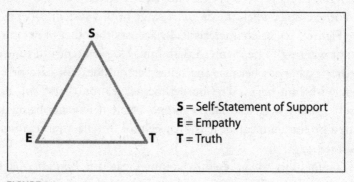

FIGURE 5-1

situation and emphasizes that the person with BPD is ultimately accountable for his life and that others' attempts to help cannot preempt this primary responsibility. While *Support* and *Empathy* are subjective statements confirming how the principals feel and are usually communicated first, *Truth* statements acknowledge that a problem exists and address the practical objective issue of what can be done to solve it. "Well, what do you think we can do about it?" is one essential *Truth* response. Other characteristic *Truth* expressions refer to actions that the speaker feels compelled to take in response to borderline behaviors. These *Truth* statements should be expressed in a neutral matter-of-fact fashion ("Here's what happened . . . These are the consequences . . . This is what I can do . . . What are you going to do?"). But they should be stated in a way that avoids blaming and sadistic punishing ("This is a fine mess you've gotten us into!" "You made your bed; now lie in it!"). *Truth* is also intended to begin consideration of possible solutions and to counter expressions of hopelessness and helplessness. The *Truth* part of the SET system is the most important and the most difficult for the borderline person to accept, since so much of his world view excludes or rejects realistic consequences.

Communication with the borderline individual should attempt to include all three messages. However, even if all three parts are stated, he may not integrate all of them. Predictable responses result when one of these levels is either not clearly stated or is not "heard."

For example, when the *Support* stage of this system is bypassed (see Figure 5-2), he characteristically accuses the other of not caring or not wanting to be involved with him. He then tends to tune out further exchanges because the other person does not care or may even wish him harm. The borderline accusation that "You don't care!" usually suggests that the *Support* statement is not being integrated or communicated. It is then helpful to reflect more *Support* assurances.

The inability to successfully communicate the *Empathy* part of the message (see Figure 5-3) leads to feelings that the other person does not understand what the borderline individual is going through.

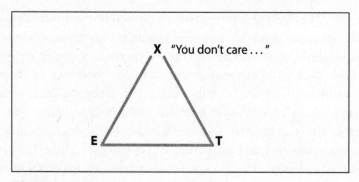

FIGURE 5-2

("You don't know how I feel!") Here, he will justify his rejection of the communication by saying he is being misunderstood. Since the other person cannot appreciate the pain, that person's responses can be devalued. When either the *Support* or the *Empathy* overtures are not accepted, further communications are not heard. Therefore, it is often necessary to reinforce *Support* and/or *Empathy* statements when you are accused of not caring or not understanding.

When the *Truth* element is not clearly expressed (see Figure 5-4), a more dangerous situation emerges. A borderline individual will interpret others' acquiescence in ways he finds most comfortable for his needs, usually as confirmation that others really can be responsible for him when he cannot, or that his own perceptions are

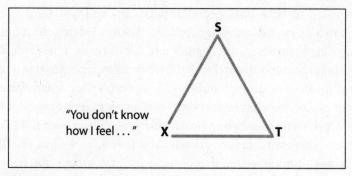

FIGURE 5-3

universally shared and supported. The borderline individual's fragile merger with these other people eventually disintegrates when the relationship is unable to sustain the weight of his unrealistic expectations. Without clearly stated *Truth* and confrontation, he continues to be overly entangled with others. His needs gratified, he will perceive that all is well, or at least that things will get better without further effort on his part. Indeed, the evidence for this enmeshment is often a striking temporary absence of conflict. He will exhibit less hostility and anger. However, when his unrealistic expectations are eventually frustrated, the relationship collapses in a fiery maelstrom of anger and disappointment.

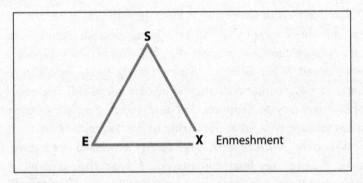

FIGURE 5-4

The UP extension to the SET framework is intended as a continuous reminder that relationships require *Understanding* and *Perseverance*. Understanding borderline pathology and symptoms allows for patience in pursuing improvement. Acknowledging the anguish of an illness, however, is recognition of adjustments to be made, not absolution from responsibility. Persevering in treatment and in a relationship, despite disappointments, is necessary for improvement. Often one of the most important contributors to improved health is the fact that the community surrounding the person with BPD—his doctors, therapists, family, friends, and lovers, as well as the BPD individual himself—consistently hung in there despite the frustrations along the way. It is helpful for all involved in the relationships,

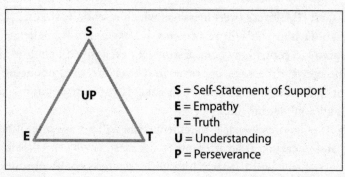

S = Self-Statement of Support
E = Empathy
T = Truth
U = Understanding
P = Perseverance

FIGURE 5-5

through spoken and unspoken communications, to continue to sustain these sentiments (see Figure 5-5).

Borderline Dilemmas

The SET-UP principles can be used in a variety of settings in attempts to defuse unstable situations. Following are some typical borderline predicaments in which the SET strategy may be used.

Damned If You Do and Damned If You Don't

Borderline confusion often results in contradictory messages to others. Frequently, the person with BPD will communicate one position with words but will express a contradictory message with behavior. Although she may not be consciously aware of this dilemma, she frequently places a friend or relation in a no-win situation in which she condemns him, no matter which way he goes. ("Tell me, which one of these dresses makes me look fatter?" . . . "Why do *you* think I'm mad at you?")

CASE 1: GLORIA AND ALEX. Gloria tells her husband Alex that she is forlorn and depressed. She says she plans to kill herself but forbids him from seeking help for her.

In this situation, Alex is confronted with two contradictory messages: (1) Gloria's overt message, which essentially states, "If you care about me, you will respect my wishes and not challenge my autonomy to control my own destiny and even die, if I choose"; and (2) the opposite message, conveyed in the very act of announcing her intentions, which says, "For God's sake, if you care about me, help me, and don't let me die."

If Alex ignores Gloria's statements, she will accuse him of being cold and uncaring. If he attempts to list reasons why she should not kill herself, she will frustrate him with relentless counterarguments and will ultimately condemn him for not truly understanding her pain. If he calls the police or her doctor, he will be rejecting her requests and proving that she cannot trust him.

Because Gloria doesn't feel strong enough to take responsibility for her own life, she looks to Alex to take on this burden. She feels overwhelmed and helpless in the wake of her depression. By drawing Alex into this drama, she is making him a character in her own scripted play, with an uncertain ending to be resolved not by herself, but by Alex. She faces her ambivalence about suicide by turning over to him the responsibility for her fate.

Further, Gloria splits off the negative portions of her available choices and projects them onto Alex, preserving for herself the positive side of the ambivalence. No matter how Alex responds, he will be criticized. If he does not actively intercede, he is uncaring and heartless and she is "tragically misunderstood." If he tries to stop her suicide attempts, he is controlling and insensitive, while she is bereft of her self-respect.

Either way, Gloria envisions herself a helpless and self-righteous martyr—a victim who has been deprived by Alex of achieving her full potential. As for Alex, he is damned if he does and damned if he doesn't!

SET-UP principles may be helpful in confronting a difficult situation like this. Ideally, Alex's responses should embrace all three sides of the SET triangle. Alex's S statement should be a declaration of his commitment to Gloria and his wish to help her: "I am very concerned about how bad you are feeling and want to help because

I love you." If the couple can identify the specific areas of concern that are adding to her anguish, he could suggest solutions and proclaim his willingness to help: "I think some of this might be related to the problems you've been having with your boss. Let's discuss some of the alternatives. Maybe you could ask for a transfer. Or if the job is causing you this much difficulty, I want you to know that it's okay with me if you want to quit and look for another job."

The *E* statement should attempt to convey Alex's awareness of Gloria's current pain and his understanding of how such extreme circumstances might lead her to contemplate ending her life: "The pressure you've been under these past several months must be getting unbearable. All of this agony must be bringing you to the edge, to a point where you feel like you just can't go on anymore."

The most important part of Alex's *T* statement should identify his untenable "damned if he does and damned if he doesn't" dilemma. He should also attempt to clarify Gloria's ambivalence about dying by acknowledging that in addition to that part of her that wants to end her life, another part of her wishes to be saved and helped. Alex's *T* responses might be something like: "I recognize how bad you are feeling and your thoughts about dying. I know you said that if I cared at all for you, I should just leave you alone. But if I cared, how could I possibly sit back and watch you destroy yourself? Your alerting me to your suicidal plans tells me that as much as you may wish to just give up, there is at least some part of you that doesn't want to die. And it is to that part that I feel I must respond. I want you to come with me to see a doctor to help us with these problems."

Depending on the immediacy of the circumstances, Alex should insist that Gloria be psychiatrically evaluated soon, or if she is in imminent danger, he should take her to an emergency room or seek help from police or paramedics.

At this juncture Gloria's fury may be exacerbated as she blames Alex for forcing her into the hospital. But *Truth* statements should remind Gloria that she is there not so much because of what Alex did, but because of what Gloria did—threatening suicide. The borderline individual may frequently need to be reminded that others' reactions to her are based primarily on what *she* does, and that *she* must take responsibility for the consequences, rather than blaming others for realistic responses to her behavior.

When the immediate danger has passed, subsequent *T* statements should refer to Gloria's unproductive patterns of handling stress and the need to develop more effective ways of dealing with her life. *Truth* considerations should also include how Gloria's and Alex's behaviors affect each other and their marriage. Over time they may be able to work out a system of responding to each other, either on their own or within therapy, that will fulfill the needs of both.

This kind of problem is especially common within families of borderline patients who display prominent self-destructive behaviors. Delinquent or suicidal adolescents and alcoholic and anorexic patients may present similar no-win dilemmas to their families. They actively resist help while behaving in obviously self-destructive ways. Usually, direct confrontation that precipitates a crisis is the only way to help. Some groups, such as Alcoholics Anonymous, recommend standardized confrontational situations in which family, friends, or coworkers, often together with a counselor, confront the patient with his addictive behavior and demand treatment.

Tough Love groups believe that true caring forces the individual to face the consequences of his behaviors rather than protecting him from them. Tough Love groups for parents of teenagers, for example, may insist that an adolescent drug abuser either be hospitalized or be barred from the home. This type of approach emphasizes the *Truth* element of the SET-UP triangle but may ignore the *Support* and *Empathy* segments. Therefore, these systems may be only partially successful for the person afflicted with BPD who may go through the motions of change that *Truth* confrontations force on him. Underneath, however, the lack of nurturing and trust provided by *Support* and *Empathy* hinders his motivation for dedicated and lasting change.

Feeling Bad About Feeling Bad

Borderline individuals typically respond to depression, anxiety, frustration, or anger by superimposing more layers of these same feelings. Because of his perfectionism and tendency to perceive things in black-and-white extremes, he attempts to obliterate unpleasant feelings rather than understand or cope with them. When he finds that he cannot simply erase these bad feelings, he becomes even more frustrated or guilty. Since feeling bad is unacceptable, he feels bad about feeling bad. When this makes him feel even worse, he becomes caught in a seemingly bottomless downward spiral.

One of the goals for his therapists and other close relations is to crack through these successive layers to locate the original feeling and help him accept it as part of himself. The borderline individual must learn to allow himself the luxury of "bad" feelings without rebuke, guilt, or denial.

CASE 2: NEIL AND FRIENDS. Neil, a fifty-three-year-old bank officer, has had episodes of depression for more than half his life. Neil's parents died when he was young, and he was reared mostly by his much older unmarried sister, who was cold and hypercritical. She was a religious zealot who insisted he attend church services daily and frequently accused him of sinful transgressions.

Neil grew up to become a passive man, dominated by his wife. He was reared to believe that anger was unacceptable and denied ever feeling angry at others. He was hardworking and respected at his job but received little affection from his wife. She rejected his sexual advances, which frustrated and depressed him. Neil would initially get angry at his wife for her rejections, then feel guilty and get angry at himself for being angry, and then lapse into depression. This process permeated other areas of Neil's life. Whenever he was mistreated, he felt it was deserved. If he responded with resentment or other negative feelings, he would pressure himself to end them. Since he could not control his inner feelings, he became increasingly disappointed and frustrated with himself. His depression worsened.

Neil's friends tried to comfort him. They told him they were behind him and were available whenever he wanted to talk. They empathized with his discomfort at work and his problems in dealing with his wife. They pointed out that "he was feeling bad over feeling bad," and that he should pull himself together. This advice, however, didn't help; in fact, Neil felt worse because he now felt he was letting his friends down on top of everything else. The harder he tried to stop his negative feelings, the more he felt like a failure, and the more depressed he became.

SET-UP statements from his friends could help Neil confront this dilemma. Neil received much *Support* and *Empathy* from his friends, but their *Truth* messages were not helpful. Rather than trying to erase his unpleasant emotions (an all-or-none proposition), Neil must understand the necessity of accepting them as real and appropriate, within a nonjudgmental context. Instead of adding layers of more self-condemnation, which allows him to continue to wallow in the muck of "woe is me," he must instead confront the criticism and work to change.

Further *Truth* statements would acknowledge the reasons for Neil's passive behavior and the behaviors of his wife and others in his life. He must recognize that, to some degree, he places himself in a position of being abused by others. Although he can work to change this situation in the future, he must now deal with the way things are currently. This means recognizing that he is angry, that he has reasons to be angry, and that he has no choice but to accept his anger, for he cannot make it disappear, at least not right away. Though he may regret the presence of unacceptable feelings, he is powerless to change them (a dictum similar to those used in Alcoholics Anonymous). Accepting these uncomfortable feelings means accepting himself as an imperfect human being and relinquishing the illusion that he can control uncontrollable factors. If Neil can accept his anger or his sadness or any unpleasant feeling, the "feeling bad about feeling bad" phenomenon will be short-circuited. He can move on to change other aspects of his life.

Much of Neil's professional success has resulted from trying harder. Studying harder usually results in better grades. Practicing harder usually results in a better performance. But some situations in life require the opposite. The more you grit your teeth and clench your fists and try to go to sleep, the more likely you will be awake all night. The harder you try to make yourself relax, the more tense you may become. The more you try to not be anxious, the more anxious you become.

Someone trapped in this dilemma will often break free when he least expects it—when he relaxes, becomes less obsessive and self-demanding, and learns to accept himself. It is no coincidence that the borderline character who seeks a healthy love relationship more often finds it when he is least desperate for one and more engaged in self-fulfilling activities. For it is at this point that he is more attractive to others and less pressured to grasp at immediate and unrealistic solutions to loneliness.

The Perennial Victim

A person with BPD frequently gets involved in predicaments in which he becomes a victim. Neil, for example, perceives himself as a helpless character upon whom others act. Borderline behavior is frequently provocative or dangerous and may in some way invite persecution. The woman who continually chooses men who abuse her is typically unaware of the patterns she is repeating. The split view of the borderline self includes a special entitled part and an angry unworthy part that masochistically deserves punishment, although he may not be consciously aware of one side or the other. In fact, a pattern of this type of "invited" victimization is often a solid indication of BPD pathology.

Although being a victim is most unpleasant, it can also be a very appealing role. Indeed, sometimes there can be a fear of giving up that identity role, expressed by persistent self-sabotaging behavior, in an unconscious resistance to "getting better." A helpless waif, buffeted by the turbulent seas of an unfair world, is very attractive to some people. A match between an overwhelmed and inconsolable damsel and one who feels a strong urge to rescue and take care of others satisfies needs for both parties. Borderline identity finds a "kind stranger" who promises complete and total protection. And the partner fulfills his own desire to feel strong, protective, important, and needed—to be the one to "take her away from all this."

In this situation the roles of the hero and the forlorn waif are mutually reinforcing. The hero feels powerful and develops a sense of purpose in protecting his charge. The oppressed borderline woman feels more secure and can avoid responsibility. They may cling to these roles. He may feel threatened if she appears more independent, and she may become fearful if he exhibits vulnerability.

CASE 3: ANNETTE. Born to a poor black family, Annette lost her father at a very young age when he abandoned the household. A succession of other men briefly occupied the "father" chair in the home. Eventually her mother remarried, but her second husband was also a drinker and carouser. When Annette was about eight, her stepfather began sexually abusing her and her sister. Annette was afraid to tell her mother, who gloried in the family's finally achieving some financial security. So Annette continued to keep her stepfather's abuse a secret—"for her mother's sake."

At seventeen, Annette became pregnant and married the baby's father. She managed to graduate from high school, where her grades were generally good, but other aspects of her life were in turmoil: her husband drank and ran around with other women. After a while, he began beating her. She continued to bear more of his children, complaining and enduring—"for the children's sake."

After six years and three children, Annette's husband left her. His departure prompted a kind of anxious relief—the wild ride was finally over, but concerns over what to do next loomed ominously.

Annette and the kids tried to make things work, but she felt constantly overwhelmed. Then she met John, who was about twenty-five years older (he refused to tell her his exact age) and seemed to have a genuine desire to take care of her. He became the good father Annette never had. He encouraged and protected her. He advised her on how to dress and how to talk. After a while, Annette became more self-confident, got a good job, and began enjoying her life. A few months later, John moved in—sort of. He lived with her on weekends but slept away during the week because of work assignments that made it "more convenient to sleep at the office."

Deep inside, Annette knew John was married, but she never asked. When John became less dependable, stayed away more, and generally became more detached, she held in her anger. On the job, however, this anger surfaced, and she was passed over for many promotions. Her supervisors said that she lacked the academic qualifications of others and that she was abrasive, but Annette wouldn't accept those explanations.

Incensed, she attributed the rejections to racial discrimination. She became more and more depressed and eventually entered the hospital.

In the hospital, Annette's racial sensitivities exploded. Most of the doctors were white, as were most of the nurses and most of the other patients. The hospital decor was "white" and the meals were "white." All of the anger that had built up over the years was now focused on society's discrimination against blacks. By concentrating exclusively on this global issue, Annette avoided her own personal demons.

Her most challenging target was Harry, a white music therapist on staff at the hospital. Annette felt that Harry insisted on playing only "white" music, and that his looks and whole demeanor embodied "whiteness." Annette vented her fury on this therapist, and she would stalk away angrily from the music therapy sessions.

Although Harry was frightened by the outbursts, he sought out Annette. His *Support* statement reflected his personal concern about Annette's progress in the hospital program. Harry expressed his *Empathy* for Annette by voicing his recognition of how frustrating it feels to be discriminated against, and cited his own experiences as one of the only Jews in his educational program. Then Harry attempted to confront the *Truth*, or reality, issues in Annette's life, pointing out that railing against racial discrimination in society and her company, *though justified and important*, was overwhelming her need to make changes in her personal mindset. Annette's need to remain a victim, Harry said, shielded her from assuming any responsibility for what happened in her life. She could feel justified in cursing society rather than bravely investigating her own role in continuing to be used by others. By wrapping herself in a veil of righteous anger, Annette was avoiding any kind of frightening self-examination or confrontation that might induce change, and thereby was perpetuating her impotency and helplessness. This left her incapable of making changes "for *her* sake."

At the next music therapy session, Annette did not stalk out of the room. Instead, she confronted Harry and the other patients. She suggested different songs to play. At the following meeting the group agreed to play some gospel songs of Annette's choosing. Later, Harry complimented Annette on her openness to hear what he was trying to communicate (*Understanding*), and her willingness to hang in there with him (*Perseverance*) while they worked together.

Harry's responses, exemplifying SET-UP principles, would also have been useful for Annette's boss, her friends—anyone who faced her angry outbursts on a regular basis.

SET-UP communication can free a person with BPD or anyone who is locked into a victim role by pointing out the advantages of being a victim (being cared for, appearing blameless for bad results, disavowing responsibility) and the disadvantages (abdicating autonomy, maintaining obsequious dependency, remaining fixated and immobile amid life's dilemmas). The borderline "victim" must, however, hear all three parts of the message, otherwise the impact of the message will be lost. If "the Truth will set you free," then *Support* and *Empathy* must accompany it to ensure it will be heard.

Quest for Meaning

Much of dramatic borderline behavior is related to his interminable search for something to fill the emptiness that continually haunts him. Destructive relationships, binge eating, self-injuring, and drugs are some of the mechanisms the borderline person uses to combat the loneliness and to capture a sense of existing in a world that feels real.

CASE 4: RICH. "I guess I just love too much!" said Rich in describing his problems with his girlfriend. He was a thirty-year-old divorced man who had a succession of disastrous affairs with women. He would cling obsessively to these women, showering them with gifts and attention. Through them he felt whole, alive, and fulfilled. But he demanded from them—and from other friends—total obedience. In this way he felt in control, not only of them but, more important, of his own existence.

He became distraught when these women acted independently. He cajoled, insisted, and threatened. To stave off the omnipresent sense of emptiness, he attempted to control others; if they refused to comply with his wishes, Rich became seriously depressed and out of control. He turned to alcohol or drugs to recapture his sense of being or authenticity. Sometimes he picked fights with girlfriends or even with strangers when he knew he would lose the conflict. He intentionally engaged in road-rage incidents that required police intervention. Sometimes he cut himself when he feared he was losing touch with his sensory or emotional feelings. When the anger and pain no longer brought changes, he would take up with another woman who perceived him as "misunderstood" and merely needing "the love of a good woman." Then the process would start all over again.

Rich lacked insight into his dilemma, insisting that it was always "the bitch's fault." He dismissed his friends as not caring or not understanding—*Support* and *Empathy* were not being heard. The women he became involved with were initially sympathetic but lacked the *Truth* component. Rich needed to be confronted with all three aspects.

In this situation, where sadly none of the essential aspects of SET were being heard, the *S* message would continue to convey caring about Rich. The *E* part would accept without challenge Rich's feeling of "loving too much" but would also help him understand his sense of emptiness and his need to fill it.

The *Truth* message would attempt to point out the patterns in Rich's life that seem to repeat endlessly. *Truth* should also help Rich see that he uses women as he does drugs and self-mutilation—as objects or maneuvers to relieve numbness and feel whole. As long as Rich continues to search outside himself for inner contentment, he will remain frustrated and disappointed, because he cannot control outside forces and especially others as he can himself. For instance, despite his most frenzied efforts to regulate her, a new girlfriend will eventually retain some independence outside the realm of Rich's control. Similarly, he could lose a new job, through no fault of his own, due to economic factors that may eliminate the position. Rich *cannot* dominate these situations, but he *can* control his own creative powers, intellectual curiosity, and so on. Independent personal interests—books, hobbies, arts, sports, exercise—can serve as reliable and enduring sources of satisfaction, sources that cannot easily be taken away.

Search for Constancy

Adjusting to a world that is continually inconsistent and untrustworthy is a major problem for someone with BPD. His universe lacks pattern and predictability. Friends, jobs, and skills can never be relied upon. He must keep testing and retesting all of these aspects of his life; he is in constant fear that a trusted person or situation will change into the total opposite—absolute betrayal. A hero becomes a devil; the perfect job becomes the bane of his existence. The borderline person cannot conceive that individual or situational object constancy (see chapter 2 and Appendix B) can endure. He has no laurels on which to rest. Every day he must begin anew, trying desperately to prove to himself that the world can be trusted. Just because the sun has risen in the east for thousands of years does not mean it will happen today. He must see it for himself each and every day.

CASE 5: PAT AND JAKE. Pat was an attractive twenty-nine-year-old woman in the process of divorcing her second husband. As with her first husband, she accused him of being an alcoholic and of abusing her. Her lawyer, Jake, saw her as an unfortunate victim in need of protection. He called her frequently to be sure she was all right. They began to have lunch together. As the case proceeded, they became lovers. Jake moved out of his house and away from his wife and two sons. Though not yet divorced, Pat moved in with him.

At first Pat admired Jake's intelligence and expertise. Where she felt weak and defenseless, he seemed "big and strong." But over time she became increasingly demanding. As long as Jake was protective, Pat cooed. But when he began to make demands, she became hostile. She resented his going to work and particularly his involvement in other divorce cases. She resisted his visits to his children and accused him of choosing them over her. She would initiate brutal arguments that often culminated in her rushing out of the house to spend the night with a male "platonic friend."

Pat lacked object constancy (see chapter 2 and Appendix B). Friendships and love relationships had to be constantly tested because she never felt secure with any human contact. Her need for reassurance was insatiable. She had been through countless other relationships in which she first appeared ingenuous and in need of caretaking and then tested them with outrageous demands. The relationships all ended with precisely the abandonment she feared; then she would repeat the process in her next romance.

At first, when Pat perceived Jake as supportive and reassuring, she idealized their relationship. But when he exhibited signs of functioning separately, she became enraged, cursing and denigrating him. When he was at the office, she would call him incessantly because, as she said, she was "forgetting him." To her friends, Jake sounded like two completely different people; for Pat, he was.

SET confrontations of object inconstancy require recognition of this borderline dilemma. *Support* statements must convey that caring is constant, unconditional. Unfortunately, with BPD it is difficult for Pat to grasp that she does not need to demand acceptance continuously. She is in constant fear that *Support* could be withdrawn if at any point she displeases. Thus, attempts at reassurance are never-ending and never enough.

The *Empathy* message should confirm an understanding that Pat has not yet learned to trust Jake's continual attempts at comfort. Jake must communicate his awareness of the horrific anxieties Pat is experiencing and how frightening it is for her to be alone.

Truth declarations must include attempts to reconcile the split parts. Jake has to explain that he cares for Pat all the time, even when he is frustrated by her. He must also declare his intention not to allow himself to be abused. Capitulation to Pat's demands will only result in more demands. Trying to please and satisfy Pat is an impossible task, for it is never finished—new insecurities will always arise. *Truth* will probably mandate ongoing therapy for both of them, if their relationship is to continue.

The Rage of Innocence

Borderline rage is often terrifying in its unpredictability and intensity. It may be sparked by relatively insignificant events and explode without warning within a context of normal pleasant interactions. It may be directed at previously valued people. The threat of violence sometimes accompanies this anger. All of these features make borderline rage much different from typical anger.

In an instant, Pat could transform from docile, dependent, and childlike to demanding, screaming, and inconsolable. On one occasion she tenderly suggested that she and Jake have a quiet romantic lunch together. But when Jake told her he first had to go to the office, she suddenly began screaming at him, inches from his face, accusing him of ignoring her needs. She viciously attacked his manhood, his failures as a husband and father, and his profession. She threatened to report him to the bar association for misconduct. When Jake's attempts to placate her failed, he would silently walk away, which infuriated Pat even more. When he returned later on, both would act as if nothing had ever happened.

SET-UP principles must first of all address safety issues. Volatility must be contained. In the scenario above, Jake's *Support* and *Empathy* messages should come first, though Pat will probably reject them as insincere. In such cases it is imprudent for Jake to continue to argue that he cares and understands that she is upset. He must move immediately to *Truth* statements, which must first mandate that neither of them will physically harm the other. He must firmly tell her to back off, to allow some physical distance. He can inform her of his wish to communicate calmly with her. If she will not allow this, he can state his intention of leaving until the situation quiets down, at which point they can resume discussions. He must try to avoid physical conflict, despite Pat's provocations. Although unconsciously Pat may actually want Jake to physically overpower her, this need is based on unhealthy experiences from her past and will likely later be used to criticize him more.

Truth statements made during angry confrontations are often better directed toward the underlying dynamics than toward the specifics of the clash. Further debate about whether taking Pat to lunch is more important than going to the office will probably be unproductive. However, Jake might address Pat's apparent need to fight and her possible wish to be overpowered and hurt. He might also confront Pat's behavior as a need to be rejected. Is she so fearful of rejection that she is precipitating it in order to "hurry up and get it over with"? The primary *Truth* message is that this behavior is driving Jake away. He may ask if this is really what Pat wants.

The Need for Consistency—Setting Limits

All *Truth* statements must indeed be true. For the borderline person, already living in a world of inconsistencies, it is much worse to make idle threats about the unenforced consequences of an action than to passively allow inappropriate behaviors to continue. In *Fatal Attraction*, for example, Alex Forrest, the main female character (played by Glenn Close) in the iconic 1987 film, exhibited several "textbook" borderline traits in the extreme, and for decades has served as the prototype of the dramatic (versus the comic) "crazy ex." Entering into an affair with Dan Gallagher (Michael Douglas), a well-ensconced married man, she refuses to let go, even after it is obvious Dan will not leave his wife. By the end of the movie, Dan, his family, and Alex are destroyed or close to it. Alex was used to resisting rejection by manipulating others. For Dan to say he was going to end the relationship without unequivocally doing so was destructive. Of course, he didn't understand that following the termination of an intense relationship, Alex is unable to "just be friends"—an in-between relationship that the borderline character finds intolerable.

Because people with BPD have such difficulty with equivocation, intentions must be backed up with clear, predictable actions. A parent who threatens his adolescent with revocation of privileges for certain behaviors and then does not carry out his promises exacerbates the problem. A therapist who purports to set limits for therapy—establishing fees, limiting phone calls, etc.—but then does not follow through invites increased borderline testing.

Borderline people are often reared in situations in which their threats and dramatic actions are the only ways to achieve what is sought. Just as the borderline individual perceives acceptance as conditional, so rejection can also be seen this way. He feels that if only he is attractive enough or smart enough or rich enough or demanding enough, he will ultimately get what he wants. The more there is acquiescence to testing behavior, the more he will employ such maneuvers.

CASE 6: KEVIN. Mr. and Mrs. Hopkins were stymied in their efforts to help Kevin, their twenty-nine-year-old son. Except for his years at a local college, during which he intermittently lived in a nearby dorm, Kevin had always lived at home. Although he achieved good grades in school and was liked by teachers and employers, Kevin had always been a loner, with few friends. He avoided family get-togethers and exhibited severe temper outbursts when stressed. Mr. and Mrs. Hopkins were cautious around their son, fearing to upset him.

After quitting another job, he spent most of his time in his room, watching TV and playing video games. He refused his parents' pleas to seek help or employment or to consider pursuing an advanced degree. Kevin prepared meals separately, ate in his room, and avoided contact with his parents. They could hear him at times screaming at himself but feared intervening.

Mr. and Mrs. Hopkins begged, demanded, and threatened, all to no avail. When they tried to take the TV out of the room, Kevin became physically aggressive and threatened suicide, since he had nothing else to do. His room was a mess, and he refused to help with household chores. Every so often, a friend would call and invite Kevin out. Kevin would then demand money for the evening, which his parents readily gave him, encouraged that he was willing to leave his room. Kevin slept until the afternoon and stayed out late when he did leave the house. Liquor bottles began to pile up in the garbage.

Mr. and Mrs. Hopkins began to argue more. Mr. Hopkins demanded that they throw Kevin out of the house, but Mrs. Hopkins feared Kevin couldn't survive on his own. Then the family endured a series of misfortunes. Mrs. Hopkins was diagnosed with breast cancer. Mr. Hopkins's business went through a financial setback. Both parents were more stressed and grew distant from each other. Mr. Hopkins continued to fume, but both silently agreed that it was easier to just give in to Kevin's lifestyle for the time being. Still, they worried: What will happen to our son when we're gone?

One late afternoon, Kevin confessed to his mother that he had just swallowed a handful of aspirin. He passively objected to his mother's calling for an ambulance, but quietly assented to be taken to the hospital. Discharged after a few days on antidepressant medicine, Kevin agreed to see a therapist.

For the next several months, things were better. Kevin got a job he liked as a teaching assistant. He helped around the house and ate dinner with his parents. He spent more time with friends. But after a while, Kevin and his family recalibrated to the previous equilibrium. He took his medications irregularly and began missing therapy appointments. He spent more time isolated in his room.

When Kevin's therapist suggested that the whole family see a family therapist together, Mr. and Mrs. Hopkins were disappointed but not surprised when Kevin didn't show up for the initial appointment. His parents were at odds on a number of issues involving Kevin, but they and the therapist all agreed on several points:

- The situation was interfering with his parents' relationship.

- The environment at home was intolerable.

- The longer it continued, the more problems Kevin would encounter down the road.

- Disrupting the current equilibrium would cause upheaval, including the risk for impulsive self-destructive behavior. (However, the risk would become greater as time went on.)

- Mr. and Mrs. Hopkins must agree on what limits would be set and what demands would be made.

- They must expect Kevin to challenge these limits and therefore be prepared to proceed with the proposed consequences.

Mr. and Mrs. Hopkins, consulting with the therapist, were at first far apart with their expectations, but they were able to find a compromise position they could both support. In a meeting of all four of them together, they presented Kevin with a written contract. It outlined their expectations over a two-month time period: Kevin was to perform a number of specific tasks in the house per week, continue with his job or find another or enroll in an educational program. If he did not fulfill the specific commitments, he would have to leave the house. Mr. and Mrs. Hopkins provided the names and numbers of shelters and of family friends who had agreed to temporarily house him. His parents would continue a set amount of financial support for described needs for a specified period of time.

During the discussion Mr. and Mrs. Hopkins explained that they

loved Kevin very much, wanted to help him feel better, and complimented him on staying with his current job (*Support*). They recognized how unhappy he was and understood that he must be dissatisfied
with his current situation (*Empathy*). They then shared their concern about the health of all three of them and made it clear that they
could not tolerate continuing the current situation. They also related
their concern that by not confronting these issues they were inadver-
tently contributing to Kevin's discontent. Finally, they acknowledged that they had had similar conversations with Kevin in the past
but had never followed through on proposals. They fully understood
that Kevin might not be able to comply with the requests, and they
were prepared to assist him in leaving (*Truth*). Their acknowledgment of Kevin's BPD diagnosis and his follow-through over the past
months of dedication to his health (and into the future) demonstrated the UP part of their communication.

Despite Kevin's heated response to their calmly presented proposal, he angrily signed the contract. Although initially Kevin was
able to fulfill the requests, by the second month, he was expressing dissatisfaction with his job and started missing work, staying in
his room. He was given gentle reminders in advance. Then on the
appointed two-month date, Kevin was told he had to leave the
house. Disbelief ("You've got to be kidding") mutated into pleading ("You can't do this to me!"), then changed into fury ("You can
take your stupid contract and stick it! I'm better off out of here
anyway!").

Over the next several months Kevin stayed with a friend, then a
cousin, then an aunt. Once, when he vaguely mentioned to his aunt
that he'd be better off dead, she took him to the emergency room for
evaluation. There he denied suicidal feelings and admitted he was
just angry and hated his living situation. Ongoing contacts with his
parents became less hostile. After finding another teaching position,
Kevin agreed he wanted to make changes in his life and asked to
return home. Within the year he had moved in with a roommate
he'd met at work and was supporting himself.

Who Am I This Time?

Like Play-Doh, the BPD individual can model herself into many configurations. While Play-Doh is composed of flour, water, salt, borax, and mineral oil, the BPD identity is fabricated from insecurity, fear, and dread. This chameleon aspect of BPD reveals her remarkable sensitivity toward others, deriving an impression of what she feels the other person wants her to be. She can sincerely slip into the protest crowd on either side of the barricade, argue both sides of the debate, yet without the context of others, she cannot divine her own, independent stance. If Dalí's surrealistic paintings represent psychotic illnesses, then BPD is the artist's trompe l'oeil—deception of the eye—in which the artificial cannot be distinguished from the real person. Like Woody Allen's famous film character Zelig, she can transform into whomever you want her to be. In the process, however, she may lose the sense of who she really is.

CASE 7: CHRISTIE AND MARTIN. Martin couldn't help noticing Christie each week at church. A seminary student, he was actively engaged in studies and assisting in services. He noticed the pretty girl who came to Sunday services alone each week, sat quietly in an aisle seat near the back, and left immediately after final blessings. Finally, after one service at which he sat with other congregants in the back, he caught up with Christie as she hurried down the steps.

She spoke softly, looking down, remarking how much she enjoyed the pastor's sermons. For the next few weeks Martin made a point of catching Christie every Sunday after church and finally worked up the nerve to ask her to brunch with him. As they talked more, shy Christie became more open. She told Martin she was a secretary at an investment firm, lived with her cat, and enjoyed movies.

Although Martin thought Christie liked him, she declined his invitations to go out Saturday night. In fact, she said, she was busy most weekends, as her boss had many foreign business transactions on Fridays and Saturdays. Just as Martin was about to give up on the relationship, Christie suggested they see a new movie together that would be opening Thursday. After that, Thursdays, and some Tuesdays, became their date nights, along with Sunday brunch. Months went by and Martin was in love. He could picture Christie— attractive, demure, soft-spoken, yet intelligent—as a perfect companion as he pursued his goals in the ministry.

Then everything changed. Martin was attending a bachelor party for a neighbor when two women came to the house in policeman uniforms that were immediately discarded to reveal scanty lingerie. They announced they were at the party to "arrest" the bachelor, sat on his lap, and gyrated erotically to heavy metal music. Martin couldn't believe it—one of the women looked just like Christie! Her hair was much longer and her makeup much heavier, but it was her. She met his glance briefly, her eyes first widening in surprise, then narrowing in detachment. After half an hour of flirtatious dancing and talking to the other men, the women abruptly announced it was time to leave, picked up their cop uniforms and music, and left.

Afterward, Martin and Christie avoided any contact at church. When he managed a clandestine glimpse of Christie, he felt the pain of missing this woman he cared for. But then his brain conjured up the indelible image of the brazen Christie at the bachelor party. The horrifying picture nestled in his hippocampus warred with the passion in his amygdala. The logic of his prefrontal cortex kept him away. But then many months later he decided he needed to reconcile these two disparate images of Christie.

Chasing her down the steps after church, he finally got her to stop and talk to him. He tearfully confessed how much he had cared for her and how upset he was when he saw her at the party. Christie agreed to meet him again, and over time she shared her feelings and related her struggles and past problems. Martin learned that she and her younger, developmentally disabled sister had been sexually abused by an uncle who assumed custody when their parents died. She struggled to support herself and her sister, who was now in a nursing home.

Christie described how she developed different sides of her personality to manage her obligations. She could be active and forceful at her job at the investment firm, flirtatious and seductive when moonlighting at bachelor parties. But she also felt deep religious, spiritual connections. "I had to keep those parts of me separate," she told Martin. "That's why I couldn't see you on weekends—I was doing other work. I had to stay *that* Christie for a while, and she was different from the Christie you knew."

Martin decided he wanted to try to continue their relationship. He presented *Support* statements of his caring for her and his wish to continue being together. He expressed *Empathy* in acknowledging the difficulties in her early years and the strength she has had to succeed for herself and care for her sister. *Truth* statements included his conviction that the real Christie was the woman he had known before—caring and sensitive. He declared his concern for her safety in her weekend jobs. He felt her work degraded her. Martin stated his conviction that she could find other less compromising ways to supplement her income. Finally, he told her he couldn't continue being with her if she continued with that work.

Christie's initial reaction was anger and defiance. She resented what she felt was Martin's attempt to control her. "Who do *you* want me to be?" she screamed. "I'm tired of trying to be what everyone wants me to be! My priority is taking care of my sister and me and I do what I need to do. And I am who I am!"

Martin recognized Christie wasn't hearing *Empathy* statements and again verbalized his understanding of her stressors. He convinced her to have brunch with him to talk more. At the café Christie conceded that her weekend activities were "the only time I feel in control. It's when I manipulate others instead of others always controlling me."

After a while she acknowledged she felt trapped in her life. "I don't like who I've become, but it's how I cope," she confessed. "You're a good person, Martin. You know what you want in your life and deserve it. I wish it were different, but I'm not there yet. You know the kind of woman you want to be with. I don't know who I am, but right now I know I'm not that person. I don't know if I ever could be." And with that, Christie got up and walked out of his life . . . and back into hers. Sometimes borderline coping is the only way to survive.

Lies, Damned Lies, and Delusions

Perhaps the least prominent of the nine defining criteria for BPD is transient, stress-related paranoid thoughts or dissociative symptoms. Many have endured such experiences in very minor ways: For a brief moment you may have had the feeling that the two giggling strangers across the street were laughing at you. Or you may have experienced a kind of dissociative incident when driving the familiar route home from work: Lost in thought, you pulled into your driveway, not having been consciously aware of the trip or remembering how you arrived home. With BPD, these experiences are more severe and last longer than a split second or a brief instant, though usually not more than one or two days. Recovery may be surprisingly quick. Onset of suspiciousness or feelings of unreality can be abrupt and more striking and frightening to those around the BPD person. At such critical times obtaining the assistance of a professional is necessary.

CASE 8: MARNIE AND ROBIN. Marnie and Robin bonded quickly. Both women were hired as paralegals at a law firm at around the same time. Both were in their late twenties. Both had nice boyfriends. And their personalities were complementary. While Robin was somewhat introverted, Marnie was more outgoing, with high energy and an infectious laugh. When Robin's lease was coming due, Marnie invited her to move in with her. There was plenty of room, and they could commute to work together.

Now that they were living together, Robin began to see more sides of Marnie. At times she would get sullen and irritable, especially when work was more hectic. Although Marnie's boyfriend, Gavin, seemed pleasant, on some evenings Robin could hear Marnie screaming at him over the phone. Sure, Marnie could be a little moody, but Robin was surprised to learn that Marnie had been hospitalized twice before for "breakdowns" and saw her psychiatrist intermittently. She identified that the phone number on the side of the refrigerator belonged to him. "He keeps my batteries charged, and he would miss me if I stopped pestering him," Marnie joked.

Robin became concerned when Marnie began working with the lawyers on the firm's biggest case. Marnie was staying later and later at the office, Ubering home late at night. She brought work home with her. She was catching just a few hours of sleep before heading back to the office. After another phone argument with Gavin, Marnie emerged from her room crying and declared that they had broken up. As Robin tried to console her, Marnie pulled away. "Well, screw him, I've got a lot of work to do," she grumbled and went back to her desk. Over the next few days, she fluctuated between sadness and steely intensity with work.

A few nights later, Robin returned to the apartment to find Marnie standing by the door blankly staring off into space. "Are you okay?" Robin asked.

"He wants to destroy me!" Marnie responded.

Marnie went on to describe hearing Gavin's voice, saying he was going to let everyone know about the *real* Marnie, the evil, disgusting, destructive Marnie. "I don't feel real," she sobbed. "He's telling everyone I'm a fake. Everyone is fake. You don't care. No one cares."

Robin was shocked and frightened. She watched Marnie wander around the room with a blank look on her face. With a dull nod Marnie agreed to let Robin call her psychiatrist's office. While they waited for a return call, Robin offered *Support*. "I'm your friend," Robin said nervously. "I care. I want to help you."

Within minutes the doctor called back. Relieved, Robin answered, explained what was happening, and then put the phone on speaker as the doctor spoke to Marnie. "I'm glad you called. I've been concerned," the doctor said, expressing *Support*. "You told me last time how much stress you've been under with work and the breakup. With all that's been happening to you and all the stress you've been under, it's understandable how you would feel everything just closing in on you," he remarked with *Empathy*.

"But it's all gone. It's too late. Everyone is pretending. They're trying to destroy me," Marnie said, sobbing. "Don't you believe me?"

The doctor responded with *Truth*. "I believe what you are saying, and I believe you are suffering terribly and need help." He instructed Robin to take Marnie to the hospital, where she was admitted.

After two days in the hospital Marnie returned home. Robin was dismayed that her roommate appeared completely recovered in such a brief time. "I just needed a bit of a tune-up," Marnie explained. "Some adjustment of my meds, some sleep, and some food got me back together. I must have kind of freaked you out when I went cuckoo there. I'm sorry. You're a good friend, Robin." Marnie went on to explain she was seeing her doctor more regularly and had already arranged a less stressful schedule at work. "I'm learning to recognize when stress is getting to be too much and when to get help."

Although the SET-UP principles were originally developed for working with borderline patients, they can be useful for dealing with others. When communication is stalled, SET-UP can help individuals focus on messages that are not being successfully transmitted. If a person feels that he is not supported or respected or that he is misunderstood, or if he refuses to address realistic problems, specific SET steps can be taken to shore up these flagging areas. In today's complex world, a set of clear communication principles including both love and reason is necessary to overcome the tribulations of borderline chaos. A productive relationship also requires *Understanding* and *Perseverance*. Understanding the underlying dynamics of the communication and the needs of the partner reinforces SET principles. Perseverance is necessary to effect change over the long haul. For many with BPD, having a consistent unflappable figure in their lives, whether it be a neighbor, a friend, or a therapist, may be one of the most important requirements for healing. Such a figure may contribute little except for consistency and acceptance (in the face of frequent provocations), yet furnish the borderline loved one with a model of constancy in her otherwise chaotic world.

Chapter Six

Family and Friends: How to Cope

But he's a human being, and a terrible thing is happening to him. So attention must be paid. He is not to be allowed to fall into his grave like an old dog. Attention must be finally paid to such a person.

—From *Death of a Salesman*, by Arthur Miller

No one knew quite what to do with Ray. He had been in and out of hospitals and had seen many doctors over the years, but he could never remain long in treatment. Nor could he keep a job for very long. His wife, Denise, worked in a dentist's office and spent most of her leisure time with her friends, generally ignoring Ray's complaints of chest pains, headaches, backaches, and depression.

Ray was the only child of wealthy protective parents. When he was nine, his father's brother committed suicide. Although he never knew his uncle very well, Ray understood that his parents were greatly affected by the suicide. After this event, his parents became even more protective and would insist he stay home from school whenever he felt ill. At the age of twelve, Ray announced he was depressed and began seeing what evolved into a parade of therapists.

An indifferent student, he went on to college, where he met Denise. She was the only woman who had ever shown any interest in him, and after a short courtship, they were married. Both quit college and dutifully went to work but relied on Ray's parents to subsidize their household income and Ray's continuing therapy.

The couple moved frequently; whenever Denise got bored with a job or a location, they would move to a different part of the country. She would quickly acquire a new job and new friends, but Ray had great difficulty and would remain out of work for many months.

As they both began drinking more, their fighting intensified. When they bickered, Ray would sometimes leave and return to live with his parents, where he would stay until the family began to quarrel; then he would come home to Denise.

Frequently, Ray's wife and parents would tell him how fed up they were with his moodiness and multiple medical complaints, but then he'd threaten to kill himself and his parents would become panic-stricken. They insisted he see new doctors and flew him around the country to consult with various experts. They arranged hospitalizations in several prestigious institutions, but after a short time Ray always signed himself out against medical advice, and his parents would send him plane fare home. They continuously vowed to withhold further financial support but never stuck to their word.

Friends and jobs became an indistinguishable blur of unsatisfying encounters. Whenever a new acquaintance or occupation disappointed him in any way, Ray quit. His parents wrung their hands; Denise basically ignored him. Ray continued spinning out of control with no one to restrain him, including himself.

Recognizing BPD in Friends and Relations

On the surface, someone with borderline personality disorder can be very difficult to identify, despite the underlying volcanic turbulence. Unlike many people afflicted with other mental disorders—such as schizophrenia, bipolar (manic-depressive) disease, alcoholism, or eating disorders—the adult with BPD can usually function extremely well in work and social situations without appearing overtly pathological. Indeed, some of the hallmarks of borderline behavior are the sudden, unpredictable, and "out of nowhere" eruptions of anger, extreme suspiciousness, or suicidal depression from someone who has appeared so normal.

The unpredictable outbursts are usually very frightening and mystifying—both to the person with BPD himself and to those closest to him. Because of the sudden and extreme nature of more prominent symptoms, the concerned party can be easily misled and not recognize that it is a common manifestation of BPD rather than a separate primary illness. For example, a person who attempts to kill himself by overdosing or cutting his wrists may be diagnosed with depression and prescribed antidepressant medications and brief supportive psychotherapy. If the patient is suffering only from clinical depression, this regimen should improve his condition and he should recover relatively quickly and completely. If, however, the destructive behaviors are a manifestation of BPD, his self-harming will continue, unabated by the treatment. Even if he suffers from both depression *and* BPD (a common combination), this approach will only partially treat the illness and further problems will ensue. If the borderline features are not recognized, the continuation of suicidal or other destructive behaviors, despite treatment, becomes puzzling and frustrating for the patient, the doctor, and everyone concerned.

Abby, a twenty-three-year-old fashion model, was treated in a chemical dependency unit for alcoholism. She responded very well to this program, but as she continued to abstain from alcohol, she became increasingly compulsively bulimic. She then entered an eating disorder unit, where she was again successfully treated.

A few weeks later, she began experiencing severe panic attacks in stores, offices, even while driving in her car, and eventually became afraid to leave her house. In addition to these phobias, she was becoming more depressed. As she considered entering a phobia clinic, a psychiatric consultant recognized all of her symptoms to be representative of BPD and recommended instead that she enter a psychiatric unit specializing in borderline conditions. Where her previous treatments had focused exclusively on alcoholism or bulimia, this hospitalization took a more holistic view of her life and treatment.

Eventually, Abby was able to connect her problems to her continued ambivalent relationship with her parents, who had interfered with her attempts to separate, mature, and be more independent.

She realized that her various illnesses were really means to escape her parents' demands without guilt. Her bulimia, drinking, and anxieties occupied all her energy, distracting her from addressing the conflicts with her parents. What's more, her "sick" role excused her from even feeling obligated to work on this relationship. Ironically, the illnesses also kept her *attached* to her parents: Because they had serious marital problems (her mother was addicted to pain medications and her father was chronically depressed), she stayed connected to them by replicating their pathological roles.

After a brief hospitalization, she continued individual outpatient psychotherapy. Her mood improved and her anxieties and phobias dissolved. She also continued to abstain from alcohol and purging.

Abby's case illustrates how a seemingly all-consuming prominent behavior may actually represent and camouflage underlying BPD, in which one or more of its features—unstable relationships, impulsivity, mood shifts, intense anger, suicidal threats, identity disturbances, feelings of emptiness, or frantic efforts to avoid abandonment—result in psychiatric symptoms that might mistakenly lead to incomplete diagnosis or even misdiagnosis.

Coping and Helping

It is important to keep in mind that BPD is an illness, not a willful attempt to get attention. The borderline individual lacks boots, much less the bootstraps with which to pull himself up. It is useless to get angry or to cajole and plead with him to change; without help and motivation, he cannot easily modify his behavior.

However, this does not imply that he is helpless and should not be held responsible for his conduct. Actually, the opposite is true. He must accept, without being excused or protected, the real consequences of his actions, even though initially he may feel powerless to alter them. In this way, BPD is no different from any other handicap. The individual confined to a wheelchair will elicit sympathy, but he is still responsible for finding wheelchair accessibility to the places he wishes to go, and for making sure his vehicle is in good enough condition to take him there.

The extremes of borderline behavior typically lead others to respond with either a hard-nosed "You lazy good-for-nothing SOB, pull yourself together and fly right" retort or a cajoling "You poor baby, you can't do it; I'll take care of you" pat on the head. All must be aware of how their interactions may encourage or inhibit borderline responses. Those who interact with a person with BPD must attempt to walk a very thin line between, on the one hand, providing reassurance of her worthiness and, on the other, confirming the necessary expectations. They must try to respond supportively, but without overreacting. Affection and physical touching, such as hugging and holding a hand, can communicate that she is a valued person, but if it is exploitative, it will hinder trust. If caring results in *over*protectiveness, she stops feeling responsible for her behavior. A delicate balance of *Support* and *Empathy* with *Truth* is the ideal approach (see chapter 5).

In most settings, concentrating on the *Truth* segments of SET-UP principles can allow for reasonable action guidelines. But when suicide is threatened, it is usually time to contact a mental health professional or suicide-prevention facility. Suicide threats should not be allowed to become emotional blackmail, whereby the friend or relation is manipulated to behave as the borderline individual demands. Threats should be taken seriously and met with prompt predictable realistic reactions, such as demanding that she obtain professional help (a *Truth* response).

Jack, a forty-one-year-old single man, worked part time while attempting to return to school. His widowed mother continued to support him financially, and whenever he failed at work or school or with a relationship, she would reinforce his helplessness by insisting he could not succeed in achieving his goals and suggesting he return "home" to live with her. Therapy involved helping Jack understand his inclination to remain helpless and reap the inherent benefits of this helplessness and enabling him to understand his mother's need to maintain control and her role in perpetuating his dependency.

Sometimes it takes only one actor in the drama to initiate change. Jack's mother can respond to his dependency with SET-UP responses that express her caring (*Support*), understanding (*Empathy*), and acknowledgment of reality (*Truth*)—the need for Jack to take more responsibility for his own actions. If his mother is unwilling to alter her behavior, Jack must be the one to recognize her role in his problems and distance himself from her. The action of either Jack or his mother can induce change in the relationship that allows healthier interactions.

Special Parenting Problems

Most who suffer with BPD describe childhoods with characteristic features. Frequently there is a history of emotional, physical, or sexual abuse. Often one parent was missing or repeatedly absent, had time-consuming outside interests, hobbies, or career demands, or abused alcohol or drugs.

If both parents did live in the home, their relationship was often marked by discord. There was frequently a lack of consensus about child-rearing, and as a result one parent, usually the mother, assumed the primary parenting role. Such parents are rarely capable of presenting a united collaborative front to their children. For such children, the world abounds with inconsistencies and invalidation. When the child requires structure, he receives contradictions; when he needs firmness, he gets ambivalence. Thus, the future borderline adult is deprived of the opportunity to develop a consistent core identity.

The mother of a borderline individual may be blatantly mentally ill, but more often her pathology is quite subtle. She may even be perceived by others as the perfect mother because of her total "dedication" to her children. Deeper observation, however, reveals her over-involvement in her children's lives, her encouragement of mutual dependencies, and her unwillingness to allow her children to mature and separate naturally. It has often been observed that borderline mothers have borderline children.

Attempting to maintain consistent child-rearing after separation or divorce is especially challenging. Consistency among all supervisory figures—parents and stepparents—is the most important feature in establishing child-rearing rules with definitive boundaries. However, this may be difficult for the borderline parent, who may consciously or unconsciously use the children to continue the battle with her estranged spouse. The other parent should try to minimize conflicts by being highly selective in choosing his or her battles. Trying to defend oneself or debate accusations will not alter the resentment and will only confuse the child(ren). Contradicting or undermining directives of the other parent simply adds to the chaos. Often the best approach is to redirect the conversation away from the personal relationship by acknowledging mutual dedication to the children and focusing only on what's best for the kids. Usually, common ground can be found and conflict can be minimized.

Early Separations

Separations from parents, particularly during the first few years of life, are common in the borderline individual's biography. On the surface, these separations may appear insignificant, yet they have profound effects. For example, the birth of a sibling takes the mother away from her normal activities for a few weeks, but when she returns, she is no longer as responsive to the older child; in the eyes of the older child, his mother has disappeared, replaced by someone who now is focused almost exclusively on the younger sibling. For the healthy child in a healthy environment, this trauma is easily overcome, but for the pre-borderline child in a borderline setting, it may be one of a series of losses and perceived abandonments. Extended illnesses, frequent travels, divorce, or the death of a parent also deprive the developing infant of consistent mothering at crucial times, which may interfere with his abilities to develop trust and constancy in his unstable and unreliable world.

The Trauma of Child Abuse

Severe emotional, physical, and/or sexual abuse is a common trauma in the history of someone with borderline personality disorder. One report revealed that 71 percent of BPD patients reported past traumatic abuse. This analysis of ninety-seven different studies determined that individuals with BPD experienced childhood adversity at almost fourteen times the rate reported by nonclinical controls. The most common form of mistreatment was physical neglect, followed by emotional abuse. About one-third of these borderline patients experienced physical or sexual abuse.[1]

When a child is abused, he invariably blames himself because (consciously or subconsciously) that is the best of the available alternatives. If he blames the adult, he will be terrified by his dependency on incompetents who are unable to take care of him. If he blames no one, pain becomes random and unpredictable and thus even more frightening because he has no hope of controlling it. Blaming himself makes the abuse easier to understand and therefore possible to control—he can feel that he somehow causes the abuse and so will be able to find a way to end it, or he will give up and accept that he is "bad."

When the abused child learns early in life that he is bad, that he causes bad things to happen, he begins to expect punishment and may feel secure only when being punished. Later, self-mutilation may sometimes be his way of perpetuating this familiar, secure feeling of being chastised. He may see abuse as a kind of love and repeat the abuse with his own children. As an adult, he remains locked in the child's confusing world, in which love and hate commingle, only good and bad exist with no in-between, and only inconsistency is consistent.

Child abuse can take subtler forms than physical violence or deviant sexuality. Emotional abuse—expressed as verbal harassment, sarcasm, humiliation, or frigid silence—can be equally devastating.

Stephanie could never please her father. When she was young, he called her "Chubby" and laughed at her clumsy tomboy attempts to please him by playing sports. She was "stupid" when her grades were less than perfect or when she accidentally broke dishes while trying to clear the kitchen. He ridiculed her strapless gown on prom night and, on graduation day, insisted that she "would amount to nothing."

As an adult, Stephanie was always unsure of herself, never trusting flattering comments and hopelessly trying to please people who were impossible to please. After a long string of destructive relationships, Stephanie finally met Ted, who seemed caring and supportive. At every turn, however, Stephanie tried to sabotage the relationship by testing his loyalty and questioning his commitment, convinced that no one whom she valued could value her.

Ted needed to understand Stephanie's background and recognize that trust could only realistically be established over long periods of time. Not everyone is willing to wait. Ted was, and the couple was rewarded with a mutually supportive long-term relationship.

BPD Through the Life Cycle

A large UK/U.S. collaborative study demonstrated that significant borderline symptoms exhibited by age twelve were predictive of pervasive impaired functioning in transitioning to adulthood at age eighteen.[2] Although some pediatricians have declared that they can recognize, by their early behavior, which young children will become borderline adults, BPD is generally first recognized in adolescence and early adulthood.

BPD in Adolescence

By definition, the struggles of adolescence and BPD are very similar: Both the typical adolescent and the adolescent with BPD struggle for individual identity and separation from parents, seek bonds with friends and identification with groups, try to avoid being left alone, tend to go through dramatic mood changes, have anger outbursts, and are generally prone to impulsivity. The teenager's easy distract-ibility and oblivious daydreaming are analogous to borderline dis-sociative experiences and difficulties with committing to a goal and following through. Adolescents' eccentric dress styles, primitive eat-ing habits, and pounding music are usually attempts to carve out a distinctive identity and relate to specific groups of peers, efforts similar to those teenagers struggling with BPD.

A normal adolescent may listen to gloomy music, write pessimis-tic poetry, glorify suicidal celebrities, dramatically scream, cry, and threaten. However, the normal adolescent does not cut his wrists, binge and purge several times a day, become addicted to drugs, or attack his mother; it is these behavioral extremes that foreshadow the development of BPD. Some parents will deny the seriousness of an adolescent's problems (a drug overdose, for example) by dismiss-ing them as accidental or seeing them as a typical teenager's bid for attention. Though it is true that children often seek attention in dra-matic ways, neither suicide attempts nor any destructive behaviors are "normal." They instead suggest the possibility of incipient bor-derline personality or another disorder and should be evaluated by a professional. Compared to teenagers with other psychiatric disorders, borderline adolescents experience some of the most severe pathology and dysfunction. Borderline adolescents exhibit higher lifetime rates of sexually transmitted infections and medical problems. They are more likely to abuse cigarettes, alcohol, and other drugs.[3]

Usually others—parents, teachers, employers, friends—will rec-ognize when the normal teenager crosses the border into borderline behavior, even before the adolescent herself does. Continuous drug abuse, serial tumultuous relationships, or anorexic fasting are indi-cators that deeper problems may be involved. Even though the temp-tation is to look at and treat these as separate destructive behaviors, the teen's whole style of functioning, rather than individual symp-toms, should be the focus of examination. This is especially crucial when considering the potential for suicide.

Suicide is a leading cause of death among teenagers and is par-ticularly prevalent in children who are depressed, abuse drugs, act impulsively or violently, and maintain few support systems—all prominent features of BPD.[4,5] Threats of self-harm should *always* be taken seriously. Attempts to self-mutilate or harm oneself "only for attention" can go tragically awry. Parents who try to distinguish "real suicide" from "attention-seeking" miss the point—both are seriously pathological behaviors and require treatment, often hospitalization.

Confronting destructive behavior in a borderline adolescent is complicated by divorce and stepparenting. Even if bitterness persists between the divorced parties, they must cooperate in dealing with their child. All parties and guardians must act together in order to deal with the "You're not my real father/mother" and other objections to limit-setting rules.

BPD in Young Adulthood

The borderline adult in his twenties is facing the new challenges of being a grown-up. He is pondering potentially lifelong commitments in the areas of work and relationships, and is considering what kind of person he wants to be. Now that he is beyond parental and educational supervisory influences, he is thrust into a context of autonomous freedom. The human brain continues to mature into the mid-twenties, so he may continue to be captive to his adolescent impulsivity, moodiness, and anxiety as he makes life-altering decisions.

The Maturing Borderline Adult

Most people diagnosed with BPD, with or without treatment, improve over time. Many recover fully. Higher functioning borderline adults who do not fully recuperate may still have successful careers, assume traditional family roles, and have a cadre of friends and support systems. They may live generally satisfactory lives within their own separate corner of existence, despite recurrent frustrations with themselves and others who inhabit that niche.

Those with BPD who are lower functioning, however, have more difficulty maintaining a job and friends, and may lack family and support systems; they may inhabit lonelier and more desperate "black holes" within their own personal universe.

An element of unpredictability and erratic behavior may persist. This may be more obvious in the lonely, isolated individual, but those who know, for example, a supposedly contented family man well can also detect inconsistencies in his behavior that belie the superficial rationality. At work, even the successful businessperson or professional may be perceived by those working closely with him to be a bit strange, even if they can't quite identify what it is that projects that aura of imbalance. Alternatively, the successful businessperson may appear completely normal at work, but exhibit abusive or irrational behavior at home.

As many borderline adults grow older, they may "mellow out." Impulsivity, mood swings, and self-destructive behaviors seem to diminish in dramatic intensity. Some sense of identity and connection has been established. This pattern might be an objective reflection of change or a subjective evaluation of those living or working with him; friends and lovers may have adjusted to his erratic actions over time and no longer notice or respond to the outrageousness.

Maybe it is because he has settled into a more routine lifestyle that no longer requires periodic outbursts—drinking binges, suicide threats, or other dramatic gestures—to achieve his needs. Perhaps with age he loses the energy or stamina to maintain the frenetic pace of borderline living. Or perhaps there is simply a natural healing process that takes place for some as they mature. In any event, most of those with BPD get better over time, with or without treatment. Indeed, most could be considered "cured" in the sense that they no longer fulfill five of the nine defining criteria (see chapter 1). One should keep in mind that long-term prognosis for this devastating disease is very hopeful (see chapter 7).

Thus, those sharing life with a loved one with BPD can expect his behaviors to become more tolerable over time. At this point the unpredictable reactions become more predictable and therefore easier to manage, and it becomes possible for him to learn how to love and be loved in a healthier fashion.

The Aging Borderline Parent

When BPD symptoms such as moodiness, anger, fears of abandonment, and poor outside relationships persist into later life, maintaining tolerable contacts is difficult, especially with a borderline parent. In such strained situations, an adult child nevertheless probably prefers to maintain some kind of relationship, but one that doesn't continuously upset him. After all, she is his mother!

A borderline parent can provoke guilt when her needs are not met. If she has alienated others, her children may be her only social connections. In such situations, you should try to maintain consistent limits in what support you can provide. Encouraging other activities and contacts can be helpful, even if the parent does not follow through consistently.

Lois's mother called Lois frequently, complaining of severe headaches, loneliness, and an overall disgust with life. With her father long dead and her siblings estranged from the family, Lois was the "good daughter," the only child who cared, and the only family member who maintained any contact.

Lois felt guilty when her mother was alone and in pain. Despite Lois's love for her mother and the feelings of guilt her mother triggered, Lois began feeling angry when she saw her mother becoming progressively more helpless and unwilling to take care of herself. Lois began to recognize that she was being taken advantage of by her mother's increasing dependency. But when Lois expressed her anger, her mother just became more tearful and helpless, and Lois felt even guiltier, and the cycle repeated again. Only when Lois untangled herself from this interlocking system and maintained consistent contact on her own terms was her mother forced to achieve a healthier self-sufficiency.

BPD in the Workplace

In the workplace environment, borderline coworkers are often perceived as strange or eccentric. They tend to isolate themselves, avoid personal contacts, and keep others away with an aura of surliness, suspicion, or eccentricity. Some habitually complain of physical ailments or personal problems or occasionally have fits of paranoia and rage. Still others may act perfectly normal at work but seem awkward or uncomfortable around coworkers outside the workplace. A Dutch study demonstrated that workers with BPD (and even others with some, but not sufficient, borderline symptoms to justify the formal BPD diagnosis) were significantly impaired in work performance. These employees had more job insecurity, more problems with decision-making, less coworker support, and greater stress.[6]

Many employers have implemented employee assistance programs (EAPs), in-house counselors, and referral departments initially designed to help employees deal with alcohol and drug abuse problems. Today, many EAP wellness programs are also available to help workers confront other emotional problems, as well as legal and financial difficulties.

Many EAP counselors are well equipped to identify features of alcohol or drug abuse, or of prominent psychiatric illnesses such as depression or psychosis, but they may be less familiar with the more intricate symptoms of BPD. Even when the employee's supervisor, coworkers, counselor, and even the employee himself are aware of some dysfunctional or disruptive behaviors, the borderline employee might not be referred for treatment because his behaviors cannot be clearly associated with a more commonly recognized disorder.

The prospective employer may suspect borderline characteristics in an applicant who has a history of frequent job changes. These terminations will often be explained by personality conflicts (which, indeed, is often accurate). Other job separations may be sparked by a significant change—a new supervisor, a new computer system, or an adjustment in job description—that disrupted a very structured (perhaps even monotonous) routine.

Because the borderline worker may be very creative and dedicated, he can be a valuable employee. When functioning on a higher level, he can be colorful, stimulating, and inspiring to others. Most function optimally in a well-defined, structured environment in which expectations are clearly delineated. Others do well in unregulated positions where they can be more imaginative and creative.

Coworkers will interact more easily with a borderline colleague when they recognize his tendency to see the world as black or white and accept his preference for systematic structure. When directions are precise and the expected results are unambiguous, the borderline workmate will respond with less stress. Coworkers should avoid kidding around with him and should stay away from good-natured teasing, which the borderline colleague may easily misconstrue. It may be helpful to intercede if he becomes the target of others' jokes. Frequent compliments for good work and matter-of-fact noncritical recognition of mistakes along with suggestions for improvement can aid his functioning in the workplace.

Similarly, when the borderline colleague holds a management or executive position, employees need to recognize and learn to deal with his black-or-white thinking. Employees should learn to expect and accept his changeability with an understanding that mitigates frustration. They should avoid entanglement in logical arguments over minor issues because consistency may not always be possible. They should look for allies elsewhere in the organization to provide reliable feedback and evaluations. United employees can address the boss regarding more substantive concerns.

BPD at Play

At play, the individual with BPD is typically unpredictable and sometimes very disconcerting. He may have great difficulty with recreation and play, exhibiting a seriousness all out of proportion to the relaxed nature of the activity. He may be your newly assigned tennis doubles partner who at first seems nice enough, but as the game goes on becomes increasingly frustrated and angry. Though you continually remind him that it's just a game, he may stomp around, curse himself, throw the racket, and swear to give up the sport. He may be your son's Little League coach who works well with your kids, but suddenly becomes wildly abusive to the teenage umpire or angrily cruel to his own son—seen as an extension of himself—who strikes out with the bases loaded. Although these examples may describe borderline-like traits in some people who in fact are not borderline, when these behaviors are extreme or continue in a consistent pattern, they may be indications of a true borderline personality.

This intensity interferes with his ability to relax and have fun. Others' attempts at humor may frustrate him and make him angry. It is virtually impossible to kid him out of it. If you elect to continue playing tennis with your borderline partner, judicious use of SET-UP principles may make the experience more tolerable (see chapter 5).

Understanding Your Own Emotions

When you join someone with BPD on her roller-coaster ride, you also must expect to experience a variety of emotions, especially guilt, fear, and anger. When self-destructive, she may appear helpless and project responsibility for her behavior onto others, who may all too readily accept it. Guilt is a strong inhibitor of honest confrontation. Similarly, fear of physical harm—to her, others, or yourself—may also be a powerful deterrent to initiating interactions. Anger is a common reaction when, as frequently occurs, you feel manipulated or simply don't like or understand a certain behavior.

Understanding and *Perseverance* (the UP in the SET-UP communication paradigm presented in chapter 5) are important components in maintaining any relationship. They are particularly important in managing a commitment to someone with BPD. Utilizing SET and other described techniques of communication may help manage the turbulence. At the same time, you must continuously assess your own feelings. Titrate your frustration with your caring, and the tincture of time may allow you to sustain a healthy relationship.

Coping with Individual Borderline Symptoms

In chapter 2 and in our other book[7] we examine the nine defining criteria for BPD. But there are many faces to what we recognize as borderline personality disorder. Formal diagnosis requires validation of any five of the nine designated criteria. These permutations allow for 256 possible different combinations of symptoms and conceivably 256 different presentations of BPD. A borderline patient with prominent rage, wild mood swings, and self-destructive impulsivity may present quite differently from a BPD patient whose primary symptoms are fears of abandonment, feelings of emptiness, and an unstable self-image. Though SET-UP techniques can be very helpful in a general way for communicating with borderline individuals, formulating a *single* effective strategy for coping with *specific* borderline expressions might be close to impossible. Below are techniques for dealing with specific borderline symptoms, some of which were described in the primary author's previous book.[8]

Coping with Abandonment Fears (Criterion 1)

The mirror image of borderline rage that pushes people away is the borderline fear of isolating abandonment. (Indeed, these two features are signified in the title of this book!) The dread of being alone bleeds into other BPD symptoms, such as impaired relationships, a disrupted sense of identity, and feelings of emptiness. To evade abandonment a loved one with BPD may demand constant reassurance and exhibit clinging neediness.

- *Employ transitional objects.* Like Princess Diana (see chapter 3), who often traveled with a favored stuffed animal, representations of connection can be helpful when there is a separation. Providing a photo or an article of clothing can be soothing and reassuring to someone with BPD at times when she feels alone. Encouraging her to play "our song," or wear your sweater during the day can also be comforting.

- *Prepare.* For many with BPD, the future, especially an undesirable future event, such as a spouse's brief business trip, is pushed out of consciousness. Don't avoid discussing a situation that you know will be upsetting to her. Instead, periodically remind her about the trip and supplement the reminder with positive news: "Let's go out to a club together the night before I leave on that business trip."

  Encourage alternative comfort sources when you are not available, such as making arrangements with her friends, attending club meetings, or going to workout sessions, etc.

- *Establish balanced, disciplined boundaries.* You may never fully satisfy the demands of a needy borderline loved one, but try to establish limits that you can fulfill consistently, i.e., a level of connection that you can reliably maintain: "Dad, I know you're disappointed that I'm not able to come visit every night, but I am arranging to come over every Thursday evening so we can have dinner together."

Coping with Relationship Instability (Criterion 2)

His black-or-white BPD view of the world makes it difficult to sustain smooth relationships. His perception of you may mutate from angel to demon over a trivial remark. This erratic view of the world and others is a reflection of an unstable sense of who he is (Criterion 3).

- *Neither a hero nor a scapegoat be.* When you are being perceived as an "angel," accept without debate positive idealizing. Offering a humble "Aw shucks, I'm not that wonderful" protestation only invites frustration for the BPD victim; on the other hand, don't promote a savior mission nor accept a villain role.

Early in the relationship, Lindsey constantly told Nelson how wonderful he was and how—unlike her previous, hateful boyfriends—"understanding" he was. Inflated by her idealization, Nelson promised to "take her away from all this heartache" and protect her. He talked sternly to her parents and her boss. He managed her disarrayed finances. He urged her to change her hair and clothing styles. Predictably, after a period of continued idolization, Lindsey felt manipulated and became furious with Nelson, who was mystified by his transformation into a "controlling" brute.

- *Take responsibility but challenge unreasonable vilification.* Try to understand your borderline partner's abrupt shifts in attitude. Acknowledge that he is upset with you and why. But don't automatically concede demonization if it's not true. After enduring repeated attacks, you might say, "I understand you're frustrated and angry at me for not picking you up at the airport, but you know I have picked you up many times before and this time I just couldn't get away from work."

After pointing out your previous airport runs, don't continue to be defensive. Further explanations risk elevating anger. Sometimes the best approach is simply saying, "I'm sorry I disappointed you," and letting it go.

- *Prepare.* Preparing for a likely confrontation can be helpful. Anticipating how your borderline partner might respond and practicing how you might react helps keep your emotions in check. Rehearsing potential interactions keeps SET responses and other approaches handy.

Coping with Identity Disturbance (Criterion 3)

"I don't really know who I am" is a common BPD mantra. Developing a reliable, consistent sense of identity is a challenge for someone with BPD. She often feels she is "faking it" when interacting with others—she can be a chameleon, a Democrat among Democrats, a Republican among Republicans, and so on. Yet all alone, in the middle of the night, she does not know what she really believes. She may have difficulty in sustaining goals and interests. She may be unable to commit—to jobs, educational goals, relationships—which may be associated with feelings of emptiness (Criterion 7). At the opposite end of the spectrum, she may compensate for her identity void by clinging to a cultish organization whose dogmatic culture prescribes how she should think, feel, and act.

- *Explain the "no-win" dilemma.* In some situations, when who she is and what she wants is constantly wavering, her only consistent affects may be frustration and antagonism. At such times it doesn't matter what you say or do—you're damned if you do, damned if you don't. You can't really win such no-win predicaments.

  Explicating the dynamics of the situation using SET as a tool can be helpful: "I know you were mad when I said I was going out with the guys tonight. But then you got mad and said I was 'guilting' you when I said I'd stay home. Look, you know you're the most important part of my life (*Support*), and I know you've been going through a lot lately with your dad (*Empathy*). Since you may be annoyed with me no matter what I do, I'm going to stay home; and it's not out of guilt in spite of what you think (*Truth*). It's because you are important to me and this has been a tough time for you (*Support, Empathy*)."

- *Deflect.* When you anticipate you may be entering a no-win domain, ferret out your partner's stance first. "I'm not sure about that. What do you think?"

- *Use paradox.* Twenty-two-year-old Nora dropped out of college three times. She would have one good semester, then get discouraged, start missing classes, and take Incomplete grades. Each time her parents had pressured her to reenroll. This time her father consciously took a different approach. "Maybe college isn't for you. You might just be happier in life finding a nice job," he told her. Initially, Nora was offended and angry. She knew she was intelligent enough for college, and also understood that without more education she would be unable to secure satisfying work. Her father's remarks also stimulated Nora's "I'll show you" side. A few weeks later she defiantly informed him she was returning to school and had applied for a student loan to help finance it. She also told him this time she was going to finish. Which is just what her father had hoped for.

- *Join a team.* Join in a group activity with your borderline partner—a sports group, a church activity, a charitable campaign, or a community project. All of these promote social interactions and stimulate interests that define identity.

- *Be positive, consistent, and* there. Unstable identity stems from inconsistencies in life. Because of past experiences, she may doubt that you will do what you say you will do. Your being a reliable source who can emphasize positive attributes, without ignoring negative features to work on, is important for your borderline partner.

Coping with Self-Destructive Impulsivity (Criterion 4)

BPD is the only medical diagnosis that is partly defined by self-defeating impulsivity. Impulsive acts can be extremely frustrating for the borderline individual's friends and relations, particularly if the behaviors are self-destructive. Impulsivity is especially unnerving when it emerges (as it often does) at a relatively stable point in his life. Indeed, self-defeating behaviors may emanate precisely because his life *is* settling down, and he feels uncomfortable in a crisis-free state.

Larry, for example, was in a marriage that was comfortably boring. Married for over twenty years, he and his wife, Phyllis, rarely interacted. She reared their sons while Larry toiled for a large company. His life was a self-imposed prison of daily routine and compulsive behaviors. He took hours to dress, in order to arrange his clothing just so. At night before bed, he engaged in rituals to maintain a sense of control—the closet doors had to be opened in a special way, the bathroom sink had to be carefully cleaned, and the soap and toilet articles arranged in a certain pattern.

But within this tightly regimented routine, Larry would impulsively get drunk, pick fights, or abruptly leave town for an entire day without warning. On one occasion he impulsively overdosed on his heart medicine "to see what it felt like." Usually he would absorb Phyllis's anger by turning somber and quiet, but sometimes he would blame her for his need to "get away" and pick a fight over some trivial matter.

He would remain dry for several months, and then just as he was receiving praise for abstaining, he would get abusively and loudly drunk. His wife, friends, and counselors pleaded and threatened, but to no avail.

- *Predict.* After a period of sobriety, Phyllis might remind Larry, in a neutral way, that in the past when things have gone well, he has built up pressures that have exploded into drinking binges. By pointing out previous patterns, a close friend or relation can help him become more aware of feelings that preview the onset of destructive impulsivity. This can be accompanied by *Support* statements, so they are not interpreted as antagonistic "there you go again" criticism. In such a way, he learns that behaviors that he has perceived as chaotic and unpredictable can actually be anticipated, understood, and thereby controlled. However, even if he does feel criticized, predicting can stimulate a contrariness that motivates him to not repeat destructive patterns "just to show you!"

Walking the borderline individual through the likely results of behavior can sometimes mitigate it. When his fifteen-year-old daughter angrily threatened to run away again with her forbidden boyfriend, Terry responded in a matter-of-fact manner: "Oh, dear. I really wish you wouldn't. Because you know then we'll have to call the police, who will find you and Jordan, and he will get arrested again. And then you'll have to go to the hospital again, which I know you hate. And they'll probably want to keep you longer this time. I would really rather talk some more with you than go through all of that."

- *Be part of a routine.* At vulnerable times, arrange healthy activities you can do together—yoga classes, educational or religious classes, AA meetings, and so forth.

- *Focus on the anger and self-hatred.* Pleading with the borderline loved one not to go out on another drinking binge is probably fruitless. But asking why he is so angry and why he must deal with it in such a self-defeating way may have more impact. Getting him to talk rather than act out is great progress.

In therapy, Larry began to see that his seemingly unpredictable behaviors represented anger at others but mostly at himself. He realized how he would become abusive to his wife or begin drinking when he was frustrated with himself. This impulsive behavior would result in guilt and self-chastisement, which in turn served to expiate his sins. As Larry began to value himself more highly and respect his own ideals and beliefs, his destructive activities diminished.

Coping with Suicidal and Self-Mutilating Behaviors (Criterion 5)

Suicidal threats and gestures must always be taken seriously and referred to a professional for help. The risk of suicide in BPD approaches 10 percent, which is almost a thousand times the suicide rate in the general population.[9] Although many borderline symptoms abate with age (see The Maturing Borderline Adult earlier in this chapter), the risk of suicide persists throughout life, and some studies suggest it increases with age.[10] A previous history of self-harm is the strongest risk factor for subsequent suicide.

Although both genders with BPD attempt suicide in similar proportions, men are several times more successful and are usually more impaired.[11,12] Elderly suicidal patients with a history of previous suicide attempts are likely to exhibit persistent borderline and related traits. Older patients who attempted suicide for the first time are less likely to exhibit character pathology but show increased obsessiveness and a desire to control their environment. These traits, while possibly adaptive earlier in life, at a later period, when combined with depression and a feeling of loss of control, may contribute to a sense of hopelessness and increased suicidal ideation.[13]

Non-suicidal self-injury (NSSI) refers to self-mutilating behavior, such as cutting, burning, and head-banging. In BPD, these behaviors may serve to relieve tension, self-punish, overcome feelings of detachment or dissociation, establish a sense of control, or indulge a need for dangerous excitement. Confronting self-mutilating behavior can be especially challenging for family and friends. During pregnancy, self-harming fantasies have been associated with increased depression after birth and a poorer mother-infant relationship.[14] NSSI usually begins in adolescence, in which the worldwide prevalence is 18 percent.[15] Although this symptom is a defining criterion for BPD, some have suggested that NSSI should be a separate disorder. A section of DSM-5, "Conditions for Further Study," proposes distinctive separate diagnostic criteria for an NSSI diagnosis. (For further discussion of DSM-5 and alternative diagnostic models, see Appendix A.)

- *Seek help.* Suicidal threats or actions should always be taken seriously. Call a health professional, an emergency service, a support hotline, or others for backup.

- *Safeguard the environment.* Remove or minimize potentially destructive objects. Discard containers of medicine no longer used or prescribed. Eliminate unnecessary sharp instruments. Remove or sequester guns and other weapons.

- *Explore alternative actions to distract from or replace self-harming.* Join in intense exercise or other physical activity. Molding clay or banging on a piano or other musical instrument can reduce tension. A stimulating soak in a hot tub or an ice bath may help. Sometimes the act of holding ice cubes provides the desired stinging sensations but is far less harmful. For many BPD individuals, the sight of blood is the goal and can be partially simulated by marking forcefully (to elicit some discomfort) parts of the body with a red Magic Marker.

Coping with Mood Instability (Criterion 6)

Individuals with BPD are very sensitive to people and things around them. Affective changes are usually reactive to environmental circumstances and can whipsaw from one emotion to another. Negative responses, in particular, can be intense. A study using a specialized functional MRI (fMRI) examined brain reactions to negative stimuli. Results demonstrated increased sensitivity in BPD patients. While others were more likely to habituate (get used to) the same repeated distressing stimuli, those with BPD became more emotionally reactive and displayed brain patterns of continued stressful reactions.[16]

Rapid mood changes can be equally perplexing to a person with BPD and to those around him. From an early age, Meredith had always been aware of her moodiness. When things were going well, she could soar to great heights of excitement and joy, only to plummet, without warning, to the lower reaches of despair. Her parents indulged her moodiness by tiptoeing softly around her, never challenging her irritability. In school, friends would come and go, put off by her unpredictability. Some called her "the manic-depressive" and tried to kid her out of her surliness.

Her husband Ben said he was attracted to her "kindness" and "sense of fun." But Meredith could change dramatically, from playful to suicidal. Similarly, her interactions with Ben would change from joyful sharing to gloomy isolation. Her moods were totally unpredictable, and Ben was never sure how he would find her upon his return at the end of the day. At times he felt that he should enter their home by putting his hat on a stick and poking it into the doorway to see if it would be embraced, ignored, or shot at.

For Meredith, these shifts in mood, unresponsive to a variety of medications, were distressing. In therapy, however, her assigned task was to recognize such swings and what circumstances might trigger them, take responsibility for having them, and learn to adapt by compensating for their presence. When in a state of depression, she could subsequently identify it and learn to explain to others around her that she was in a down phase and would try to adapt as well as she could. If she was with people to whom she could not comfortably explain her situation, Meredith could maintain a low profile and actively try to avoid dealing with some of the demands on her. A major goal involved establishing constancy—consistent, reliable attitudes and behaviors—toward herself and others.

Ben was locked into a typical borderline "damned if you do and damned if you don't" scenario. Confronting her swings of depression would prompt more withdrawal and anger, but ignoring them might imply lack of concern. So in this seemingly hopeless quagmire, he was given the following useful tips by the couple's therapist with good results:

- *Explain the "no-win" dilemma* (see Coping with Identity Disturbance earlier in this chapter).

- *Procrastinate productively.* Living in the present is often proposed as a desirable precept for most people. But the borderline experience of perceptions and feelings exists completely in the *right now.* And the current *right now* can change moment by moment, with no context or comparisons. What came before or may occur later does not taint what she feels at the moment.

She may be demanding and impatient and insist on a response *right now*, even though the response may soon be countermanded, disavowed, or denigrated. In some situations, it may be useful to stall rather than to commit to a demand during a time of high emotionality. Useful possible rejoinders are: "I know you're concerned about this, but let me check my schedule first." "I understand you want to do this soon, but I need to see if I can rearrange some things." "I'm caught up in some things now; let me get back to you."

- *Establish more consistency.* Often the borderline individual may not be aware of the inconsistent attitudes that complicate her life. Gently illuminating contradictory attitudes and working together to adapt a consistent view can be helpful. "When we finally hired that special instructor for tennis lessons, you were excited, but some days you're enthusiastic, and other times you've said you really dislike him and don't want to go back. I'm okay either way, but we really need to talk it over and finally decide if we should continue or not."

Coping with Chronic Feelings of Emptiness (Criterion 7)

Borderline emptiness is extremely painful. The borderline individual lacks a sense of purpose or value. He feels he has nothing to give and is unworthy of receiving love or attention. Like many of the defining criteria for BPD, feelings of alienated emptiness may be linked to other symptoms, such as a blurred sense of self (Criterion 3), moodiness (Criterion 6), and fears of abandonment (Criterion 1). All-consuming feelings of emptiness may cause the borderline individual to withdraw. Avoiding disconnection and isolation is an important goal.

- *Encourage physical activity.* Get him out of the house. Walk, jog, or join an exercise class together. Physical exertion and outside activity drag him away from the black hole into which he is pulled.

- *Encourage new interests.* Hobbies, music, or reading provide intellectual stimulation that can fill in some of the emptiness.

- *Encourage social engagement.* Joining community groups, church groups, volunteer organizations, or social clubs or enrolling in classes can mitigate the isolation.

Coping with Anger (Criterion 8)

Angry outbursts may emerge without warning and seem way out of proportion to the situation. These outbursts become predictably unpredictable in frequency. You may not observe a gradual progression of frustration by the borderline loved one. You probably won't hear the whistle or see the train lights coming down the tracks until it is running over you, loud and destructive. She may go from calm to fury in a flash over what you may consider a trivial remark or incident. The sudden explosion may be as shocking to her as it is to you. Keeping cool and not getting pulled into exchanging angry words with her can be difficult. If you allow your buttons to be pushed, she may deny her own role and project it onto you: "I'm not angry. You're the one who's angry!" Enduring the "I hate you!" part of BPD can be most challenging to the relationship.

- *Let the dust settle.* Wait for the tirade to finish before jumping in with responses. Then wait a beat, to let the flash of silence contrast with the loudness of the outburst.

- *De-escalate.* As she becomes louder, try to lower the volume of your voice. As she becomes more physically animated, try to control your own physical expressions.

- *Refocus.* Ignoring the source of anger will further inflame the situation, but diverting the confrontation to a related area can help settle things down.

    Allison was screaming at Michael, upset that he was working more and spending less time with her and their baby, who had been awakened by the noise and was now crying. After she finished her tirade, Michael, in a soft voice, utilized SET statements, expressed his intent to adjust his schedule, and then focused on his admiration for Allison's devotion as a mother and her desire to maintain a soothing, healthy family environment. In this way, Michael shifted attention to Allison's priorities as a mother and away from the marital tension.

- *Fight fair.* Don't retaliate with confidential or sensitive rejoinders: "Are you going to hit me now, like your father would?" Don't dismiss frustrated anger as illness or hormones: "Did you take your medicine today?" "Are you having your period?"

- *Stay safe.* If you feel there is risk of physical violence, leave the scene. Arrange safety for minors and separation for others not involved. Borderline rage often cannot be reasoned with, so discussion and debate are unnecessary and may only inflame the situation. Instead, you should try to cool off the conflict by acknowledging the difference in opinion and agreeing to disagree. Further discussion can come later when the atmosphere is more settled.

Coping with Paranoid or Dissociative Symptoms (Criterion 9)

In contrast to the psychotic aspects seen in other psychiatric illnesses, such as schizophrenia, borderline reality distortions often emerge suddenly at stressful times—much like borderline rage outbursts or mood changes. A person with BPD psychosis usually appears detached and disoriented. He feels separated from reality and may feel others are not real. He may express paranoid fears. Despite opinions to the contrary, patients with BPD are rarely dangerous to others.

- *Maintain a safe, comfortable environment.* Preserve calm, familiar surroundings with known, trusted others. Move away from potential weapons and choose a position in the room where you have ready access to an exit if you feel threatened.

- *Talk the other person down.* Keep interactions nonthreatening by using a low, reassuring voice. Since episodes are usually precipitated in relation to stressful events, be consoling.

- *Avoid direct challenges.* Don't argue or try to talk him out of his experience. You don't have to confirm his delusion, but you can acknowledge your acceptance of what he is perceiving.

- *Get help.* Even if you are able to calm things down, arrange for professional follow-up.

What Not to Say

Borderline individuals can be very sensitive to words. So far, with SET and these other approaches we have emphasized what to say during borderline challenges. But it is also important to understand what *not* to say, what words or actions might exacerbate the situation.

- *Avoid derogatory phrases.* After a casual remark like, "Don't be silly!" or "That's crazy," the BPD individual may focus on the critical word and erupt with a response like "So now you think I'm crazy!"

- *Avoid demeaning or directly contradictory expressions.* Challenging his perception may merely inflame the situation. "That's not how it happened" or "You're overreacting" are phrases that undermine *Empathy* expressions and invite more conflict.

- *Don't deny your responsibility.* Attempts to redirect your meaning ("You're misinterpreting what I said!" "I was only kidding!" "Can't you take a joke?") will sound like you're shifting the blame on to him and will stimulate more defensiveness. Be accountable for your behavior.

- **Don't lie.** Be gentle with *Truth*, but don't lie. Inconsistencies and lies are frequent aspects of borderline experiences. An uncovered falsehood undermines the necessity of establishing credibility and trust.

- **Eventually let it go.** Don't keep plowing the same ground. Just as a child may continuously whine ("But why . . . ?"), the borderline individual may persistently argue a point. If you find yourself repeating the same words, try to move on: "I know you're still not satisfied, but we've been over and over this. Let's let it go for now. I need your help on another matter."

- **Be careful with humor.** It is usually best to avoid humor. Borderline sensitivity may interpret lighthearted kidding as trivializing or humiliating ridicule. Only in a long-standing relationship in which playful whimsy has been established can levity be helpful. Accepted humor can allow a step back and can develop perspective. In such cases, pointing out the macabre, darkly humorous side of the situation employs context that can defuse intensity. "The ridiculous crap your wife has been pulling over this divorce must be terribly frustrating, but some of this seems almost like a bad situation comedy, where Lucy has just lost it. If it weren't so upsetting, it would almost be weirdly funny!"

So far in this book we have presented the *what* and the *why* of BPD. We have presented SET-UP and other strategies that model how personal interactions can progress. The following chapters explore more of the *how* of BPD—how professional treatment works and what modalities are available.

Chapter Seven

Seeking, Finding, and Engaging in Therapy

I'm gonna give him one more year, and then I'm going to Lourdes.

—From *Annie Hall*, by Woody Allen, about his psychiatrist

Dr. Smith, a nationally known psychiatrist, had called me about his niece. She was depressed and in need of a good psychotherapist. He was calling to say that he had recommended me.

Arranging an appointment was difficult. She could not rearrange her schedule to fit my openings, so I juggled and rearranged my schedule to fit hers. I felt pressure to be accommodating and brilliant so that Dr. Smith's faith in me would be justified. I had just opened my practice and needed some validation of my professional skills. Yet I knew that these feelings were a bad sign: I was nervous.

Julie was strikingly attractive. Tall and blond, she easily could have been a model. A law student, she was twenty-five, bright, and articulate. She arrived ten minutes late and neither apologized for nor even acknowledged this slight on her part. When I looked closely, I could see that her eye makeup was a little too heavy, as if she were trying to conceal a sadness and exhaustion inside.

Julie was an only child, very dependent on her successful parents, who were always traveling. Because she couldn't stand being alone, she cruised through a series of affairs. When a man would break off the relationship, she'd become extremely depressed until embarking on the next affair. She was now "between relationships." Her most recent man had left her, and "there was no one to replace him."

It wasn't long before her treatment fell into a routine. As a session would near its end, she'd always bring up something important, so our appointments would end a little late. The phone calls between sessions became more frequent and lasted longer.

Over the next six weeks we met once a week, but then mutually agreed to increase the frequency to twice a week. She talked about her loneliness and her difficulties with separations, and she continued to feel hopeless and alone. She told me that she often exploded in rage against her friends, though these outbursts were hard for me to imagine because she was so demure in my office. She had problems sleeping, her appetite had decreased, and she was losing weight. She began to talk about suicide. I prescribed antidepressant medications for her, but she felt even more depressed and was unable to concentrate in school. Finally, after three months of treatment, she reported increasing suicidal thoughts and began to visualize hanging herself. I recommended hospitalization, which she reluctantly accepted. Clearly, more intense work was needed to deal with this unremitting depression.

The first time I saw the anger was the day of her admission, when Julie was describing her decision to come to the hospital. Crying softly, she spoke of the fear she had experienced when explaining her hospitalization to her father.

Then suddenly her face hardened, and she said, "Do you know what that bitch did?" A moment passed before I realized that Julie was now referring to Irene, the nurse who had admitted her to the unit. Furiously, Julie described the nurse's lack of attention, her awkwardness with the blood pressure cuff, and a mix-up with a lunch tray. Her ethereal beauty mutated into a face of rage and terror. I jumped when she pounded the table.

After a few days, Julie was galvanizing the hospital unit with her demands and tirades. Some of the nurses and patients tried to calm and placate her; others bristled when she threw tantrums (and objects) and walked out of group sessions. "Do you know what *your* patient did this morning, Doctor?" asked one nurse as I stepped onto the floor. The emphasis was clearly on the *your,* as if I were responsible for Julie's behavior and deserved the staff's reprimands for not controlling her. "You're overprotective. She's manipulating you. She needs to be confronted."

I immediately came to my own—and Julie's—defense. "She needs support and caring," I replied. "She needs to be re-parented. She needs to learn trust." How dare they question my judgment! Do I dare question it?

Throughout the first few days, Julie complained about the nurses, the other patients, the other doctors. She said I was understanding and caring and I had much greater insight and knowledge than the other therapists she had seen.

After three days, Julie insisted on discharge. The nurses were skeptical; they didn't know her well enough. She hadn't talked much about herself either to them or in group therapy. She was talking only to her doctor, but she insisted her suicidal thoughts had dissipated and she needed "to get back to my life." In the end I authorized the discharge.

The next day she wobbled into the emergency room drunk with cuts on her wrist. I had no choice but to readmit her to the ward. Though the nurses never actually said, "I told you so," their haughty looks were unmistakable and insufferable. I began to avoid them even more than I had until that point. I resumed Julie's therapy on an individual basis and dropped her from group sessions.

Two days later she demanded discharge. When I turned down the request, she exploded. "I thought you trusted me," she said. "I thought you understood me. All you care about is power. You just love to control people!"

Maybe she's right, I thought. Perhaps I am too controlling, too insecure. Or was she just attacking my vulnerability, my need to be perceived as caring and trusting? Was she just stoking my guilt and masochism? Was she the victim here, or was I?

"I thought you were different," she said. "I thought you were special. I thought you really cared." The problem was, I thought so, too.

By the end of the week the insurance company was calling me daily, questioning her continued stay. Nursing notes recorded her insistence that she was no longer self-destructive, and she continued to lobby for discharge. We agreed to dismiss her from the hospital, but have her continue in the day hospital program, in which she could attend the scheduled groups during the day and go home in the afternoon. On her second day in the outpatient program, she arrived late, disheveled, and hung over. She tearfully related the previous night's sleazy encounter with a stranger in a bar. The situation was becoming clearer to me. She was begging for limits and controls and structure but couldn't acknowledge this dependency. So she acted outrageously to make controls necessary, and then got angry and denied her desire for them.

I could see this, but she couldn't. Gradually I stopped looking forward to seeing her. At each session, I was reminded of my failure, and I found myself wishing that she would either get well or disappear. When she told me that maybe her old roommate's doctor would be better for her, I interpreted this as a wish to run away from herself and the real issues she faced. I knew that a change at this point would be counterproductive for her, but silently I hoped that she would change doctors for *my* sake. She still talked of killing herself, and I guiltily fantasized that it would be almost a shameful relief for me if she did. Her changes had changed me—from a masochist to a sadist.

During her third week in the day hospital, another patient hanged himself while home over the weekend. Frightened, Julie flew into a rage. "Why didn't you and these nurses know he was going to kill himself?" she screamed. "How could you let him do it? Why didn't you protect him?"

Julie was devastated. Who was going to protect *her*? Who would make the pain go away? I finally realized that it would have to be Julie. No one else lived inside her skin. No one else could totally understand and protect her. It was starting to make some sense to me, and after a while, to Julie.

She could see that no matter how hard she tried to run away from her feelings, she could not escape being herself. Even though she wanted to run away from the bad person she thought she was, she had to learn to accept herself, flaws and all. Ultimately she would see that just being Julie was okay.

Julie's anger at the staff gradually migrated toward the suicide patient, who "didn't give himself a chance." When she saw his responsibility, she began to see hers. She discovered that people who really cared about her did not let her do whatever she wanted, as her parents had done. Sometimes caring meant setting limits. Sometimes it meant telling her what she didn't want to hear. And sometimes it meant reminding her of her accountability to herself.

It wasn't much longer before all of us—Julie, the staff, and I—began working together. I stopped trying so hard to be likable, wise, and unerring; it was more important to be consistent and reliable—to *be there*.

After several weeks, Julie left the hospital outpatient program and returned to our office therapy. She was still lonely and afraid, but she didn't need to hurt herself anymore. Even more important, she was accepting the fact that she could survive loneliness and fear but could still care about herself.

After a while, Julie found a new man who really seemed to care about her. As for me, I learned some of the same things Julie did—that distasteful emotions determine who I am to a great extent and that accepting these unpleasant parts of myself helps me better understand my patients.

Beginning Treatment

Therapists who treat borderline personality disorder often find that the rigors of treatment place a great strain on their professional abilities, as well as on their patience. Treatment sessions may be stormy, frustrating, and unpredictable. The treatment period proceeds at a snail-like pace and may require years to achieve true change. Many borderline patients drop out of therapy in the first few months.

Treatment is difficult because the borderline patient responds to it in much the same way as to other personal relationships. She will see the therapist as caring and gentle one moment, deceitful and intimidating the next.

In therapy, the patient with BPD can be extremely demanding, dependent, and manipulative. It is not uncommon for her to phone or text incessantly between sessions and then appear unexpectedly at the therapist's office, threatening bodily harm to herself unless the therapist meets with her immediately. Angry tirades against the therapist and the process of therapy are common. Often she can be very perceptive about the therapist's sensitivity and eventually goad him into anger, frustration, self-doubt, and hopelessness, just as she does with others in her life.

Given the wide range of possible contributing causes of BPD and the extremes of behavior involved, there is a predictably wide range of treatment methods. According to the American Psychiatric Association's "Practice Guideline for the Treatment of Patients with Borderline Personality Disorder," "The primary treatment for borderline personality disorder is psychotherapy, complemented by symptom-targeted pharmacotherapy."[1] Psychotherapy can take place in individual, group, or family therapy settings. It can proceed in or out of a hospital setting. Therapy approaches can be combined, such as individual and group. Some therapy approaches are more psychodynamic—that is, they emphasize the connection between past experiences and unconscious feelings and current behaviors. Other approaches are more cognitive and directive, focused more on changing current behaviors than on exploring unconscious motivations. Some therapies are time-limited, but most are open-ended.

Some treatments are usually avoided. Strict behavior modification is seldom utilized. Classical psychoanalysis on the couch with use of free association in an unstructured environment can be devastating for the borderline patient, whose primitive defenses may be overwhelmed. Because hypnosis can produce an unfamiliar trance state resulting in panic or even psychosis, it is also usually avoided as a therapeutic technique.

Goals of Therapy

All treatment approaches strive for a common goal: more effective functioning in a world that is experienced as less mystifying, less harmful, and more pleasurable. The process usually involves developing insight into the unproductiveness of current behaviors. This is the easy part. More difficult is the process of applying the self-understanding to rework old reflexes and to develop new ways of dealing with life's stresses.

The most important part of any therapy is the relationship between the patient and the therapist. This interaction forms the foundation for trust, object constancy, and emotional intimacy. The therapist must become a trusted figure, a mirror to reflect a developing consistent identity. Starting with this relationship, the borderline individual learns to extend to others appropriate expectations and trust.

The ultimate goal of the therapist is to work toward losing (not keeping) his patient. This is accomplished by directing the patient's attention to certain areas for examination, not by controlling him. Though the therapist serves as the navigator, pointing out landscapes of interest and helping to re-route the itinerary around storm conditions, it is the patient who must remain firmly in the pilot's seat. Family and loved ones are also sometimes included on this journey. A major objective is for the patient to return home and improve relationships, not to abandon them.

Some people are fearful of psychiatry and psychotherapy, perceiving the process as a form of "mind control" or behavior modification perpetrated on helpless, dependent patients who are molded into robots by bearded Svengali-like mesmerists. Popular culture, especially cinema, frequently portrays the "shrink" as either a bumbling fool, more in need of treatment than his patients, or as a brilliant, nefarious criminal. Unfortunately, just as some people erroneously believe that you can be hypnotized against your will, so some believe you can be "therapized" against your will. Perhaps the most notorious example of such failed attempts to "brainwash" has emerged with so-called conversion or reparative therapy. This discredited pseudoscientific practice utilizes mostly spiritual or painful behavioral techniques in attempts to convert someone with a homosexual or bisexual orientation to heterosexuality. Conversion therapy has been disavowed by most formal psychological organizations and has been banned in several states. The aim of psychotherapy is to help a patient individuate and achieve more freedom and personal dignity. Irrational fears about the process may deprive people of opportunities to escape self-imposed captivity and achieve self-acceptance.

Length of Therapy

Because of the past prominence of psychoanalysis, which characteristically requires several years of intensive frequent treatment, most people view any form of psychotherapy as being extended and drawn out, and therefore very expensive. The addition of medications and specialized treatments to the therapeutic armamentarium are responses to the need for practical and affordable treatment methods. Broken bones heal and infections clear up, but some scars on the psyche may require longer treatment.

If therapy terminates quickly, one may question if it was too superficial. If it extends for many years, one may wonder if it is merely intellectual game-playing that enriches psychotherapists while financially enslaving their naïve and dependent patients.

Currently, there is no evidence that longer BPD therapy programs are superior to shorter treatments.[2] So how long should therapy last? The answer depends on the specific goals. Resolution of specific targeted symptoms—such as depression, severe anxiety, or temper outbursts—may be accomplished in relatively brief time spans, such as weeks or months. If the goal is more profound restructuring, a longer duration will be required. Over time BPD is usually "cured." This means that the patient, by strict definition, no longer exhibits five of the nine defining DSM-5 criteria (see chapter 2). However, some individuals may continue to suffer from disabling symptoms, which can require continued treatment.

Therapy may be interrupted. It is not unusual for borderline patients to engage in several separate rounds of therapy, with different therapists and different techniques. Breaks in therapy may be useful to solidify ideas, or to try out new insights, or merely to catch up with life and allow time to grow and mature. Financial limitations, significant life changes, or just a need for a respite from the intensity of treatment may mandate a time-out. Sometimes years of therapy may be necessary to achieve substantive changes in functioning. When the changes come slowly, it can be difficult to determine whether more work should be done or if what has been accomplished is "as good as it gets." The therapist must consider both the borderline patient's propensity to run from confrontations with his unhealthy behaviors and his tendency to cling dependently to the therapist (and others).

For some, therapy may never formally end. They may derive great benefit from continuing intermittent contacts with a trusted therapist. Such arrangements would be considered "refueling stops" on the road to greater independence, provided the patient does not rely on these contacts to drive his life.

How Psychotherapy Works

As we shall see later in this and the next chapter, there are several established therapeutic approaches for the treatment of BPD. They may proceed in individual, group, or family settings. Most of these are derived from two primary orientations: *psychodynamic psychotherapy* and *cognitive behavioral therapy (CBT)*. In the former, discussion of the past and present are utilized to discover patterns that may forge a more productive future. This form of therapy is more intensive, with sessions conducted one or more times a week and usually continuing for a longer period. Effective therapy must employ a structured consistent format with clear goals. Yet there must also be flexibility to adapt to changing needs. Cognitive behavioral approaches focus on changing current thinking processes and repetitive behaviors that are disabling; this type of therapy is less concerned about the past. Treatment is more problem-focused and often time-limited. Some therapy programs combine both orientations.

Whatever the structure, the therapist tries to guide clients to examine their experience and serves as a touchstone for experimenting with new behaviors. Ultimately, the patient begins to accept his own choices in life and to change his self-image as a helpless pawn moved by forces beyond his control. Much of this process emerges from the primary relationship between therapist and patient. Often, in any therapy, both develop intense feelings, called *transference* and *countertransference*.

Transference

Transference refers to the patient's unrealistic projections onto the therapist of feelings and attitudes previously experienced from other important persons in the patient's life. For example, a patient may get very angry with the doctor, based not on the doctor's communications, but on feelings that the doctor is much like his mother, who in the past elicited much anger from him. Or a patient may feel she has fallen in love with her therapist, who represents a fantasied all-powerful protective father figure. By itself, transference is neither negative nor positive, but it is always a distortion, a projection of past emotions onto current objects.

Borderline transference is likely to be extremely inconsistent, just as is true of other aspects of the patient's life. He may see the therapist as caring, capable, and honest one moment, deceitful, devious, and unfeeling the next. These distortions make the establishment of an alliance with the therapist quite difficult. Yet establishing and sustaining this alliance is the most important part of any treatment.

In the beginning stages of therapy, the borderline patient both craves and fears closeness to the therapist. He wants to be taken care of but fears being overwhelmed and controlled. He attempts to seduce the doctor into taking care of him and rebels against his attempts to "control his life." As the therapist remains steadfast and consistent in withstanding his tirades, object constancy (see chapter 3) develops—the borderline individual begins to trust that the therapist will not abandon him. From this beachhead of trust, he can venture out with new relationships and establish more trusting contacts. Initially, however, such new friendships can be difficult to sustain, because in the past, he may have perceived the development of new alliances as a form of disloyalty. He may even fear that his mate, friend, or therapist may become jealous and enraged if he broadens his social contacts.

As the therapy progresses, he settles into a more comfortable, trusting dependency. As he prepares for termination, however, there may again be a resurgence of turmoil in the relationship. He may pine for his previous ways of functioning and resent needing to proceed onward; he may feel like a tiring swimmer who realizes he has already swum more than halfway across the lake, and now rather than return to the shore he departed from must continue on to the other side before resting.

At this point the borderline patient must also deal with his separateness and recognize that he, not the therapist, has effected change. Like Dumbo, who first attributes his flying ability to his "magic feather" but then realizes it is due to his own talents, the borderline individual must begin to recognize and accept his own abilities to function independently. And he must develop new coping mechanisms to replace the ones that no longer work.

As he improves, the intensity of the transference diminishes. The anger, impulsive behaviors, and mood changes—often directed at, or for the benefit of, the therapist—become less severe. Panicky dependency may gradually wither and be replaced by a growing self-confidence; anger erupts less often, replaced by greater determination to be in charge of one's own life. Impatience and caprice diminish, because he begins to develop a separate sense of identity that can evolve without the need for parasitic attachment.

Countertransference

Countertransference refers to the therapist's own emotional reactions to the patient, which are based less on realistic considerations than on the therapist's past experiences and needs. An example is the doctor who perceives the patient as more needy and helpless than is truly the case because of the doctor's need to be a caretaker, to perceive himself as compassionate, and to avoid confrontation.

The borderline patient is often very perceptive about others, including the therapist. This sensitivity often provokes the therapist's own unresolved feelings. The doctor's needs for appreciation, affection, and control can sometimes prompt her into inappropriate behavior. She may be overly protective of the patient and encourage dependency. She may be overly controlling, demanding that the patient carry out her recommendations. She may complain about her own problems and induce the patient to take care of her. She may extract information from the patient for financial gain or mere titillation. She may even enter into a sexual relationship with the patient "to teach intimacy." The therapist may rationalize all these as necessary for a "very sick" patient, but in reality they are satisfying her own needs. It is these countertransference feelings that result in most examples of unethical behavior between a trusted doctor or therapist and patient.

A patient with BPD can provoke feelings of anger, frustration, self-doubt, and hopelessness in the therapist that mirror his own. Goaded into emotions that challenge her professional self-worth, the therapist may experience genuine countertransference hate for the patient and view him as untreatable. Treatment of borderline personality disorder can become so frustrating and infuriating that some professionals invoke the term *borderline* inaccurately as a derogatory label for any patient who is extremely irritating or who does not respond well to therapy. In these cases, *borderline* more accurately reflects the countertransference frustration of a therapist than a scientific diagnosis of her patient.

The Patient-Therapist Fit

All of the treatments described in this book can be productive approaches to the borderline patient, though no therapeutic technique has been shown to be consistently superior to another or uniformly curative in all cases. The only factor that seems to correlate consistently with improvement is a positive, mutually respectful relationship between patient and therapist.

Even when a doctor is successful in treating one or many borderline patients, this does not guarantee automatic success in treating others. The primary determining factor of success is usually a positive, optimistic feeling shared between the participants—a kind of patient-therapist fit.

A good fit is difficult to define precisely, but refers to the abilities of both the patient and the therapist to tolerate the predictable turbulence of therapy, while maintaining a sturdy alliance as therapy proceeds.

The Therapist's Role

Because treatment of BPD may entail a combination of several therapies—individual, group, and family psychotherapies, medications, and hospitalization—the therapist's role in treatment may be as varied as the different therapies available. The doctor may be confrontational or nondirective; he may either spontaneously exhort and suggest or initiate fewer exchanges and expect the patient to assume a heavier burden for the therapy process. More important than the particular doctor or treatment method is the feeling of comfort and trust experienced by both patient and therapist. Both must perceive commitment, reliability, and true partnership from the other.

To achieve this feeling of mutual comfort, both patient and doctor must understand and share common objectives. They should agree upon methods and have compatible styles. Most important, the therapist must recognize when he is treating a borderline patient.

The therapist should suspect that he is dealing with BPD when he takes on a patient whose past psychiatric history includes contradictory diagnoses, multiple past hospitalizations, or trials of many medications. The patient may report being kicked out of previous therapies and becoming persona non grata in the local emergency room, having frequented the ER enough times to have earned a nickname (such as "Overdose Eddie") from the medical staff.

The experienced doctor will also be able to recognize his countertransference reactions to the patient. Borderline individuals usually elicit strong emotional reactions from others, including therapists. If early on in the evaluation, the therapist experiences strong feelings of wanting to protect or rescue the patient, of responsibility for the patient, or of extreme anger toward the patient, he should recognize that his intense responses may signify reactions to someone with BPD. Then the therapist's task is to be aware of his feelings, regulate them, and use them in therapy to better understand the patient.

Choosing a Therapist

Therapists with differing styles may perform equally well with borderline patients. Conversely, doctors who possess special expertise or interest in BPD and who generally do well with borderline patients cannot guarantee success with every patient.

A patient can choose from a variety of mental health professionals. Though psychiatrists, in their medical training, often have years of experience in psychotherapy techniques (and, as physicians, are the primary professionals capable of dealing with concurrent medical illnesses, prescribing medications, and managing hospitalization), other skilled professionals—psychologists, social workers, counselors, psychiatric nurse clinicians—may also attain expertise in psychotherapy with borderline patients.

In general, a therapist who works well with BPD possesses certain qualities that a prospective patient can usually recognize. He should be experienced in the treatment of BPD and remain tolerant and accepting in order to help the patient develop object constancy. He should be flexible and innovative, in order to adapt to the contortions through which therapy with a borderline patient may put him. He should possess a sense of humor, or at least a clear sense of proportion, to present an appropriate model for the patient and to protect himself from the relentless intensity that such therapy requires.

Just as the doctor evaluates the patient during the initial assessment interviews, so should the patient evaluate the doctor to determine if they can work together effectively.

First, the patient should consider whether she is comfortable with the therapist's personality and style. Will she be able to talk with him openly and candidly? Is he too intimidating, too pushy, too wimpy, too seductive?

Second, do the therapist's assessment and goals coincide with the patient's? Treatment should be a collaboration in which both parties share the same view and use the same language. What should therapy hope to achieve? How will you know when you get there? About how long should it take?

Finally, are the recommended methods acceptable to the patient? There should be agreement on the type of psychotherapy advocated and the suggested frequency of meetings. Will the doctor and patient meet individually or together with others? Will there be a combination of approaches, which might include, say, individual therapy on a weekly basis, along with intermittent conjoint meetings with the spouse? Will therapy be more exploratory or more supportive? Will medications or hospitalization likely be employed? What kinds of medicines and which hospitals?

This initial assessment period usually requires at least one interview, often more. Both the patient and the clinician should be evaluating their ability and willingness to work with the other. Such an evaluation should be recognized as a kind of no-fault interchange. It is irrelevant and probably impossible to blame the therapist or the patient for the inability to establish rapport. All that is necessary is to determine whether a therapeutic alliance is possible. However, if a patient continues to find every psychotherapist she interviews unacceptable, her commitment to treatment should be questioned. Perhaps she is searching for the "perfect" doctor who will take care of her or whom she can manipulate. Or she should consider the possibility that she is merely avoiding therapy and should perhaps choose an admittedly imperfect doctor and get on with the task of getting better.

Obtaining a Second Opinion

Once therapy is under way, it is not unusual for treatment to stop and start, or for the form of therapy to change over time. Adjustments may be necessary because the borderline patient may require changes in his treatment as he progresses.

Sometimes, however, it is difficult to distinguish when therapy is stuck from when it is working through painful issues; it is sometimes difficult to separate dependency and fear of moving on from the agonizing realization of unfinished business. At such times, the question of whether to proceed along the same lines or to take a step back and regroup will arise. Should treatment begin to involve family members? Should group therapy be considered? Should therapist and patient reevaluate medications? At this point a consultation with another doctor may be indicated. Often the treating therapist will suggest this, but sometimes the patient must consider this option on his own.

Although the patient may fear that a doctor is offended by a request for a second opinion, a competent and confident therapist will not object to, or be defensive about, such a request. It is, however, an area for exploration in the therapy itself, in order to assess whether the patient's wish for a second evaluation might constitute a running away from difficult issues or represent an unconscious angry rebuke.

Alternatively, it may be the doctor who recommends assessment by another caregiver. In such cases, the patient may feel offended and rejected, and the therapist must make clear that the patient will be able to return to her doctor after the consultation and is not being summarily handed over to a new therapist. A second opinion may be helpful for both the patient and the doctor in providing a fresh outlook on the progress of treatment.

Getting the Most from Therapy

Appreciating treatment as a collaborative alliance is the most important step in maximizing therapy. The borderline patient frequently loses sight of this primary principle. Instead, she sometimes approaches treatment as if the purpose were to please the doctor or to fight with him, to be taken care of or to pretend to have no problems. Some patients look at therapy as the opportunity to get away, get even, or get an ally. But the real goal of treatment should be to *get better.*

The person with BPD may need frequent reminders of the parameters of therapy. He should understand the ground rules, including the doctor's availability and limitations, the time and resource constraints, and the agreed-upon mutual goals.

The patient must not lose sight of the fact that he is bravely committing himself, his time, and his resources to the frightening task of trying to understand himself better and to effect alterations in his life pattern. Honesty in therapy is therefore of paramount importance for the *patient's* sake. He must not conceal painful areas or play games with the therapist to whom he has entrusted his care. He should abandon his need to control, or his wish to be liked by, the therapist. In the borderline quest to satisfy a presumed role, he may lose sight of the fact that it is not his obligation to please the therapist but to work with him as a partner.

Most important, the patient should always feel that he is actively collaborating in his treatment. He should avoid either assuming a totally passive role, deferring completely to the doctor, or becoming a competitive, contentious rival, unwilling to listen to contributions from the therapist. Molding a viable relationship with the therapist becomes the borderline's first and, initially, most important task in embarking on a journey toward mental health.

Finding the Right Therapist

As noted above, various mental health providers, such as psychiatrists, psychologists, social workers, and nurse practitioners, are clinicians who are capable of providing good treatment. Online sources can provide some objective biographical information about practitioners, such as training background, years of experience, and licensing. You can easily determine location accessibility, insurance coverage, and fees. Most national organizations of these professions offer location directories. Personal endorsements or online recommendations (including those provided in the Resources section of this book) may provide direction, but because of the special individualized relationship between patient and therapist, they should not replace your own judgment. Ultimately, as described earlier in this chapter, a few visits may be required to determine if your provider-patient relationship is a good fit.

Therapeutic Approaches

Many clinicians divide therapy orientations into exploratory and supportive treatments. Though these styles overlap, they are distinguished by the intensity of therapy and the techniques utilized. As we will see in the next chapter, a number of therapy strategies are used for the treatment of BPD. Some employ one style or the other; some combine elements of both.

Exploratory Therapy

Exploratory psychotherapy is a modification of classical psycho-analysis. Sessions are usually conducted one or more times per week. This form of therapy is more intensive than supportive therapy (see below) and has a more ambitious goal—to adjust personality structure. The therapist provides little direct guidance to the patient, utilizing confrontation instead to point out the destructiveness of specific behaviors and to interpret unconscious precedents in the hopes of eradicating them.

As in less intensive forms of therapy, a primary focus is on the here and now. Genetic reconstruction, with its concentration on child-hood and developmental issues (see chapter 3), is important, but emphasized less than in classical psychoanalysis. The major goals in the early overlapping stages of treatment are to diminish behaviors that are self-destructive and disruptive to the treatment process (including prematurely terminating therapy), to solidify the patient's commitment to change, and to establish a trusting, reliable relation-ship between patient and doctor. Later stages emphasize the processes of formulating a separate, self-accepting sense of identity, establish-ing constant and trusting relationships, and tolerating aloneness and separations (including those from the therapist) adaptively.[3,4]

Transference in exploratory therapy is more intense and pro-minent than in supportive therapy. Dependency on the therapist, together with idealization and devaluation, are experienced more passionately, as in classical psychoanalysis.

Supportive Therapy

Supportive psychotherapy is usually conducted on a once-weekly or less often basis. Direct advice, education, and reassurance replace the confrontation and interpretation of unconscious material typi-cally used in exploratory therapy. Many therapists explain their diag-nosis of BPD and encourage patients to educate themselves about it.

This approach is meant to be less intense and to bolster more adaptive defenses than exploratory therapy. In supportive psycho-therapy the doctor may reinforce suppression, discouraging discussion of painful memories that cannot be resolved. Rather than question the roots of minor obsessive concerns, the therapist may encourage them as "hobbies" or minor eccentricities. For example, a patient's need to keep his apartment spotless may not be dissected as to causes, but be acknowledged as a useful means to retain a sense of mastery and control when he is feeling overwhelmed. This contrasts with psychoanalysis, in which the aim is to analyze defenses and then eradicate them.

Focusing on current, more practical issues, supportive therapy tries to quash suicidal and other self-destructive behaviors rather than to explore them fully. Impulsive actions and chaotic interpersonal relationships are identified and confronted, without necessarily acquiring insight into the underlying factors that caused them.

Supportive therapy may continue on a regular basis for some time before dwindling to an as-needed frequency. Intermittent contacts may continue indefinitely, and the therapist's continued availability may be very important. Therapy gradually terminates when other lasting relationships form and gratifying activities become more important in the patient's life.

In supportive therapy, the patient tends to be less dependent on the therapist and to form a less intense transference. Though some clinicians argue that this form of therapy is less likely to institute lasting change in borderline patients, others have induced significant behavioral modifications in borderline patients with such treatment.

Group Therapies

Group therapy comes in several forms. Focused discussion groups or self-help groups such as Alcoholics Anonymous progress without a therapist. Some therapy groups are designed primarily to teach coping skills. Others focus on interpersonal interactions designed to build trust. Treating someone with BPD in a group makes perfect sense. Group psychotherapy allows the borderline patient to dilute the intensity of feelings directed toward one individual (such as the therapist) by recognizing emotions stimulated by others. In a group he can more easily control the constant struggle between emotional closeness and distance; unlike individual therapy, in which the spotlight is always on him, he can attract or avoid attention in a group. Confrontations by other group members may sometimes be more readily accepted than those from the idealized or devalued therapist, because a peer may be perceived as someone "who really understands what I'm going through." The borderline person's demanding nature, egocentrism, isolating withdrawal, abrasiveness, or social deviance can all be more effectively challenged by group peers. In addition, he may accept more readily the group's expressions of hope, caring, and altruism.[5,6,7]

The progress of other group members can serve as a model for growth. When a group patient attains a goal, he serves as an inspiration to others in the group, who have observed his growth and have vicariously shared his successes. The rivalry and competition so characteristic of borderline relationships are vividly demonstrated within the group setting and can be identified and addressed in ways that would be inaccessible in individual therapy. In a mixed group of higher functioning and lower functioning BPD and non-BPD patients, all participants may benefit. Healthier patients can serve as models for more adaptive ways of functioning. And for those patients who have difficulty expressing emotion, the borderline patients can reciprocate by demonstrating greater access to emotion. Finally, a group provides a living, breathing experimental laboratory in which the borderline individual can attempt different patterns of behavior with other people, without the risk of penalties from the outside world.

However, the features that make group therapy a potentially attractive treatment for BPD individuals are the very reasons many such patients resist group settings. The demand for individual attention, the envy and distrust of others, and the contradictory wish for and fear of intense closeness all contribute to the reluctance of many borderline patients to enter group treatment. Those who are higher functioning can tolerate these frustrations of group therapy and use the "in vivo" experiences to address defects in interrelating. Lower functioning patients with BPD, however, often will not join, and if they do, they will not stay.

The borderline patient may experience significant obstacles in psychodynamic group therapy. His self-absorption and lack of empathy often prevent involvement with others' problems. If his concerns are too deviant or the material too intense, he may feel isolated and disconnected. For example, a patient who discusses childhood incest or deviant sexual practices or severe drug abuse may fear that he may shock the other group members. And indeed, some members may have difficulty relating to upsetting material. Some may share the feeling that their needs are not being met by the therapist. In such situations they may attempt to take care of one another in the ways that they fantasized they could be cared for. This may lead to contacts between patients outside of the group setting and perpetuation of dependency needs as they try to "treat" each other. Romances or business dealings between group members usually end disastrously, because these patients will not be able to use the group objectively to explore the relationship, which is often a continuation of unproductive searches to be cared for.

Elaine, a twenty-nine-year-old woman, was referred for group therapy after two years of individual psychotherapy. The oldest of four daughters, Elaine was sexually abused by her father, starting around age five and continuing for over ten years. She perceived her mother as weak and ineffectual and her father as demanding and unable to be pleased. In adolescence, she became the caretaker for the whole family. As her sisters married and had children, Elaine remained single, entering college and then graduate school. She had few girlfriends and dated infrequently. Her only romantic relationships involved two married, much older work supervisors. Most of her off-work time was devoted to organizing family functions, caring for ill family members, and generally taking care of family problems.

Isolated and depressed, Elaine sought individual therapy. Recognizing the limitations in her social functioning, she later requested a referral for group therapy. There she quickly established a position as the helper for the others, denying any problems of her own. She often became angry with the therapist, whom she perceived as not helpful enough to the group members.

The group members encouraged Elaine to examine issues she had previously been unable to confront—her constant scowling and intimidating facial expressions and her subtly angry verbal exchanges. Although this process took many frustrating months, she was eventually able to acknowledge her disdain for women, which became obvious in the group setting. Elaine realized that her anger at the male therapist was actually transferred anger from her father and recognized her compulsive attempts to repeat this father-daughter relationship with other men. Elaine began to experiment in the group with new ways of interacting with men and women. Simultaneously, she was able to pull back from the suffocating immersion in her family's problems.

Most standardized therapies (see chapter 8) combine group with individual treatment. Some approaches, such as mentalization-based therapy (MBT), are psychodynamic and exploratory, with less direction from the therapist. Others, such as dialectical behavioral therapy (DBT) and Systems Training for Emotional Predictability and Problem Solving (STEPPS), are more supportive, behavioral, and educational, emphasizing skills development, lectures, "homework" assignments, and advice, as opposed to nondirective interactions.

Family Therapies

Family therapy is a logical approach for the treatment of some borderline patients, who often emerge from disturbed relationships with parents only to engage in persistent conflicts that may eventually entangle the borderline patient's own spouse and children.

Though family therapy is sometimes implemented with outpatients, it is often initiated at a time of crisis or during periods of hospitalization. At such a point the family's resistance to participating in treatment may be more easily overcome.

The families of borderline individuals often balk at treatment for several reasons. They may feel guilt over the patient's problems and fear being blamed for them. Also the bonds in borderline family systems are often very rigid; family members are often suspicious of outsiders and fearful of change. Though family members may be colluding in the perpetuation of the patient's behaviors (consciously or unconsciously), the attitude of the family is often "Make him better, but don't blame us, don't involve us, and most of all, don't change us."

Still, it is imperative to gain some support from the family, for without it, therapy may be sabotaged. For adolescents and young adults, family therapy involves the patient and his parents, and sometimes his siblings. For the adult borderline who is married or involved seriously in a romantic relationship, family therapy will often include the spouse or lover and sometimes the couple's children. (Unfortunately, many health insurance policies will not cover treatment that is labeled *marriage therapy* or *family treatment*.)

The dynamics of borderline family interaction usually reflect one of two extremes—either very strongly entangled or very detached. In the former case, it is important to build an alliance with all family members, for without their support the patient may not be able to maintain treatment independently. When the family is estranged, the therapist must carefully assess the potential impact of family involvement. If reconciliation is possible and healthy, it may be an important goal; if, however, it appears that reconciliation may be detrimental or hopelessly unrealistic, the patient may need to relinquish fantasies of reunion. In fact, mourning the loss of an idealized family interrelationship may become a major milestone in therapy.[8] Family members who resist an exploratory psychotherapy may nevertheless be willing to engage in a psycho-educational format, such as presented in the STEPPS therapy program (see chapter 8).

Debbie, a twenty-six-year-old woman, entered the hospital with a history of depression, self-mutilation, alcoholism, and bulimia.

Family assessment meetings revealed an ambivalent but basically supportive relationship with her husband. The course of therapy began to focus on previously undisclosed episodes of sexual abuse by an older neighbor boy, starting when the patient was about eight years old. In addition to sexually abusing her, this boy had also forced her to share liquor with him and then would make her drink his urine from the bottle, which she would later vomit. He had also assaulted her when she tried to refuse his advances.

These past incidents were reenacted in her current pathology. As these memories unfolded, Debbie became more conscious of long-standing rage at her passive alcoholic father and at her weak, disinterested mother, whom she perceived as unable to protect her. Although she had previously maintained a distant, superficial relationship with her parents, she now requested an opportunity to meet with them in family therapy to reveal her past hurts and disappointment in them.

As she predicted, her parents were very uncomfortable with these revelations. But for the first time Debbie was able to confront her father's alcoholism and her disappointment in him and in her mother's detachment. At the same time, all confirmed their love for one another and acknowledged the difficulties in expressing it. Although she recognized there would be no significant changes in their relationship, Debbie felt she had accomplished much and was more comfortable in accepting the distance and failures in the family interactions.

Therapeutic approaches to family therapy are similar to those for individual treatment. A thorough history is important and may include the construction of a family tree. Such a diagram may stimulate exploration of how grandparents, godparents, namesakes, or other important relatives may have influenced family interactions across generations. For example, the effects on second and third generations of Holocaust survivors is an area that has stimulated much interest in scientific studies and popular literature.[9]

As in individual and group therapy, family therapy approaches may be primarily supportive-educational or exploratory-reconstructive. In the former, the therapist's primary goals are to ally with the family; minimize conflicts, guilt, and defensiveness; and unite them in working toward mutually supportive objectives. Exploratory-reconstructive family therapy is more ambitious, directed more toward recognizing the members' complementary roles within the family system and attempting actively to change these roles.

At one point in her therapy, Elaine (discussed in the Group Therapy section earlier) focused on her relationship with her parents. After confronting them with the revelation of her father's sexual abuse, she continued to feel frustrated with them. Both parents refused further discussion about the abuse and discouraged her from continuing her treatment. Elaine was puzzled by their behavior. Sometimes they were very dependent and clinging; other times she felt infantilized, especially when they continually referred to her by her childhood nickname. Elaine requested family meetings, to which they reluctantly agreed.

During these meetings Elaine's father eventually admitted that her accusations were true, though he continued to deny any detailed recollection of his assaults. Her mother realized that in many ways she had been emotionally unavailable to her husband and children and recognized her own indirect responsibility for the abuse. Elaine learned for the first time that her father had also been sexually abused during his childhood. The therapy succeeded in releasing skeletons from the family closet and establishing better communication within the family. Elaine and her parents began for the first time speaking to one another as adults.

Artistic and Expressive Therapies

Individual, group, and family therapies require patients to express their thoughts and feelings with words, but the borderline patient is often somewhat handicapped in this area, more likely to exhibit inner concerns through actions rather than through words. Expressive therapies utilize art, music, literature, physical movement, and drama to encourage communication in nontraditional ways.

In art therapy, patients are encouraged to create drawings, paintings, collages, self-portraits, clay sculpture, dolls, and so on that express inner feelings. Patients may be presented with a book of blank pages, in which they are invited to draw representations of a variety of experiences, such as inner secrets, closeness, or hidden fears. Music therapy uses various melodies and lyrics to stimulate feelings that may otherwise be inaccessible. Music often unlocks emotions and promotes meditation in a calm environment. Body movement and dance use physical exertion to express emotions. In another type of expressive therapy called psychodrama, patients and the "therapist-director" act out a patient's specific problems. Bibliotherapy is another therapy technique in which patients read and discuss literature, short stories, plays, poetry, movies, and videos. Edward Albee's *Who's Afraid of Virginia Woolf?* is a popular play to read and perform, because its emotional scenes provide a catharsis as patients recite lines of rage and disappointment that reflect problems in their own lives.

Nicole's chronic depression was related to sexual abuses that she had endured at an early age from her older brother and that she had only recently begun to remember. At twenty-five and living alone, she was flooded with recollections of these early encounters and eventually required hospitalization as her depression worsened. Because she felt overwhelmed by guilt and self-blame, she was unable to verbalize her memories to others or allow herself to experience the underlying anger.

During an expressive therapy program that combined art and music, the therapists worked with Nicole to help her become more aware of the fury that she was avoiding. She was encouraged to draw what her anger felt like, while loud, pulsating rock music played in the background. Astonishing herself, she drew penises, which she then disfigured. Initially fearful and embarrassed about these drawings, she soon became more aware and accepting of her rage and obvious wish for retaliation.

As she discussed her emotional reactions to the drawings, Nicole began to describe her past abuse and the accompanying feelings. Eventually she began to talk more openly, both individually with doctors and in groups, which afforded her the opportunity to develop mastery over these frightening experiences and to place them in proper perspective.

Psycho-educational Therapies

Educating patients and families about their illness has a long tradition in medicine. Learning about an illness (such as diabetes or schizophrenia) and how best to treat and cope with it are important elements in treatment. Information may emanate from treatment facilities, books, or websites. One example of a formalized psycho-educational group program (PEG) for borderline patients was developed at McLean Hospital in collaboration with Italian doctors. This six-week program presented information on defining diagnostic criteria for BPD, genetic and environmental contributors, associated disorders (such as depression), prognosis considerations, and treatment approaches. Borderline patients exposed to this psycho-educational therapy, compared to a control group in supportive therapy, showed significant improvement and less worsening on measured scales.[10]

Hospitalization

Borderline patients constitute as much as 20 percent of all hospitalized psychiatric patients, and BPD is far and away the most common personality disorder encountered in the hospital setting.[11] Borderline propensities for impulsivity, self-destructive behaviors (suicide, drug overdoses), and brief psychotic episodes are the usual acute precipitants of hospitalization.

The hospital provides a protected, structured milieu to help contain and organize the often-chaotic world of BPD. The support and involvement of other patients and staff present the borderline patient with important feedback that challenges some of his perceptions and validates others.

The hospital minimizes his conflicts in the external world and provides greater opportunity for intensive self-examination. It also allows a respite from the intense relationships between the borderline individual and the outside world (including with his therapist), and permits diffusion of this intensity onto other staff members within the hospital setting. In this safe and more neutral milieu, the patient can reevaluate his personal goals and program of therapy.

At first the borderline inpatient typically protests his admission, but by the time of his discharge, he may be fully ensconced in the hospital setting, often fearful of discharge. He has an urgent need to be cared for, yet at the same time may become a leader of the ward trying to control and "help" other patients. At times he appears overwhelmed by his catastrophic problems; on other occasions he displays great creativity and initiative.

Characteristically, the hospitalized borderline patient creates a fascinating pas de deux of splitting and projective identification (see chapter 2 and Appendix B) with staff members. Some staff perceive him as a pathetic but appealing gamin; others see him as a calculating, sadistic manipulator. These disparate views emerge when the patient splits staff members into all-good (supportive, understanding) and all-bad (confrontive, demanding) projections, much like he does with other people in his life. When staff members accept the assigned projections—both "good" ("You're the only one who understands me") and "bad" ("You don't really care; you're only in it for the paycheck")—the projective identification circle is completed: conflict erupts between the "good" staff and the "bad" staff.

Amid this struggle the hospitalized patient with BPD recapitulates the interpersonal patterns of his external world: a seductive wish for protection, which ultimately leads to disappointment, then to feelings of abandonment, and finally to self-destructive behaviors and emotional retreat. In the hospital setting he has the opportunity to work through these conflicts.

Acute Hospitalization

Since the 1990s, increasing costs of hospital care and more stringent restrictions by insurance companies have restructured hospital-based treatment programs. Most hospital admissions today are precipitated by acute, potentially dangerous crises, including suicide attempts, violent outbursts, psychotic breaks, or self-destructive episodes (drug abuse, uncontrolled anorexia/bulimia, etc.). Insurance companies usually limit inpatient stays to a few days. Most will cover the hospital charges only when there is continued, documented "danger to self and/or others."

During short-term hospitalization, a complete physical and neurological assessment is performed. The hospital milieu focuses on structure and limit-setting. Support and positive rapport are emphasized. Treatment concentrates on practical, adaptive responses to turmoil. Vocational and daily living skills are evaluated. Conjoint meetings with family, when appropriate, are initiated. A formalized contract between patient and staff may help solidify mutual expectations and limits. Such a contract may outline the daily therapy program, which the patient is obligated to attend, and the patient's specific goals for the hospitalization, which the staff agrees to address with him.

The primary goals of short-term hospitalization include resolving the precipitating crises and terminating destructive behaviors. For example, the spouse of a patient who has thoughts of shooting himself will be asked to remove guns from the house. Personal and environmental strengths are identified and bolstered. Important treatment issues are uncovered or reevaluated, and modifications of psychotherapy approaches and medications may be recommended. Deeper exploration of these issues is limited on a short-term inpatient unit, and is more thoroughly pursued on an outpatient basis or in a less intensive program, such as partial hospitalization (discussed later in this chapter). Since the overriding concern is to return the patient to the outside world as quickly as possible and avoid regression or dependence on the hospital, plans for discharge and aftercare commence immediately upon admission.

Long-Term Hospitalization

While acute hospitalization is measured in days, long-term hospital care usually extends over months. Today, extensive hospitalization has become quite rare and is reserved for the very wealthy or for those with exceptional insurance coverage for psychiatric illness. In many cases where continued longer-term care is indicated, but confinement in a twenty-four-hour residence is not necessary, therapy can continue in a less restrictive milieu, such as partial hospitalization. Proponents of long-term hospitalization recognize the dangers of regression to a more helpless role, but argue that true personality change may require extensive and intensive treatment in a controlled environment. Indications for long-term confinement include chronically low motivation, inadequate or harmful social supports (such as enmeshment in a pathological family system), severe impairments in functioning that preclude holding a job or being self-sufficient, and repeated failures at outpatient therapy and short hospitalizations. Such features make early return to the outside environment unlikely.

During longer hospitalizations, the milieu may be less highly structured. The patient is encouraged to assume more shared responsibility for treatment. In addition to current practical concerns, the staff and patient explore past archetypal patterns of behavior and transference issues. The hospital can function like a laboratory, in which the borderline patient identifies specific problems and experiments with solutions in his interactions with staff and other patients.

Eventually, Jennifer (see chapter 1) entered a long-term hospital. She spent the first few months in the closet—literally and figuratively. She would often sit in her bedroom closet, hiding from the staff. After a while she became more involved with her therapist, getting angry at him and attempting to provoke his rage. She alternately demanded and begged to leave. As the staff held firm, she talked more about her father—how he was like her husband, how he was like all men. Jennifer began to share her feelings with the female staff, something that had always been difficult because of her distrust of and disrespect for women. Later during the hospitalization, she decided to divorce her husband and give up custody of her son. Although these actions hurt her, she considered them "unselfish selfishness"—trying to take care of herself was the most self-sacrificing and caring thing she could do for those she loved. She eventually returned to school and obtained a professional degree.

The goals of longer hospitalization extend those of short-term care—not only to identify dysfunctional areas but also to modify these characteristics. Increased control of impulses, fewer mood swings, greater ability to trust and relate to others, a more defined sense of identity, and better tolerance of frustration are the clearest signs of a successful hospital treatment. Educational and vocational objectives may be achieved during an extensive hospitalization. Many patients are able to begin a work or school commitment while transitioning from the hospital. Changes in unhealthy living arrangements—moving out of the home, divorce, etc.—may be completed.

The greatest potential hazard of long-term hospitalization is regression. If staff do not actively confront and motivate the patient, the borderline individual can become mired in an even more helpless position, in which he is even more dependent on others to direct his life.

The old stereotype of the psychiatric hospital as a "snake pit," populated by a wildly hallucinating population draped in pale nightshirts and futilely battling the ravages of stupefying drugs and shock treatment (such as the facility portrayed in Ken Kesey's *One Flew Over the Cuckoo's Nest*), is no longer relevant. Today, hospitals are regularly inspected and regulated to meet established care standards by federal agencies such as the Joint Commission on Accreditation of Healthcare Organizations (JCAHO). Several reputable hospital programs are listed in the Resources section of this book.

Partial Hospitalization

Partial (or day) hospital care is a treatment approach in which the patient attends hospital activities during part or most of the day and then returns home in the evening. Partial hospital programs may also be held in the evening, following work or school, and may allow sleeping accommodations when alternatives are not available. This approach is appropriate for individuals who are not a danger to themselves or others and require less active supervision.

This approach allows the patient with BPD to continue involvement in the hospital program, benefiting from the intensity and structure of hospital care, while maintaining an independent living situation. Hospital dependency occurs less frequently than in long-term hospitalization. Because partial hospitalization is usually much less expensive than traditional inpatient care, it is usually preferred for cost considerations.

Borderline patients who require more intensive care but not twenty-four-hour supervision, who are in danger of severe regression if hospitalized, who are making a transition out of the hospital to the outside world, who must maintain vocational or academic pursuits while requiring hospital care, or who experience severe financial limitations on care may all benefit from this approach. The hospital milieu and therapy objectives are similar to those of the associated inpatient program.

The Rewards of Treatment

As we shall see in the next two chapters, treatment of BPD usually combines standardized psychotherapeutic approaches and medications targeting specific symptoms. While at one time BPD was thought to be a diagnosis of hopelessness and irritation, we now know that the prognosis is generally much better than previously thought. And we know that most of these patients leave the chaos of their past and go on to productive lives.

The process of treatment may be arduous. But the end of the journey opens up new vistas.

"You always spoke of unconditional acceptance," said one borderline patient to her therapist, "and somewhere in the recent past I finally began to feel it. It's wonderful. . . . You gave me a safe place to unravel—to unfold. I was lost somewhere inside my mind. You gave me enough acceptance and freedom to finally let my true self out."

Chapter Eight

Specific Psychotherapeutic Approaches

There is a Monster in me. . . . It scares me. It makes me go up and down and back and forth, and I hate it. I will die if it doesn't let me alone.

—From the diary of a borderline patient

True life is lived when tiny changes occur.

—Leo Tolstoy

Borderline personality disorder is the only major psychiatric illness for which there are more evidence-based studies demonstrating efficacy from psychosocial therapies than for pharmacological (drug) treatments. Thus, unlike the treatment for most other disorders, medications are viewed as secondary components to psychotherapy. Not only have several psychotherapy approaches been shown to be effective, the arduous and sometimes extensive endeavor of psychotherapy has also been shown to be cost-effective for the treatment of personality disorders.[1]

Psychotherapy as a treatment for BPD has come a long way since the publication of this book's first two editions. Spurred by rigorous research and constant refinement by clinicians, two primary schools of therapy with variations have emerged—the cognitive behavioral and psychodynamic approaches. In each category, several distinct strategies have been developed, each supported by its own set of theoretical principles and techniques. Several psychotherapy strategies combine group and individual sessions. Though some are more psychodynamic and some are more behavioral, most combine elements of both. All embrace communication that reflects SET-UP features that were developed by the primary author and discussed in detail in chapter 5: *Support* for the patient, *Empathy* for his struggles, confrontation of *Truth* or reality issues, together with *Understanding* of issues and a dedication to *Persevere* in the treatment.

Proponents of several therapy approaches have attempted to standardize their therapeutic techniques by, for example, compiling instructional manuals to help guide practitioners in conducting the specific treatment. In this way, it is hoped that the therapy is conducted consistently and equally effectively, irrespective of the practitioner. (An obvious, though perhaps crass, analogy may be made to a franchise food company, such as Starbucks or McDonald's, which standardizes its ingredients so that its coffee or hamburgers taste the same regardless of where it is purchased or who is behind the counter.) Standardization also facilitates gathering evidence in controlled studies, which can support, or refute, the effectiveness of a particular psychotherapy approach.

The underlying theory of standardization is that just as it would make little difference which Prozac capsule the patient chose from the bottle (as long as he ingested it), it would make little difference who administered the psychotherapy, as long as the patient was in attendance. However, interpersonal interactions are surely different from taking and digesting a pill, so it is probably naive to presume that all psychotherapists following the same guidelines will produce the same results with patients. Indeed, John G. Gunderson, MD, a pioneer in the study of BPD, has pointed out that the original developers of these successful techniques are blessed with prominent charisma and confidence, which followers may not necessarily possess.[2] Additionally, many therapists might find such a constrained approach too inflexible.[3]

Although the different psychotherapy strategies emphasize distinctions, they possess many commonalities. All attempt to establish clear goals with the patient. A primary early goal is to disrupt self-destructive and treatment-destructive behaviors. All of the formal "manualized" therapies are intensive, requiring consistent contact usually one or more times per week. All of these therapies recognize the need for the therapist to be highly and specially trained and supported, and many require supervision and/or collaboration with other team members. Therapists are more vigorously interactive with patients than in traditional psychoanalysis. Because these therapies are time and labor intensive, usually expensive, and often not fully covered by insurance (e.g., insurance does not cover team meetings between therapists, as required in formal DBT—see Dialectical Behavioral Therapy on the following page), most of the studies exploring their efficacy have been performed in university or grant-supported environments. Most community and private treatment protocols attempting to reproduce a particular approach are truncated modifications of the formal programs.

It is no longer simply a matter of "finding any shrink who can cure me" (though it is possible, of course, to get lucky this way). In our complex society, all sorts of factors are and should be considered by the patient: time and expense, therapist's experience and specialization, and so on. Most important, the patient should be comfortable with the therapist and her specific approach to treatment. So the reader is advised to read the remainder of this chapter with an eye toward at least becoming familiar with specific approaches, as she will likely see them (and their acronyms) again at some point during the therapeutic process. In seeking a preferred patient-therapist fit (see chapter 7), a prospective patient may further explore some of these described approaches and seek care from a clinician who offers the favored treatment.

Cognitive and Behavioral Treatments

Cognitive behavioral approaches focus on changing current thinking processes and repetitive behaviors that are disabling; this type of therapy is less concerned about the past than psychodynamic approaches (see Psychodynamic Treatments below). Treatment is more problem focused and often time limited.

Cognitive Behavioral Therapy (CBT)

A system of treatment developed by Aaron Beck, CBT focuses on identifying disruptive thoughts and behaviors and replacing them with more desirable beliefs and reactions.[4] Active attempts to point out distorted thinking ("I'm a bad person"; "Everyone hates me") and frustrating behaviors ("Maybe I can have just one drink") are coupled with homework assignments designed to change these feelings and actions. Assertiveness training, anger-management classes, relaxation exercises, and desensitization protocols may all be used. Typically, CBT is time limited, less intensive than other protocols, and therefore usually less expensive. The following treatment programs are derived from CBT.

Dialectical Behavioral Therapy (DBT)

Developed by Marsha M. Linehan, PhD, at the University of Washington, DBT is a derivation of standard cognitive behavioral therapy that has furnished the most controlled studies demonstrating its efficacy. The *dialectic* of the treatment refers to the goal of resolving the inherent "opposites" faced by BPD patients—that is, the need to negotiate the patient's contradictory feeling states, such as loving, then hating the same person or situation. A more basic dialectic in this system is the need to resolve the paradox that the patient is trying as hard as she can and is urged to be satisfied with her efforts and her current level of functioning, and yet is simultaneously striving to change even more and do even better.[5,6]

DBT posits that borderline patients possess a genetic/biological vulnerability to emotional overreactivity. This view hypothesizes that the limbic system, the part of the brain most closely associated with emotional responses, is hyperactive in BPD. The second contributing factor, according to DBT practitioners, is an invalidating environment: that is, others dismiss, contradict, or reject the developing individual's emotions. Confronted with such interactions, the individual is unable to trust others or her own reactions. Emotions are uncontrolled and volatile. To calm these erratic emotions, DBT emphasizes *mindfulness,* the process of paying attention to what is happening at the moment, without extreme emotional reactivity, judgment, or invalidation.

In the initial stages of treatment, DBT focuses on a hierarchical system of targets, confronting first the most serious and then later the easier behaviors to change. The highest priority addressed immediately is the threat of suicide and self-injuring behaviors. The second-highest target is to eliminate behaviors that interfere with therapy, such as missed appointments or not completing homework assignments. The third priority is to address behaviors that interfere with a healthy quality of life, such as disruptive compulsions, promiscuity, or criminal conduct; among these, easier changes are targeted first. The fourth priority is to focus on increasing behavioral skills.

The structured program consists of four main components:

1. Weekly individual psychotherapy to reinforce learned new skills and to minimize self-defeating behaviors.
2. Weekly group skills therapy that utilizes educational materials about BPD and DBT, homework assignments, and discussion to teach techniques to better control emotions, improve interpersonal contacts, and nurture mindfulness. Each week, patients are given a DBT "diary card" to fill out daily. The diary is meant to document self-destructive behaviors, drug use, disruptive emotions, and the patient's efforts to cope with such daily stresses.
3. Telephone coaching (a unique feature of DBT) to help patients work through developing stresses before they become emergencies; calls can be made to on-call coaches at any time, but are deemed inappropriate if made *after* a patient has acted out in a destructive manner.
4. Weekly meetings among all members of the therapy team to enhance treaters' skills and motivation and to combat burnout.

Systems Training for Emotional Predictability and Problem Solving (STEPPS)

Another manual-based variation of CBT is STEPPS, developed at the University of Iowa. Like DBT, STEPPS focuses on the borderline patient's inability to modulate emotions and impulses. The unique modifications of STEPPS were partly built on a wish to develop a less costly program. STEPPS is a group therapy paradigm, without individual sessions. It is also designed to be shorter—consisting of twenty two-hour weekly groups (compared to the typical one-year commitment expected in DBT). This program also emphasizes the importance of involving the borderline individual's social systems in treatment. Educational training sessions "can include family members, significant others, health care professionals, or anyone they regularly interact with, and with whom they are willing to share information about their disorder."[7,8] STEPPS embodies three primary components:

1. Sessions educate about BPD and schema (cognitive distortions about oneself and others, such as a sense of unlovability, mistrust, guilt, a lack of identity, a fear of losing control, etc.).
2. Skills to better control emotions, such as problem management, distracting, and improving communication, are taught.
3. The third component teaches basic behavioral skills, such as healthy eating, a healthy sleep regimen, exercise, and goal setting.

A second phase of STEPPS is STAIRWAYS (setting goals; trusting; anger management; impulsivity control; relationship behavior; writing a script; assertiveness training; your journey; schemas revisited). This is a twice-monthly one-year extension of skills-training "seminars," which reinforce the STEPPS model. Unlike DBT, which is designed to be self-contained and discourages other therapy contributions, STEPPS is designed to complement other therapy involvement.

Schema-Focused Therapy (SFT)

SFT combines elements of cognitive, Gestalt, and psychodynamic theories. Developed by Jeffrey Young, PhD, a student of Aaron Beck's, SFT conceptualizes maladaptive behavior arising from schemas. In this model, a schema is defined as a world view developed over time in a biologically vulnerable child who encounters instability, overindulgence, neglect, or abuse. Schemas are the child's attempts to cope with these failures in parenting. Such coping mechanisms become maladaptive in adulthood. The concept of schemas derives from psychodynamic theories. SFT attempts to challenge these distorted responses and teaches new ways of coping through a process denoted as re-parenting.[9]

Multiple schemas can be grouped into five primary schema modes, with which borderline patients identify and which correlate with borderline symptoms:

1. Abandoned and Abused Child (abandonment fears)
2. Angry Child (rage, impulsivity, mood instability, unstable relationships)
3. Punitive Parent (self-harm, impulsivity)
4. Detached Protector (dissociation, lack of identity, feelings of emptiness)
5. Healthy Adult (therapist's role to model for the patient—soothes and protects the other modes)

Specific treatment strategies are appropriate for each mode. For example, the therapist emphasizes nurturing and caring for the Abandoned and Abused Child mode. Expressing emotions is encouraged for the Detached Protector mode. Re-parenting attempts to supply unmet childhood needs. Therapists are more open than in traditional therapies, often sharing gifts, phone numbers, and other personal information, projecting themselves as real, honest, and caring. Conveying warmth, praise, and empathy are important therapist features in SFT. Patients are encouraged to read about schema and

BPD. Gestalt techniques, such as role-playing, acting out dialogue between modes, and visualization techniques (visualizing and role-playing stressful scenarios) are employed. Assertiveness training and other cognitive behavioral methods are utilized. A possible danger in SFT is the boundary confrontation in re-parenting. Therapists must be extremely vigilant regarding the risk of transference and countertransference regression (see chapter 7).

Psychodynamic Treatments

Psychodynamic approaches typically employ discussion of the past and present, with the goal of discovering patterns that may forge a more productive future. This form of therapy is usually more intensive—with sessions conducted one or more times a week—than the cognitive-behavioral approach. The therapist should implement a structured, consistent format with clear goals, yet be flexible enough to adapt to changing needs.

Transference-Focused Psychotherapy (TFP)

TFP is a manual-based program that Otto Kernberg, MD, and his colleagues at Cornell have developed from more traditional psycho-analytic roots.[10,11] The therapist focuses initially on developing a contract of understanding of the roles and limitations in the therapy. Like DBT, TFP's early concerns revolve around suicide danger, interruption of therapy, dishonesty, and so on. Like other treatment approaches, TFP acknowledges the role of biological and genetic vulnerability interacting with early psychological frustrations.

A primary defense mechanism seen in borderline patients is *identity diffusion,* which refers to a distorted and unstable sense of self and consequently of others. Identity diffusion suggests a perception of oneself and others as if they were fuzzy, ghostlike distortions in a funhouse mirror, barely perceptible and insubstantial to the touch. Another feature of BPD is persistent splitting—dividing perceptions into extreme and opposite dyads of black or white, right or wrong, resulting in the belief that oneself, another, or a situation is all good or all bad. In addition, if the all-good person disappoints the borderline individual, the formerly good person can mutate into an all-bad person almost overnight.

TFP theorizes that identity diffusion and splitting are early primary elements in normal development. However, in BPD, normal, developing integration of opposite feelings and perceptions is disrupted by frustrating caregiving; in other words, the borderline individual gets stuck at an immature level of functioning (see chapter 3). Feelings of emptiness, severe emotional swings, anger, and chaotic relationships result from this black-and-white thinking. TFP typically consists of twice-weekly individual sessions, in which the relationship with the therapist is examined. This here-and-now transference experience (see chapter 7) allows the patient to experience in the moment the splitting that is so prevalent in his life experience. The therapist's office becomes a kind of laboratory in which the patient can examine his feelings in a safe, protected environment and then extend his understanding to the outside world. The combination of intellectual understanding and the emotional experience in working with the therapist can lead to the healthy integration of identity and perceptions of others.

Mentalization-Based Therapy (MBT)

Mentalization, a term elaborated by Peter Fonagy, PhD, describes how people understand themselves, others, and their environment. Using mentalization, an individual understands why she and others interact the way they do, which in turn leads to the ability to empathize with another's feelings.[12,13] The term overlaps with the concept of *psychological mindedness* (understanding the connection between feelings and behaviors) and *mindfulness* (a goal in DBT; see above). Fonagy theorizes that when the normal development of mentalization beginning in early childhood is disrupted, adult pathology develops, particularly BPD. This conceptualization is based on psychodynamic theories of a healthy attachment to a parenting figure (see chapter 3). When the child is unable to bond appropriately with a parent, he has difficulty understanding the parent's or his own feelings. He has no healthy context on which to base emotions or behaviors. Object constancy cannot be sustained. The child develops abandonment fears or detaches from others. This developmental failure may arise either from the child's temperament (biological or genetic limitations) or from the parent's pathology, which may consist of physical or emotional abuse or abandonment, or inappropriate smothering of independence, or from both.

MBT is based on the supposition that beliefs, motives, emotions, desires, reasons, and needs must first be understood in order to function optimally with others. The goal of MBT is to help the patient think through his feelings before he reacts to them. He is also encouraged to more carefully consider the thoughts and actions of others as a check against misperceptions.

Confirming data on the effectiveness of this method has been documented by Bateman and Fonagy, primarily within a daily partial hospital setting in England.[14,15] In this design, patients attend the hospital during the day, five days a week for eighteen months. Treatment includes psychoanalytically oriented group therapy three times a week, individual psychotherapy, expressive therapy consisting of art, music, and psychodrama programs, and medications as needed. Daily staff meetings are held and consultations are available. Therapists, employing a manual-based system, focus on the patient's current state of mind, identify distortions in perception, and collaboratively attempt to generate alternative perspectives in the patient about himself and others. While many of the behavioral techniques are similar to DBT, some of the psychodynamic structure of MBT overlaps with transference-focused psychotherapy (TFP). (The professional reader will note that distortions in MBT's mentalization include the concepts of identity diffusion and splitting in TFP; the difficulty with dyadic extremes recalls the dialectical paradoxes theorized in DBT.)

A Dutch study comparing the intense day hospital MBT system

described above with MBT on a less intensive outpatient basis revealed similar levels of significant improvement in symptoms with both approaches. However, the day hospital approach yielded more improvement in interpersonal functioning and quality of life and decreased self-harm.[16]

Good Psychiatric Management (GPM)

Some years ago, Dr. John G. Gunderson recognized that most borderline patients did not have access to many of these specialized programs. Furthermore, most psychiatrists and other practitioners were not able to participate in formal training curricula to allow delivery of these programs. He developed what he felt was a more practical therapy process that combined cognitive, behavioral, and psychodynamic elements that he termed "good enough" for most therapists to provide and for most borderline patients to gain improvement from. Special attention is devoted to the borderline patient's hypersensitivity in relationships.[17]

Gunderson outlined eight basic principles for practitioners of GPM (many have counterparts in SET-UP; see chapter 5):

1. *Offer psychoeducation.* Depending on the patient, discussion of the BPD diagnosis, genetic and environmental contributions, and other clinical information may be appropriate (exhibiting *Understanding* as in SET-UP).
2. *Be active, not reactive.* Be responsive, involved, and interested (which would reflect *Support* and *Empathy*).
3. *Be thoughtful.* Model the idea of thinking before acting.
4. *Be real and professional.* Acknowledge mistakes. Some personal sharing is okay.
5. *Expect change.* Stick with realistic goals and don't accept resignation (*Perseverance*).
6. *Hold patients accountable.* Expect patients to be responsible for their actions (as in the *Truth* portion of SET-UP).

7. *Focus on life outside.* Emphasize social, interpersonal, and vocational concerns.

8. *Be flexible and pragmatic.* Improvise. Adjust to the needs of the patient.

GPM's primary goal of change occurs along three primary axes:

1. *Mentalization:* Learning to "think first." Thinking before acting. Being aware of one's own feelings and identifying feelings and motivations of others (as in MBT).

2. *Social rehabilitation:* Establishing social and vocational routines. Developing better relationships. Improving the activities of daily living (as in DBT).

3. *Corrective experiences:* Expanding a reliable, trusting connection with the therapist that can be internalized as a model for outside relationships (as in TFP).

Comparing Treatments

A vignette may help demonstrate how therapists utilizing these various approaches might handle the same situation in therapy:

Judy, a twenty-nine-year-old single accountant, arrived at her therapist's office quite upset, after having an intense argument with her father, during which he called her a slut. When her doctor inquired about what prompted this slur, Judy became more upset, accusing the therapist of taking her father's side and throwing a box of tissues across the room.

A DBT therapist might focus on Judy's anger and physical outburst. He might empathize with her frustration, accept her impulsive gesture, and then work with her to vent her frustration without becoming violent. He might also discuss ways to deal with her frustration with her father.

The SFT therapist might first try to correct Judy's misperception of him and reassure her that he is not angry at her and is totally on her side.

With MBT, the doctor may try to get Judy to relate what she is feeling and thinking at this moment. He may also attempt to direct her to thinking (mentalizing) about what she supposed her father was reacting to during their conversation.

The TFP therapist may explore how Judy is comparing him to her father. He might focus on her severely changing feelings about him at that moment in therapy.

The GPM doctor might first express his own alarm at Judy's violence. He may express regret for upsetting her. He might then point out her extreme reaction to his query and explore with her other ways to discharge her anger.

Other Therapies

A number of other therapy approaches, less studied, have also been described. Most of these schools have produced manuals for therapists to follow in practice. Robert Gregory and his group at the State University of New York in Syracuse have developed a manual-based protocol, Dynamic Deconstructive Psychotherapy (DDP), specifically directed toward borderline patients who are more challenging or have complicating disorders such as substance abuse.[18] Weekly individual, psychodynamically oriented sessions are directed toward activating impaired cognitive perceptions and helping the patient develop a more coherent, consistent sense of self and others.

Alliance-Based Therapy (ABT), developed at Austen Riggs Center in Stockbridge, Massachusetts, is a psychodynamic approach that focuses specifically on suicidal and self-destructive behaviors.[19] Much like TFP, the emphasis is on the therapeutic relationship and how it impacts self-harming actions.

Intensive Short-Term Dynamic Psychotherapy (ISTDP), designed for the treatment of patients with borderline and other personality disorders, has been elaborated by a Canadian group.[20] Weekly individual sessions concentrate on unconscious emotions that are responsible for defenses and the connections between these feelings and past traumas. Treatment is generally expected to continue for a period of around six months.

Practitioners from Chile, recognizing the difficulty of providing intensive individual care for borderline patients, developed a group therapy system, Intermittent-Continuous Eclectic Therapy (ICE).[21] Weekly ninety-minute group therapy sessions are conducted in ten-session cycles. Patients may continue with further rounds, as they and their therapists choose. A psychodynamic viewpoint guides understanding of the patient, but interpretations are minimized. The first part of each session is an open, supportive period in which unstructured discussion is encouraged; the second half is arranged like a classroom, in which skills are taught to handle difficult emotions (as in DBT and STEPPS).

Which Therapy Is Best?

All of these "alphabet soup" treatment designs endeavor to standardize the therapy, most utilizing manual-based programs, and have attempted to develop controlled studies to determine efficacy. All have evolved studies demonstrating the superiority of the formalized therapy over a comparative nonspecific supportive "treatment as usual." Some research has studied comparative results among these different treatments.

One study compared the results of year-long outpatient treatments for borderline patients with three different approaches: DBT, TFP, and a psychodynamic supportive therapy.[22] Patients in all three groups demonstrated improvement in depression, anxiety, social interactions, and general functioning. Both DBT and TFP showed significant reduction in suicidal thinking. TFP and supportive therapy were more effective in reducing anger and impulsivity. TFP performed the best in reducing irritability and verbal and physical assault.

A three-year Dutch study compared results of treating borderline patients with SFT versus TFP.[23] After the first year, both treatment groups experienced comparable significant reductions in BPD symptoms and improvement in quality of life. By the third year, however, SFT patients exhibited significantly greater improvement and had fewer dropouts. A later study from the Netherlands compared the cost-effectiveness of these two psychotherapy designs.[24] This investigation attempted to measure the cost of treatment with the improvement in quality of life over time (determined by a self-administered questionnaire). Although quality of life measures after TFP were slightly higher than after SFT, the overall cost for comparable improvement was significantly more efficient with SFT.

A two-year study comparing BPD patients who had completed treatment with DBT and those with GPM showed mostly similar results.[25] Both groups exhibited significant and comparable improvement in most measured areas. Over 60 percent of patients in both groups no longer qualified for the formal BPD diagnosis. Measures of quality of life were equally and significantly improved in both groups. However, this was mitigated by persistent deficits in independent living. In both groups, over half of the patients remained unemployed and over a third remained on disability support.

A one-year follow-up study with BPD patients comparing DDP and DBT found significant symptom reduction in both groups. However, DDP treatment experienced fewer dropouts and better outcomes.[26]

Although all these studies are admirable attempts to compare different treatments, all can be criticized. Patient and therapist selection, validity of measures used, and the plethora of uncontrolled variables that impact any scientific study make attempts to compare human behavioral responses very difficult. Continued studies on larger populations may illuminate other therapeutic approaches that will be beneficial for many patients in aggregate. But given the complex variations rooted in our DNA, which make one person so different from another, unveiling the "best" treatment that will be ideal for every individual is surely impossible.

All successful therapeutic interventions have common features, particularly a reliable, trusting relationship with the therapist. And no specific approach has been proven to be consistently better than others. The treatment that demonstrates superiority in a majority of patients in a study may not be the ideal choice for *you*. This is no less true in the area of medications, where we find one size does *not* fit all. Thus, the primary point to be gleaned from these studies is not which treatment works best, but that psychotherapeutic treatment *does* work! Indeed, as the Dodo in *Alice's Adventures in Wonderland* declares after a race, "Everybody has won, and all must have prizes!"

Unfortunately, psychotherapy has been figuratively and literally devalued over the years. Psychological services in general are reimbursed at a remarkably lower rate than medical services. Insurance payment to a clinician for an hour of noninterventional interaction with a patient (e.g., diet and behavioral adjustments to diabetes, instruction on caring for a healing wound, or psychotherapy) is a fraction of the payment for a routine medical procedure (minor surgical intervention, steroid injection, etc.). For one hour of psychotherapy, Medicare and most private insurance companies pay less than one-tenth of the reimbursement rate directed for many minor outpatient surgical procedures.

As the United States continues its quest to provide health care to more people in more affordable ways, there will be temptations to mandate treatments that are shown to be grossly equivalent but less expensive. It will be important to maintain flexibility in such a system, so that we do not denigrate the *art* of medicine, which allows individuality in the sacred relationship between doctor and patient.

Future Research and Specialized Therapies for BPD

In the future, advances in genetic and biological research may suggest how therapies can be individualized for specific patients. Just as no single medicine is recognized as better than the others in treating *all* BPD patients, no single therapeutic approach has been demonstrated to be better for all, despite attempts to compare approaches. Therapists should direct specific therapy approaches to different patient needs, rather than try to apply the fictional *best* approach to everyone. For example, borderline patients who are significantly suicidal or engaged in serious self-mutilating behaviors may initially respond best to cognitive/behavioral approaches, such as DBT. Higher functioning patients may respond better to psychodynamic protocols. Financial or scheduling limitations may favor time-limited therapies, whereas repeated destructive life patterns might dictate a need for longer-term, more intensive protocols. Some therapists closely follow a specific process laid down in a manual. Others may employ an eclectic therapeutic approach that combines various methods. In order to achieve the best fit (see chapter 7), the patient should understand and be comfortable with the practitioner's approach.

Just as most medical specialties (e.g., ophthalmology) have developed subspecialty areas for complicated situations or for the parts of the organ involved (e.g., retina, cornea), optimal treatment of BPD may be heading in the same direction. Some programs, for example, have been designed specifically for patients who self-mutilate. In the future, specialized centers of care for BPD, which feature experienced, specially trained professionals and focus on specific symptoms, may offer more effective treatment regimens.

Chapter Nine

Medications: The Science and the Promise

One pill makes you larger, and one pill makes you small . . .

—From "White Rabbit," by Grace Slick of Jefferson Airplane

Doctors are men who prescribe medicines of which they know little, to cure disease of which they know less, in human beings of whom they know nothing.

—Voltaire

While psychotherapy is the recognized primary treatment for BPD, most treatment plans include recommendations for inclusion of drug therapy. However, medications often present highly charged dilemmas for borderline patients. Some are bewitched by the alluring promise of drugs to "cure" their "borderline." Others fear being transformed into zombies and resist any medication. As scientists have not yet isolated a *borderlinus* virus, no single "antibiotic" treats all aspects of BPD. However, medications are useful for treating associated symptoms (such as antidepressants for depression) and for taming self-defeating characteristics, such as impulsivity.

Despite Voltaire's plaint, doctors are learning more and more about how and why medications treat disease. New discoveries in the genetics and neurobiology of BPD help us understand how and why these medications can be effective.

Genetics

Nature-nurture arguments about the cause of physical and mental disease have raged for decades, of course, but with the expansion of knowledge of heritability, gene mapping, and molecular genetics over the past quarter century, the role of nature has become better understood. One approach to this controversy is through the use of twin studies. In this type of study, identical twins (possessing the same genetic makeup) who are adopted into different households are examined years later for the presence of the disease. If one twin exhibits BPD, the likelihood that the other, reared in a different environment, will also be diagnosed with BPD is as much as 35 percent to almost 70 percent in some studies, thus giving greater weight to the nature argument.[1] Specific borderline traits—anxiety, emotional lability, suicidal tendencies, impulsivity, anger, sensation-seeking, aggression, cognitive distortions, identity confusion, and relationship problems—can also be highly genetic.

Heritability also extends to family members. Relatives of borderline patients exhibit significantly greater rates of mood and impulse disorders, substance abuse, and personality disorders, especially BPD and antisocial personality.[2]

Our humanness emerges from the elaborate and unique chain of chromosomes that determine the individual. Although one specific gene alone does not determine our fate, a combination of DNA codings on different chromosomes do contribute to vulnerability for illness. Individual genes have been associated with Alzheimer's disease, breast cancer, and other maladies; however, other chromosomal loci and environmental factors also contribute. Molecular genetics has identified specific gene alterations (polymorphisms) that are associated with BPD. Interestingly, these genes are involved with production and metabolism of the neurotransmitters serotonin, norepinephrine, and dopamine. These neurotransmitters facilitate communication between brain cells and influence which genes are turned on or off. Alterations in these neurotransmitters have been associated with mood disorders, impulse dysregulation, dissociation, and pain sensitivity.

Neuroendocrinology

Other endocrine (hormone) neurotransmitters have been implicated in borderline pathology. NMDA (N-methyl-D-aspartate) dysregulation has been noted in BPD (as well as in some other illnesses) and implicated with dissociation, psychotic episodes, and impaired cognition.[3] Disruptions in the body's opioid (endorphin) system has been demonstrated in BPD and associated with dissociative experiences, pain insensitivity (particularly among self-mutilating individuals), and opiate abuse.[4] Acetylcholine is another neurotransmitter affecting memory, attention, learning, mood, aggression, and sexual behavior, which has been linked to BPD.[5]

Chronic or repeated stress can also disrupt the neuroendocrine balance. Stress activates the hypothalamic-pituitary-adrenal (HPA) axis, which secretes cortisol and activates the body's immune system. In the usual acute stress situation, this system activates the fight-or-flight mechanisms of the body in a productive way. An internal feedback mechanism acts like a thermostat to then turn down the axis and return the body to equilibrium. However, ongoing stress dismantles the regenerative circuit and the stress alarms continue unabated, inflicting negative impact on the body, including shrinkage in characteristic areas of the brain. This pattern has been observed in several disorders, including BPD, PTSD, major depression, and certain anxiety disorders.

Oxytocin is also produced in the hypothalamus and secreted into the bloodstream by the pituitary gland. This hormone is associated with increased social sensitivity, intimate feelings, trust, and decreased anxiety (and is sometimes referred to as the "love hormone" or the "cuddle chemical"). Some studies suggest oxytocin levels are lower in borderline women.[6]

Neurological Dysfunction

Disturbances in brain function have been frequently associated with BPD. A significant subset of borderline patients has experienced a history of head trauma, encephalitis, epilepsy, learning disability, EEG (electroencephalogram, or brain wave) abnormalities, sleep pattern dysfunction, and abnormal subtle neurologic "soft signs."[7,8]

Sophisticated brain imaging—such as fMRI (functional magnetic resonance imaging), CT (computed tomography), PET (positron emission tomography), and SPECT (single photon emission computed tomography)—has elucidated some of the anatomical and physiological deviations associated with BPD. As already noted (see chapter 3), these studies seem to imply overactivity of those parts of the brain involved with emotional response (the limbic system), which includes such deep brain structures as the amygdala, the hippocampus, and the cingulate gyrus, while demonstrating underactivity of the outer parts of the brain involved with executive thinking and control, such as the prefrontal cortex.[9] A study employing actigraphs (sophisticated wrist monitors that measure rest-activity patterns and sleep-awake circadian rhythms) determined that disturbances in these sequences correlated with increased impulsivity and mood instability in BPD, compared to bipolar patients and healthy controls.[10]

Future Considerations

With these advances in genetics and neurobiology, scientists will eventually be able to subtype more discretely different presentations of pathology, and based on this knowledge, doctors may be able to more precisely "customize" a particular drug to a particular patient. To use an analogy: Our current understanding of psychiatric illnesses is roughly similar to our understanding of infections in the early and mid-1900s, before doctors could adequately culture the infecting agent. A hundred years ago doctors could diagnose pneumonia, but they could not determine whether the infecting agent was bacterial, viral, or fungal. Seventy years ago, they could recognize bacteria, but could not establish which antibiotic would be most effective. However, when scientists discovered how to culture individual strains of bacteria and establish their sensitivities to particular antibiotics, doctors could prescribe a specific drug with the greatest likelihood of success. In other words, doctors were not simply treating infection or pneumonia; they were treating a specific strain, such as *Staphylococcus aureus*. Similarly, in the future, the hope is that we will be able to "culture" the psychiatric illness and determine the best treatment. We will be treating the individual's unique biology, not simply the diagnosis. Just as precision medicine in cancer treatment can determine specific chemotherapy approaches based on genetic biomarkers, precision psychiatry will be able to specify treatment for distinctive syndromes. As a result, the concept of off-label (in which a medicine is prescribed for a condition it is not formally approved for) will become moot, since the medicine will be directed toward a specific biological process, rather than a particular diagnosis. At such a point, diagnosis will be made by bio-physiological determinants, not by descriptions of individual symptoms. This is the ultimate goal of the NIMH's Research Domain Criteria (RDoC) for diagnosis. (See Appendix A.)

Medications

Discoveries in the exploding fields of genetics and brain physiology have led to new drugs for many physical and mental conditions. Great advances have been achieved in pharmacology, especially in the area of biotechnology; in short, numerous psychotherapeutic drugs have been developed in the last twenty years, and the evidence suggests that some have proved effective in treating some BPD symptoms. Although no medication is targeted specifically for the BPD diagnosis, research has demonstrated that three primary classes of medicines—antidepressants, mood stabilizers, and neuroleptics (antipsychotics)—ameliorate many of the maladaptive behaviors associated with the disorder.[11]

Antidepressants

Most research has examined the use of antidepressants, particularly selective serotonin reuptake inhibitors (SSRIs or SRIs). These medicines include Prozac (fluoxetine), Zoloft (sertraline), Paxil or Pexeva (paroxetine), Luvox (fluvoxamine), Celexa (citalopram), and Lexapro (escitalopram—related to citalopram). More recent medicines considered SRIs include Viibryd (vilazodone) and Brintellix (vortioxetine). Predictably, these drugs have been effective for mood instability and related symptoms of depression, such as feelings of emptiness, rejection sensitivity, and anxiety. Additionally, SRIs have been shown to decrease inappropriate anger and temper outbursts, aggressive behavior, destructive impulsivity, and self-mutilating actions, even in the absence of depressive symptoms. In many studies, higher than usual doses of these medicines (for example, greater than 80 mg of Prozac; greater than 200 mg of Zoloft per day) were necessary to have a positive effect on BPD symptoms. A related group of drugs, serotonin-norepinephrine reuptake inhibitors (SNRIs), have not been as extensively studied, but may have similar positive effects. These include Effexor (venlafaxine), Pristiq (desvenlafaxine—related to venlafaxine), and Cymbalta (duloxetine). More recently developed SNRIs are Fetzima (levomilnacipran), indicated for depression, and Savella (milnacipran), medically indicated only for fibromyalgia.

Older antidepressants, such as tricyclic antidepressants (TCAs) and monoamine oxidase inhibitors (MAOIs), have also been studied. TCAs include Elavil (amitriptyline), Tofranil (imipramine), Pamelor or Aventyl (nortriptyline), Vivactil (protriptyline), Sinequan (doxepin), Norpramin (desipramine), Asendin (amoxapine), Surmontil (trimipramine), and others. These drugs have generally been less effective and in some cases have decreased emotional control. Therefore, the patient diagnosed with BPD should be wary of prescribed drugs in the TCA class.

MAOIs—including Nardil (phenelzine), Parnate (tranylcypromine), Emsam (selegiline), and Marplan (isocarboxazid)—have shown efficacy in BPD comparable to that of SRIs. However, MAOIs tend to have more side effects, are more dangerous in cases of overdose, and require dietary and concurrent medication restrictions, and are therefore utilized much less.

Mood Stabilizers

This group of medications includes lithium, a naturally occurring element, and antiseizure drugs—Depakote (valproate), Tegretol (carbamazepine), Trileptal (oxcarbazepine—related to carbamazepine), Lamictal (lamotrigine), and Topamax (topiramate). APA guidelines recommend this group as adjunctive treatment when SRIs or other interventions are ineffective or only partially effective. These medicines, in typical doses, help stabilize mood, decrease anxiety, and better control impulsivity, aggression, irritability, and anger. Neurontin (gabapentin), Dilantin (phenytoin), Gabatril (tiagabine), Keppra (levetiracetam), Zonegran (zonisamide), and others are also in this class of drugs, but studies testing their effectiveness in BPD patients have been limited.

Neuroleptics (Antipsychotics)

These drugs are recommended for initial treatment of cognitive-perceptual distortions in borderline patients. Paranoia, dissociative symptoms, and feelings of unreality (criteria 9 in the DSM-5—see chapter 2) are primary targets. In combination with SRIs, these medicines, usually in lower than common doses, relieve feelings of anger and aggressiveness; stabilize mood; and decrease anxiety, obsessional thinking, impulsivity, and interpersonal sensitivity.

Early studies were done with older neuroleptics, such as Thorazine (chlorpromazine), Stelazine (trifluoperazine), Trilafon (perphenazine),

Haldol (haloperidol), Navane (thiothixene), and Loxitane (loxapine). Newer medicines, called atypical antipsychotics, have also demonstrated efficacy with generally less complicated side effects. These include Zyprexa (olanzapine), Seroquel (quetiapine), Risperdal (risperidone), Abilify (aripiprazole), and Clozaril (clozapine). Other medicines in this class—Invega (paliperidone—related to risperidone), Fanapt (iloperidone), Saphris (asenapine), Geodon (ziprasidone), Vraylar (cariprazine), Latuda (lurasidone), and Rexulti (brexpiprazole)—have either not been studied or have yielded inconclusive results.

Anxiolytics

Antianxiety agents, although acutely helpful for anxiety, have been shown to increase impulsivity and can be abused and addictive. These tranquilizers, primarily in the class known as benzodiazepines, include Xanax (alprazolam), Ativan (lorazepam), Tranxene (clorazepate), Valium (diazepam), and Librium (chlordiazepoxide), among others. Klonopin (clonazepam), a longer-acting benzodiazepine that may have greater effect on serotonin, has had some success in treating symptoms of aggression and anxiety and so is perhaps the only benzodiazepine that may be useful for BPD.

Opiate Antagonists

Revia or Vivitrol (naltrexone) blocks the body's release of its own endorphins, which induce analgesia and euphoric feelings. Some reports suggest that this medicine may inhibit self-mutilating behavior.

Other Medication Treatments

Homeopathic or herbal treatments have generally been unsuccessful, with the exception of omega-3 fatty acid preparation. One small study found that the substance did decrease aggressiveness and depression among women.[12]

Substances that modulate the neurotransmitter glutamate have been investigated in BPD. Two of these substrates, the amino acid N-acetylcysteine and Rilutek (riluzole)—a drug used for the treatment of amyotrophic lateral sclerosis (Lou Gehrig's disease)—were both reported to significantly diminish self-injurious behavior in two borderline patients.[13] Other glutamate modulators (including dextromethorphan, a commonly used cough suppressant) have been investigated for use in depression. The most studied is ketamine.[14] Ketamine, originally developed as an anesthetic mostly used in animals, was also exploited as a club drug known as Special K. More recently it has been approved for treatment in resistant depression. It has not been studied for BPD symptoms.

The APA's Practice Guideline recommends that medications target a specific symptom cluster. Guidelines divide BPD symptoms into three primary groups: mood instability, impulse dyscontrol, and cognitive-perceptual distortions. An algorithm of recommended treatment approaches, with alternative tactics if the previous choice is ineffective, is summarized in Table 9-1.

TABLE 9-1. Pharmacotherapy for treating BPD symptoms

Symptom	1st Choice	2nd Choice	3rd Choice	4th Choice
Mood instability	SRI	different SRI or SNRI	add NL, clonazepam; or switch to MAOI	add MS
Impulse dyscontrol	SRI	add NL	add MS; or switch to MAOI	
Cognitive-perceptual distortions	NL	add SRI or MAOI or different NL		

SRI = serotonin reuptake inhibitor; may require higher than usual doses
NL = neuroleptic; usually in low doses
MAOI = monoamine oxidase inhibitor
MS = mood stabilizer

A Word About Off-Label Use

The FDA (Food and Drug Administration) has not formally approved any drug for the treatment of BPD, so all of the medicines commonly used for treating BPD are considered off-label. Though the term *off-label* may be off-putting, if not seem downright risky to the uninitiated, off-label prescribing is quite common for a wide variety of conditions. Because a pharmaceutical company spends around $1 billion on average to bring a drug to market, many companies do not seek approval for a wide range of conditions or outside narrow dosage ranges, as these strategies might narrow the chances for FDA approval and greatly increase the cost of development. For example, even though it is known that SRIs benefit several conditions, including depression, PTSD, anxiety illnesses, and some pain disorders, the drug manufacturer may not want to absorb the extra expense of gaining FDA approval—nor risk FDA rejection—by applying for label use for all of these indications and/or broad dosage ranges. Whenever a physician prescribes a medicine for an unapproved condition, or at a dose outside of recommendations, it is considered off-label. Unfortunately, managed care agencies or health insurance companies may refuse approval of these (sometimes expensive) off-label prescriptions.

Generic Drugs

In simplest terms, a generic drug contains the same primary or active ingredient as the original formulation; generally speaking, it is almost always less expensive. However, this does not mean that a generic medication is *identical* to its brand-name counterpart. The FDA considers a generic drug "equivalent" to a branded medicine if blood levels in healthy volunteers are within 20 percent variation, a significant difference in some patients. A generic may also differ from the original in its inactive ingredients and its delivery system (e.g., tablet or capsule). Moreover, one generic may vary widely from another (theoretically, up to a 40 percent variation in blood level). The lesson here is that if a switch to a generic drug will result in significant savings, it may be worth trying. However, if symptoms recur, it is best to return to the brand-label medicine. Additionally, if you are taking a generic medicine that is working, do not change to a different generic. Also, be aware that some pharmacies and some doctors receive bonuses for switching patients to generic drugs, which, though less expensive to the patient, allows for a greater markup profit for the pharmacy. Patients should also recognize that using insurance to purchase an inexpensive generic medicine may actually be more expensive than purchasing the drug directly, independent of insurance coverage.

Other Physical Treatments

Although ECT (electroconvulsive treatment) has proved useful treatment for depression, it has not been helpful in BPD.[15] There have been a few studies of BPD with depression treated with repetitive transcranial magnetic stimulation (rTMS), a mechanism using electromagnetic stimulation of parts of the brain. These small studies have suggested improvement in BPD symptoms of anger, mood instability, impulsivity, and interpersonal sensitivity.[16]

Split Treatment

Many patients receive care from more than one provider. Often therapy may be administered by a nonmedical professional (psychologist, social worker, or counselor), while medications are administered by a physician (psychiatrist or primary care doctor). Advantages of this protocol include less expense (thus accounting for its encouragement by managed care companies), involvement of more professionals, and separation of therapy and medication issues. But this separation can also be a disadvantage, since it allows the potential for patients to split providers into "good doctors" and "bad doctors" and to become confused about the treatment. Close communication among professionals treating the same patient is essential for the process to be successful. In some cases, a psychiatrist skilled in both medical management and psychotherapy techniques may be the preferred approach.

Can BPD Be Cured?

Much like the disorder itself, professionals' opinion about the prognosis for those afflicted with BPD has whipsawed from one extreme to the other. In the 1980s, so-called Axis II personality disorders were generally thought to be enduring and stable over time. DSM-III-R at the time asserted that personality disorders "begin in childhood or adolescence and persist in stable form (without periods of remission or exacerbation) into adult life."[17] This perception was in contrast to most Axis I disorders (such as major depression, alcoholism, bipolar disorder, schizophrenia, etc.), which were thought to be more episodic and responsive to pharmacological treatment. Suicide rates in BPD approached 10 percent.[18] All of these considerations suggested that prognosis for BPD was likely to be poor.

However, it is now generally accepted that personality traits can change over time, and that these changes can emerge at any point in the lifespan.[19] Longer-term evaluations of individuals with BPD have demonstrated significant improvement over time.[20,21,22] In these studies, tracking borderline patients over a ten-year period, up to two-thirds of the patients no longer exhibited five of the nine defining criteria for BPD and therefore could be considered "cured," since they no longer fulfilled the formal DSM definition. Improvement occurred with or without treatment, although treated patients achieved remission sooner. Most patients remained in treatment, and relapses diminished over time. Despite these optimistic findings, it was also discovered that although these patients no longer could be formally designated as borderline, some continued to have difficulty with interpersonal functioning that impaired their social and vocational relationships. This suggests that the more acute and prominent symptoms of BPD (which primarily define the disorder), such as suicidal or self-mutilating behaviors, destructive impulsivity, and quasi-psychotic thinking, are more quickly responsive to treatment or time than the more enduring temperamental symptoms (fears of abandonment, feelings of emptiness, dependency, etc.). In short, although the prognosis is clearly much better than originally thought, some borderline individuals continue to struggle with ongoing issues.

Those who conquer the illness display a greater capacity to trust and establish satisfactory relationships. They have a clearer sense of purpose and a more stable understanding of themselves. In a sense, then, even if some borderline issues remain, they maintain productive lives speckled with fragmented relics of borderline personality.

Chapter Ten

Understanding and Healing

Now, *here*, you see, it takes all the running *you* can do, to keep in
the same place. If you want to get somewhere else, you must run
at least twice as fast as that!

—From *Through the Looking-Glass*, by Lewis Carroll

"I feel like I have a void in me that I can never quite fill." Elizabeth,
an attractive, witty twenty-eight-year-old woman, was originally
referred for therapy by her family doctor. She had been married for
six years to a man who was ten years older than her and had been
her boss at one time. Five months before, she had given birth to her
first child, a daughter, and was now severely depressed.

She yearned for something she could call her own, something
that would "show that the rest of the world knew I was here." Inside,
she felt her "real self" was a swamp of childish emotions, and that
she was always hiding her feelings, which were "ugly and bad."
These realizations turned into self-hate; she wanted to give up.

By her count, Elizabeth had engaged in nine extramarital affairs
over the previous six years—all with men she met through work.
They began soon after the death of her father. Most were relationships that she totally controlled, first by initiating them and later by
ending them. She had found it exciting and empowering that these
men seemed so puzzled by her advances and then by her sudden
rejections, which left her alone. Like the character Buddy in Stephen
Sondheim's *Follies,* she experienced those "God-why-don't-you-

love-me-oh-you-do-I'll-see-you-later blues." Elizabeth enjoyed the physical closeness but acknowledged she dreaded being too emotionally involved. Although she controlled these relationships, she never found them sexually satisfying; nor was she sexually responsive to her husband. She admitted that she used sex to "equalize" relationships, to stay in control; she felt safer that way. Her intellect and personality, she felt, were not enough to keep a man.

Reared in a working-class Catholic family, Elizabeth had three older brothers and a younger sister, who had drowned in a swimming accident at age five. Elizabeth was only eight at the time and had little understanding of the event except to observe her mother becoming more withdrawn.

For as long as Elizabeth could remember, her mother had been hypercritical, constantly accusing Elizabeth of being "bad." When she was a young girl, her mother insisted that she attend church with her, and forced her father to construct an altar in Elizabeth's bedroom. Elizabeth felt closer to her father, a passive and quiet man dominated by his wife. As she entered puberty, he became more distant and less affectionate.

Growing up, Elizabeth was quiet and shy. Her mother disapproved of her involvement with boys and closely watched her friendships with girls; she was expected to have "acceptable" friends. Her brothers were always her mom's favorites; Elizabeth would kid with them, trying to be "one of the guys." Elizabeth achieved good grades in high school but was discouraged from going to college. After graduation, she began working full time as a secretary.

As time went on, the conflicts with her mother escalated. Even in high school, Elizabeth's mother had denounced her as a "tramp" and constantly accused her of promiscuity even though Elizabeth had had no sexual experience. After a while, having endured the shouting contests with her mother, she saved enough money to move out on her own.

During this turmoil, Elizabeth's boss, Lloyd, separated from his wife and became embroiled in a painful divorce. Elizabeth offered solace and sympathy. He reciprocated with encouragement and support. They began dating and married soon after his divorce was finalized. Naturally, her mother berated her for marrying a divorced man, particularly one who was ten years older and a lapsed Catholic.

Her father remained detached. One year after Elizabeth married, he died.

Five years later, her marriage was disintegrating, and Elizabeth was blaming her husband. She saw Lloyd as a "thief" who had stolen her youth. She was only nineteen when she met him, and she needed to be taken care of so badly that she traded in her youth for security—the years when she could have been "experimenting with what I wanted to be, could be, should have been."

In the early stages of treatment, Elizabeth began to talk of David, her most recent and most important affair. He was twelve years older, a longtime family friend, and the parish priest. He was someone known and loved by her whole family, especially by her mother. He was the only man to whom Elizabeth felt connected. This was the only relationship that she did not control. On and off, over a period of two years, he would abruptly terminate the affair and then resurrect it. Later, she confessed to her psychiatrist that David was the father of her child. Her husband was apparently unaware of this.

Elizabeth became more withdrawn. Her relationship with her husband, who was frequently away traveling, deteriorated. She became more alienated from her mother and brothers and allowed her few friendships to lapse. She resisted attempts to include her husband in therapy, feeling that Lloyd and her doctor colluded and favored "his side." So even therapy reinforced her belief that she couldn't trust or place faith in anyone because she would only be disappointed. All her thoughts and feelings seemed to be laden with contradictions, as if she were in a labyrinth of dead-end paths. Her sexuality seemed the only way out of the maze.

Her therapist was often the target of her complaints because he was the one "in control." She would yell at him, accuse him of being incompetent, and threaten to stop therapy. She hoped he would get mad, yell back, and stop seeing her, or become defensive and plead with her to stay. But he did neither, and she railed against his unflappability as evidence that he had no feelings.

Even though she was accustomed to her husband's frequent business trips, she started to become more frightened when left alone. During these trips, for reasons not yet clear to her, she slept on the floor. When Lloyd returned, she raged constantly at him. She became more depressed. Suicide became less an option than a destiny, as if everything were leading to that end.

Elizabeth's perception of reality became more tenuous. She yearned to be "psychotic," to live in a fantasy world where she could "go anywhere" in her mind. The world would be so far removed from reality, no one—not even the best psychiatrist—could get to her and "see what's underneath."

In her daydreams she envisioned herself protected by a powerful, handsome man who actively appreciated all of her admirable qualities and was endlessly attentive. She fantasized him as a previous teacher, then her gynecologist, then the family veterinarian, and eventually her psychiatrist. Elizabeth perceived all these men as powerful, but she also knew in the back of her mind that they were unavailable. Yet in her fantasies, they were overwhelmed by her charm and drawn irresistibly to her, just as David, for a while, had been. When reality did not follow her script—when one of these men did not aggressively return her flirtations—she became despondent and self-loathing, feeling she was not attractive enough.

Everywhere she looked she saw women who were prettier, smarter, better. She wished her hair was prettier, her eyes a different color, her skin clearer. When she looked in a mirror, she did not see the reflection of a beautiful young woman but an old hag with sagging breasts, a wide waist, plump calves. She despised herself for being a woman whose only value was her beauty. She longed to be a man, like her brothers, "so my mind would count."

In her second year of outpatient therapy, Elizabeth experienced several losses, including the death of a favorite uncle to whom she had grown close. She was haunted by recurring dreams and nightmares that she could not remember when she awoke. She became more depressed and suicidal and was finally hospitalized.

With more intensive therapy, she began recalling traumatic childhood events, opening up a Pandora's box of flooding memories. She recalled severe physical beatings by her mother and then began to remember her mother's sexual abuses—episodes in which her mother had inflicted vaginal douches and enemas and fondled her in order to "clean" her vagina. These rituals began when Elizabeth was about eight, shortly after her sister's death, and persisted until puberty. Her memories included looking into her mother's face and noting a benign, peaceful expression; these were the only times Elizabeth could remember when it appeared her mother was not disapproving.

Elizabeth recalled sitting alone in the closet for many hours and often sleeping on the floor for fear of being molested in her bed. Sometimes she would sleep with a ribbon or award she had won in school. She found these actions to be comforting and continued them as an adult, often preferring the floor to her bed and spending time alone in a quiet room or a dark closet.

In the hospital Elizabeth spoke of the different sides to her personality. She described fantasies of being different people and even gave these personality fragments separate names. These personae were independent women, had unique talents, and were either admired by others or snobbishly avoided social contacts. Elizabeth felt that whenever she accomplished something or was successful, it was due to the talents of one of these separate personality segments. She had great difficulty integrating these components into a stable self-concept.

Nonetheless, she did recognize these as personality fragments, and they never took over her functioning. She suffered no clear periods of amnesia or dissociation, nor were her symptoms considered aspects of dissociative identity disorder (multiple personality)— although this syndrome is frequently associated with BPD.

Elizabeth used these "other women" to express the desires and feelings that she herself was forced to repress. Believing she was worthless, she felt these other partial identities were separate, stronger entities. Gradually, in the hospital, she learned that they were always a part of her. Recognizing this gave her relief and hope. She began to believe that she was stronger and less crazy than she had imagined, marking a turning point in her life.

But she could not claim victory yet. Like a field officer, she commanded the various sides of her personality to stand before her and concluded that they could not go into battle without a unifying resolve. Elizabeth—the core of her being—was still afraid of change, love, and success, still searched in vain for safety, still fled from relationships. Coming to accept herself was going to be more difficult than she had ever imagined.

After Elizabeth left the hospital, she continued in outpatient care. As she improved, her relationship with her husband deteriorated. But instead of blaming him or herself, as she typically did, she attempted to resolve the differences and to stay with him. She distanced herself from unhealthy contacts with family members. She developed more positive self-esteem. She began taking college courses and did remarkably well, achieving academic awards. She slept with her first award under her pillow, as she did when she was a child. Later she entered law school and received merit awards for being the top student in her class. She developed new relationships, with men and women, and found she was comfortable in these, without having to be in control. She became more content with her own femaleness.

Little by little, Elizabeth started to heal. She felt "the curtains raising." She compared the feeling to looking for a valuable antique in a dark attic filled with junk—she knew that it was in there somewhere but couldn't see it because of all the clutter. When she finally did spot it, she couldn't get to it because it was "buried under a pile of useless garbage." But now and then she could see a clear path to the object, as if a flash of lightning had illuminated the room for a brief instant.

The flashes were all too brief. Old doubts reared up like ugly faces in an amusement-park funhouse. Many times she felt as if she were going up a down escalator, struggling up one step only to roll back two. She kept wanting to sell herself short and give credit to others for her accomplishments. But her first real challenge— becoming an attorney—was almost a reality. Five years before, she wouldn't have been able to talk about school, much less have had the courage to enroll. The timbre of her depressions began to change: her depression over failing was now evolving, she recognized, into a fear of success.

Growing and Changing

"Change is real hard work!" Elizabeth often noted. It requires conscious retreat from unhealthy situations and the will to build healthier foundations. It entails coping with drastic interruption of a long-established equilibrium.

Like Darwinian evolution, individual change happens almost imperceptibly, with much trial and error. The individual instinctively resists mutation. He may live in a kind of swamp, but it is *his* swamp; he knows where the alligators are, what's in all the bogs and marshes. To leave his swamp means venturing into the unknown and perhaps falling into a colder, darker, even more dangerous swamp.

For the borderline individual, whose world is so clearly demarcated by black-and-white parameters, the uncertainty of change is even more threatening. She may clutch at one extreme for fear of falling uncontrollably into the abyss of another. The borderline anorexic, for example, starves herself out of the terror that eating— even a tiny morsel—will lead to total loss of control and irrevocable obesity.

Borderline fear of change involves a basic distrust of his "brakes." In healthier people, these psychological brakes allow a gradual descent from the pinnacle of a mood or behavior to a gentle stop in the "gray zone" of the incline. Afraid that his set of brakes won't hold, the borderline adult fears that he won't be able to stop, that he will slide out of control to the bottom of the hill.

Change, however gradual, requires the alteration of automatic reflexes. He is in a situation much like a child playing a game of "Make me blink" or "Make me laugh," struggling valiantly to stifle a blink or a laugh while another child waves his hand or makes funny faces. Such reflexes, established over many years, can be adjusted only with conscious, motivated effort.

Adults sometimes engage in similar contests of opposing an instinctual response. A man who encounters an angry barking dog in a strange neighborhood resists the automatic reflex to run away from the danger. He recognizes that if he runs, the dog will likely catch up with him and introduce an even greater threat. Instead, he takes the opposite (and usually more prudent) action—he stands perfectly still, allows the dog to sniff him, and then walks slowly on.

Psychological change requires resisting unproductive automatic reflexes and consciously and willfully choosing other alternatives—choices that are different, even opposite, from the automatic response. Sometimes these new ways of behaving are frightening, but they typically are more efficient ways of coping. Elizabeth and her psychiatrist embarked on her journey of change in regular weekly individual psychotherapy. Initial contacts focused on keeping Elizabeth safe. Cognitive techniques and suggestions colored early contacts. For several weeks, Elizabeth resisted the doctor's recommendation of starting antidepressant medicine, but soon after agreeing to the medication, she noticed significant improvement in her mood.

The Beginnings of Change: Self-Assessment

Change for someone with borderline personality disorder involves more of a progressive fine-tuning than a total reconstruction. In rational weight-loss diet plans, which almost always resist the urge to lose large amounts of weight very quickly, the best results come slowly and gradually over time, with the weight loss more likely to persist. Likewise, change in BPD is best initiated gradually, with only slight alterations at first, and as in a successful diet program, with acceptance and encouragement, despite the inevitable regressive fluctuations. Change begins with self-assessment: before plotting a new course, the BPD sufferer must first recognize his current position and understand in which direction modification must progress.

Imagine personality as a series of intersecting lines, each representing a specific character trait (see Figure 10-1). The extremes of each trait are located at the ends of the line, with the middle ground in the center. For example, on the "conscientiousness at work" line, one end might indicate obsessive over-concern or workaholism and the other end irresponsibility or apathy; the middle would be an attitude somewhere between these two extremes, such as calm professionalism. If there were a "concern about appearance" line, one end might exemplify narcissistic attention to surface looks, and the other end, total lack of interest. Ideally, one's personality makeup would look like the spokes of a perfectly round wheel, with all these lines intersecting near their midpoints in the wheel "hub."

Of course, no one is completely "centered" all the time. It is important to identify each line in which change is desired and locate one's position on that line in relation to the middle. Change then becomes a process of knowing where you are and how far you want to go toward the middle. Except at the extreme ends, no particular locus is intrinsically better or worse than another. It is a matter of knowing oneself (locating oneself on the line) and moving in the adaptive direction.

For example, if we isolate the "caring for others" line (see Figure 10-2), one end ("self-sacrificing over-concern") represents the point where concern for others interferes with taking care of oneself; such a person may need to dedicate himself totally to others in order to feel worthwhile. This position may be perceived as a kind of selfish unselfishness, because such a person's "caring" is based on subconscious self-interest. At the other end ("don't give a damn") is a narcissistic person who has little regard for others, who only looks out for number one. In the middle is a kind of balance—a combination of concern for others and the obligation to take care of one's own needs as well. A person whose compassion trait resides in this mid-

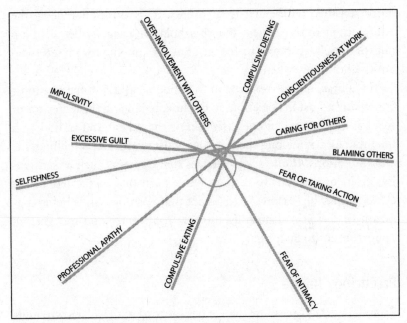

FIGURE 10-1. Personality as a series of intersecting lines.

dle zone recognizes that only by taking care of his own important needs first can he hope to help others, a kind of unselfish selfishness similar to airline pre-flight instructions that direct passengers to secure their own oxygen masks before attending to their children's.

Change occurs when one acquires the awareness to objectively place oneself on the spectrum and then compensate by adjusting behavior in a direction toward the middle. An individual who realistically locates his present position to the left of the midpoint would try to say no to others more often and generally attempt to be more assertive. One who places himself to the right of the midpoint would compensate toward the middle by choosing a course of action that is

FIGURE 10-2. The "caring for others" personality trait line.

more sensitive to the needs of others. This position reflects the admonitions of the ancient Jewish scholar and sage Hillel: "If I am not for myself, who will be for me? But if I am only for myself, who am I? If not now, when?"

Of course, no one resides "in the middle" all the time; one must constantly adjust his position on the line, balancing the teeter-totter when it tilts too far in one direction or the other. And in finding a tolerable location along the line, one must accept one's inclinations and limitations. If one acknowledges that elements such as sensitivity, guilt, or compulsive responsibility push one to the left of the center, it may be reasonable to accept that position, while being cognizant of the risk of pushing too far from center and recognizing opportunities to lean right.

Practicing Change

True change requires more than experimenting with isolated attempts to alter automatic reflexes; it involves replacing old behaviors with new habits that eventually become as natural and comfortable as the old ones. It is more than quietly stealing away from the hostile dog; it is learning how to make friends with that dog and take it for a walk.

Early on, such changes are usually uncomfortable. To use an analogy, a tennis player may decide that his unreliable backhand is in need of refinement. So he embarks on a series of tennis lessons to improve his stroke. The new techniques that he learns to improve his game initially yield poor results. The new style is not as comfortable as his old stroke. He is tempted to revert to his previous technique. Only after continuous practice is he able to eradicate his prior bad habits and instill the more effective and eventually more comfortable muscle memory. Likewise, psychological change requires the adoption of new reflexes to replace old ones. Only after persistent practice can such a substitution effectively, comfortably, and therefore permanently occur.

Learning How to Limp

If a journey of a thousand miles begins with a single step, the borderline's journey through the healing process begins with a single limp. Change is a monumental struggle in BPD, much more difficult than for others because of the unique features of the disorder. Splitting and the lack of object constancy (see chapter 2) combine to form a menacing barricade against trusting oneself and others and developing comfortable relationships.

In order to initiate change, he must break out of an impossible catch-22 position: To accept himself and others, he must learn to trust, but to trust others really means starting to trust himself—that is, his own perceptions of others. He must also learn to accept their consistency and dependability—quite a task for someone who, like a small child, believes others "disappear" when they leave the room. "When I can't see you," Elizabeth told her psychiatrist early in her treatment, "it's like you don't exist."

Like someone with an injured leg, an individual with BPD must learn to limp. If after a leg trauma, he remains bedridden, his leg muscles will atrophy and contract; if he tries to exercise too vigorously, he will reinjure the leg even more severely. Instead, he must learn to limp on it, putting just enough weight on the leg to build strength gradually, but not so much as to strain it and prevent healing (tolerating leg pain that is slight, but not overwhelming). Likewise, healing in BPD requires placing just enough pressure by challenging himself to move forward. As Elizabeth's therapy progressed, cognitive interventions gave way to a more psychodynamic approach, with more attention focused on connections between her past experiences and her current functioning. During this transition, the therapist's interventions diminished and Elizabeth became responsible for more of the direction of therapy.

Leaving the Past Behind

The borderline view of the world, like that of most people, is shaped by childhood experiences in which the family served as a microcosm of the universe. Unlike healthier individuals, however, he cannot easily separate himself from other family members, nor can he separate his family from the rest of the world. Indeed, he perceives all relationships to be like those in his family. And he continues to accept as normal the pathological interactions therein.

Unable to see his world through adult eyes, the borderline individual continues to experience life as a child—with a child's intense emotions and perspective. When a young child is punished or reprimanded, he sees himself as unquestionably bad; he cannot conceive of the possibility that mother might be having a bad day. As the healthy child matures, he sees his expanding world as more complex and less dogmatic. But in BPD he remains stuck—a child in an adult's body.

"There is always one moment in childhood when the door opens and lets the future in," wrote Graham Greene in *The Power and the Glory*. In many borderline childhoods, the responsibilities of adulthood arrive too early; the door opens ever more widely and precipitously, but he cannot face the light. Or perhaps it is the unrelenting opening that makes facing it so difficult.

Change in BPD comes when he learns to see current experiences—and review past memories—through adult "lenses." The new "vision" is akin to watching an old horror film on TV that you haven't seen in years: the movie, once so frightening on the big screen, seems tame—even silly—on a small screen with the lights on; you can't fathom why you were so scared when you saw it the first time.

When Elizabeth was well into her journey in psychotherapy, she began to look at her early childhood feelings in a different light. She began to accept them, to recognize the value of her own experience; if not for those early feelings and experiences, she realized, she would not have been able to bring the same fervor and motivation she was bringing to her new career in law. "Feelings born in my childhood," she said, "still continue to haunt me. But I'm even seeing all that in a different light. The very ways I have hated I now accept as part of me."

Playing the Dealt Hand

One of the greatest obstacles to change in BPD is the tendency to evaluate in absolute extremes. He must either be totally perfect or a complete failure; he grades himself either an A+ or, more commonly, an F. Rather than learning from his F, he wears it like a scarlet letter and so makes the same mistakes again and again, oblivious to the patterns of his own behavior, patterns from which he could learn and grow.

If the situation presented is not perfect, it is rejected. Unwilling to play the hand that is dealt him, he keeps folding every time, losing his ante, waiting to be dealt four aces. If he cannot be assured of winning, he won't play out the hand. Improvement comes when he learns to accept the hand for what it is, and recognize that, skillfully played, he can still win.

The borderline individual, like many people, is sometimes paralyzed by indecisiveness. Various alternatives seem overwhelming, and she feels incapable of making any decisions. But as she matures, choices appear less frightening and may even become a source of pride and growing independence. At that point she can recognize that she faces decisions that only she is capable of making. "I'm finding," Elizabeth noted, "that the roots of my indecisiveness are the beginning of success. I mean, the agony of choosing is that I suddenly see choices."

Boundary Setting: Establishing an Identity

One of the primary goals in treating BPD is to establish a separate sense of identity and to overcome the proclivity to merge with others. In biological terms, it is like advancing from a parasitic life form to a state of symbiosis and even independence. Either parasitism or independence can be terrifying, and most find that relying on themselves is like walking for the first time.

In biology, the parasite's existence is entirely dependent on the host organism. If the parasitic tick sucks too much blood from the host dog, the dog dies and the tick soon follows. Human relationships function best when they are less parasitic and more symbiotic. In symbiosis, two organisms thrive better together but may subsist independently. For example, moss growing on a tree may help the tree by shading it from direct sunlight and help itself by having access to the tree's large supply of underground water. But if either the moss or the tree dies, the other may continue to survive, though less well. The person with BPD sometimes functions as a parasite whose demanding dependence may eventually destroy the relationship with the person to whom he so strongly clings; when this person leaves, the individual with BPD may be destroyed. If he can learn to establish more collaborative relationships with others, all learn to live more contentedly.

Elizabeth's increasing comfort with others started with her relationship with her psychiatrist. After months of testing his loyalty by berating and criticizing him and threatening to terminate therapy, Elizabeth began to trust his commitment to her. She began to accept his flaws and mistakes, rather than see them as proof of the inevitability of his failing her. After a while, Elizabeth began to extend the same developing trust to others in her life. And she began to accept herself, imperfections and all, just as she was accepting others the same way.

As Elizabeth continued to improve, she became more confident that she would not lose her inner core. Where once she would squirm in a group of people, feeling self-conscious and out of place, she could now feel comfortable with others, letting them take responsibility for themselves and she for herself. Where once she felt compelled to adopt a role in order to fit into the group, she could now hold on to her more constant, immutable sense of self; now she could "stay the same color" more easily. Establishing a constant identity means developing the ability to stand alone without relying on someone else to define one. It means trusting one's own judgment and instincts and then acting rather than waiting for the feedback of others and then *re*acting.

Building Relationships

As the borderline individual forges a distinct core sense of identity, he also differentiates himself from others. Change requires the appreciation of others as independent persons and the empathy to understand their struggles. Their flaws and imperfections must not only be acknowledged but also be understood as separate from himself, part of the process of mentalization (see chapter 8). When this task fails, relationships falter. Princess Diana mourned the loss of her fantasy of a fairy-tale marriage to Prince Charles: "I had so many dreams as a young girl. I wanted, and hoped . . . that my husband would look after me. He would be a father figure, and he'd support me, encourage me. . . . But I didn't get any of that. I couldn't believe it. I got none of that. It was role reversal."[1]

In BPD, one must learn to integrate the positive and negative aspects of other individuals. When the borderline person wants to get close to another, he must learn to be independent enough to be dependent in comfortable, not desperate, ways. He learns to function symbiotically, not parasitically. In the healing process, he develops a constancy about himself and about others; trust—of others and of his own perceptions of others—develops. The world becomes more balanced, more in-between.

Just as is true in climbing a mountain, the fullest experience comes when the climber can appreciate all the vistas: to look up and keep his goal firmly in view, to look down and recognize his progress as he proceeds. And finally, to rest, look around, and admire the view from right where he is at the moment. Part of the experience is recognizing that no one ever reaches the pinnacle; life is a continuous climb up the mountain. A good deal of mental health is being able to appreciate the journey—to be able to grasp the Serenity Prayer invoked at most twelve-step meetings: "God grant me the serenity to accept the things I cannot change, courage to change the things I can, and wisdom to know the difference."

Recognizing the Effect of Change on Others

When an individual first enters therapy, he often does not understand that it is *he*, not others, who must make changes. However, when he does make changes, important people in his life must also adjust. Stable relationships are dynamic, fluctuating systems that have attained a state of equilibrium. When one person in that system makes significant changes in his ways of relating, others must adjust in order to recapture homeostasis, a state of balance. If these readjustments do not occur, the system may collapse and the relationships may shatter.

For example, Alicia consults a psychotherapist for severe depression and anxiety. In therapy, she rails against her dependent alcoholic husband, Adam, whom she blames for her feelings of worthlessness. Eventually she recognizes her own role in the crumbling marriage—her own need to have others become dependent upon her, her reciprocal need to shame them, and her fears of reaching for independence. She begins to blame Adam less. She develops new independent interests and relationships. She stops her crying episodes; she stops initiating fights over his drinking and irresponsibility; the equilibrium of the marriage is altered.

On the other side of the coin, Adam may now find that the situation is much more uncomfortable than it was before. He may escalate his drinking in an unconscious attempt to reestablish the old equilibrium and compel Alicia to return to her martyred, caretaking role. He may accuse her of seeing other men and try to disrupt their relationship, now intolerable to him.

Or he too can begin to see the necessity for change and his own responsibility in maintaining this pathological equilibrium. He may take the opportunity to see his own actions more clearly and reevaluate his own life, just as he has seen his wife do.

Participation in therapy may be a valuable experience for everyone affected. The more interesting and knowledgeable Elizabeth became, the more ignorant her husband seemed to her. The more open-minded she became—the more gray she was able to perceive in a situation—the more black and white he became in order to reestablish equilibrium. She felt that she was "leaving someone behind." That person was her—or more accurately, a part of her she no longer needed or wanted. She was, in her words, "growing up."

As Elizabeth's treatment wound down, she met less regularly with her doctor, yet still had to contend with other important people in her life. She fought with her brother, who refused to own up to his drug problem. He accused her of being "uppity," of "using her new psychological crap as ammunition." They argued bitterly over the lack of communication within the family. He told her that even after all the "shrinks," she was still "screwed up." She fought with her mother, who remained demanding, complaining, and incapable of showing her any love. She contended with her husband, who professed his love but continued to drink heavily and criticize her desire to pursue her education. He refused to actively participate with their children, and after a while she discovered his frequent absences were related to an affair with another woman.

Finally, Elizabeth began to recognize that she did not have the power to change others. She utilized SET-UP techniques to try to better understand these family members and to maintain protective boundaries for herself, which could shield her from being pulled into further conflicts. She began to accept them for who they were, love them as best she could, and go on with her own life. She recognized the need for new friends and new activities in her life. Elizabeth called this "going home."

Appendix A

Alternative Models for Diagnosing BPD

Despite criticism from some clinicians and researchers, the American Psychiatric Association kept the diagnostic model for BPD intact from previous editions in its *Diagnostic and Statistical Manual*, 5th ed. (2013). Section II of DSM-5 lists nine criteria, of which at least five must be exhibited by the patient to confirm a BPD diagnosis. For an in-depth discussion, see chapter 2.

This *categorical* approach has several limitations.

(1) Each criterion is granted the same weight or significance, but the qualitative degree of severity and comparative significance is not assessed. This impedes the development of more individualized treatment plans for the various distinctive presentations of BPD patients and inhibits constructing more accurate predictions of outcome.

(2) Many of these criteria apply equally to other diagnoses of personality disorder, frequently resulting in multiple diagnoses.

(3) "Personality disorder" is defined in DSM-5 as "an enduring pattern" that is "pervasive and inflexible," "stable over time," and causing "distress or impairment."[1] Yet an individual

displaying five criteria who at some point eliminates one symptom (for example, he is no longer suicidal) can no longer fulfill the requirements of the diagnosis despite continued distress. Suddenly, an "enduring," "pervasive," "inflexible," and "stable" level of personality functioning has disappeared.

(4) Finally, the categorical system lumps any five of the nine defining criteria together. Thus many patients may fulfill the categorical definition of BPD, yet appear quite different from each other and exhibit very different prominent behaviors, requiring diverse treatment approaches.

Current recommended therapies have focused on particular subtypes of BPD and may not be as useful for other core symptoms. For example, dialectical behavioral therapy (DBT) may primarily target self-defeating behaviors but be less useful when feelings of emptiness or identity confusion are more prominent. Transference-focused therapy (TFT) may emphasize interpersonal functioning but be less helpful for certain self-defeating impulsivity. See chapter 8 for further discussion of DBT, TFT, and other treatment modalities.

For these reasons *dimensional* models have been proposed. These constructs acknowledge that personality pathology is on a continuum with normality, not marooned in a divorced reality. Dimensional models focus more closely on the core features of BPD, including emotional dysregulation, destructive impulsivity, hostility, identity confusion, and interpersonal dysfunction.[2] They evaluate the levels of functioning and degree of impairment that determine when, say, normal frustration and moodiness cross over into pathological rage and emotional instability. Dimensional concepts recognize degrees of severity of symptoms resulting in different severity levels of "borderline-ishness." In contrast, the categorical system determines that a symptom, and ultimately a personality disorder, either is present or it isn't, subjectively determined by the clinician.

Alternative DSM-5 Model for Personality Disorders (AMPD)

In an attempt to address the difficulties of the categorical approach, Section III of DSM-5 describes an alternative, though much more complex, model for defining personality disorders. This view (AMPD) emphasizes a dimensional consideration of personality disorders as being on a continuum with normality and determined by the level of severity. However, the model does retain some categorical determinants that describe specific disorders.

This model embraces three primary components:

First is a measure of severity in four specific areas: (1) *identity* (critical self-image, feelings of emptiness); (2) *self-direction* (instability in goals, values); (3) *empathy* (inability to recognize feelings and needs of others); and (4) *intimacy* (unstable, conflicted relationships). The level of impairment in these areas determines if a personality disorder is present.

Second, pathological personality traits are organized into five broad domains described by twenty-five examples (trait facets). These five domains are reminiscent of our discussion in chapter 10, Figure 10-1, where we describe intersecting lines of personality traits and the wish to find a healthy middle ground.

The five domains are:

Negative Affects (anxious, depressed, angry, etc.) versus *Emotional Stability*

Detachment (avoidant, withdrawn, etc.) versus *Extraversion*

Antagonism (deceitful, manipulative, grandiose, etc.) versus *Agreeableness*

Disinhibition (impulsive, risk-taking, etc.) versus *Conscientiousness*

Psychoticism (eccentric, bizarre behavior, etc.) versus *Lucidity*

(Of course, the opposite extreme on the domain could also be pathological. Thus, *Extraversion* could mutate into mania. *Conscientiousness* could at the extreme become obsessive-compulsiveness.)

Finally, the AMPD embraces a categorical element describing six personality disorders—borderline, antisocial, narcissistic, avoidant, obsessive-compulsive, schizotypal. These correspond to those in Section II of the DSM-5, although defining criteria vary somewhat. Interestingly, four of the disorders described in Section II (paranoid, schizoid, histrionic, dependent) are eliminated in the AMPD due to a lack of studies delineating these four disorders within this model.

After establishing moderate or greater impairment in personality functioning, the model lists seven pathological "traits" that are identified with BPD. Just as in Section II, where at least five of the nine criteria for BPD are necessary to accept the diagnosis, to confirm the diagnosis of BPD, in the AMPD at least four of these seven "traits" must be demonstrated.[3]

1. *Emotional instability* (an aspect of *Negative Affects*): frequent mood changes, intense emotions out of proportion to circumstances
2. *Anxiousness* (an aspect of *Negative Affects*): panicky feelings, fears of uncertainty, fears of losing control
3. *Separation insecurity* (an aspect of *Negative Affects*): fears of rejection, fears of excessive dependency and loss of autonomy
4. *Depressivity* (an aspect of *Negative Affects*): feelings of hopelessness, pessimism, shame, unworthiness; thoughts of suicide
5. *Impulsivity* (an aspect of *Disinhibition*): impulsive reactions without goal or consideration of outcomes; difficulty following plans; self-harming when stressed
6. *Risk-taking* (an aspect of *Disinhibition*): dangerous, potentially self-damaging activities; denial of personal limitations and reality of personal danger

7. *Hostility* (an aspect of *Antagonism*): rage outbursts in response to minor slights

At least one of the exhibited criteria must be **Impulsivity, Risk-taking,** or **Hostility.**

These criteria for BPD dismiss some of those listed in Section II, particularly chronic feelings of emptiness and transient stress-related paranoid thoughts or dissociative experiences. The pattern of unstable and intense relationships with extremes of idealization and devaluation, which is often a separate, prominent feature of BPD, is only hinted at in this paradigm.

Obviously, AMPD is exceedingly more complex than the DSM-5 Section II model. It can be useful for researchers, but impractical for clinicians, and will require much refinement in the future to attain acceptance. It is, however, an initial attempt to better understand personality disorders and to develop more effective treatment of them.

ICD-11 Model of Personality Disorders

The International Classification of Diseases (ICD), published by the World Health Organization (WHO), is the most utilized model for describing all medical diseases, including psychiatric disorders worldwide. The current revision, ICD-10,[4] recognizes the diagnosis of Emotionally Unstable Personality Disorder. Two variants of this diagnosis are noted—Impulsive Type (explosive, rageful, threatening) and Borderline Type (disturbed self-image, feelings of emptiness, fears of abandonment, unstable relationships, emotional crises, and suicidal threats or self-harming acts). The eleventh iteration, proposed in April 2019, is still being modified. Formal approval and implementation are projected for 2022 or later.

The emphasis in ICD-11 is in first establishing existence of a personality disorder with significant personal dysfunction and disturbances with others, which cause substantial distress or impairment.

The next priority is in establishing the level of severity as mild, moderate, or severe.

The ICD-11 system then refers to six personality patterns, which are on a continuum with normality. With some variance these correspond to the five domains described in AMPD. A sixth designation is *Borderline Pattern*. This designation is described primarily by the criteria listed in DSM-5 Section II, although there is no required number of criteria needed to certify the diagnosis.[5] The dimensional perspectives of both DSM-5 Section III and ICD-11 anticipate that patient improvement may result in lessening of severity designation, while retaining a personality disorder diagnosis. In contrast, the DSM-5 Section II system allows only the presence or absence of a personality disorder.

Research Domain Criteria (RDoC)

The National Institute of Mental Health (NIMH) initiated the Research Domain Criteria (RDoC) as a research project. Unlike the DSM or ICD, it is not currently considered practical for clinical diagnosis. Instead, RDoC is a research tool attempting to utilize increasing knowledge of neuroscience to determine the causes and development of mental disorders.[6]

The RDoC proposes human behavior patterns that represent systems of emotion, cognition, motivation, and social interaction. These domains will be associated with new research on genes, molecules, cells, neural circuits, physiology, behavioral tendencies, self-reports, and formal testing.[7]

The identified domains that will be correlated with these new research areas are:

Negative valence (fear, anxiety, loss)

Positive valence (effort, reward-based response)

Cognitive systems (attention, perception, impulsivity, memory, language)

Social processes (communication, self-knowledge, culture, family, trauma)

Arousal and regulatory systems (sleep-wake cycles, activation)

Sensorimotor systems (motor reflex stimuli, initiation/inhibition)

New research may reveal new perceptions of BPD. Genetic connections may further illuminate elements of negativity (emptiness, fears of abandonment). Neurological circuits are related to impulsivity. Biological sensitivity to internal and external stimuli may affect social, arousal, and sensorimotor systems. It may be possible to collate specific symptoms with new science discoveries.

The DSM of the future will adopt many of these alternative assessments. As we learn more about the science of mental illness, we will be able to be more precise in diagnosis. And this will make individualized treatment more effective.

Appendix B

Evolution of the Borderline Syndrome

The concept of the borderline personality has evolved primarily through the theoretical formulations of psychoanalytic writers. Current DSM-5 criteria—observable, objective, and statistically reliable principles for defining this disorder—are derived from the more abstract, speculative writings of psychoanalytic theorists over the past hundred years.

Freud

During Sigmund Freud's era at the turn of the century, psychiatry was a branch of medicine closely aligned with neurology. Psychiatric syndromes were defined by directly observable behaviors, as opposed to unobservable, mental, or "unconscious" mechanisms, and most forms of mental illness were attributed to neurophysiological aberrations.

Though Freud himself was an experienced neurophysiologist, he explored the mind through different portals. He developed the concept of the unconscious and initiated a legacy of psychological—rather than physiological—exploration of human behavior. Yet he remained convinced that physiological mechanisms would eventually be uncovered to coincide with his psychological theories.

Over a century after Freud's landmark work, we have come almost full circle. Today, diagnostic classifications are once again defined by observable phenomena, and new frontiers of research into BPD and other types of mental illness are again exploring neurophysiological factors, while acknowledging the impact of psychological and environmental factors.

Freud's explication of the unconscious mind is the underpinning of psychoanalysis. He believed that psychopathology resulted from the conflict between primitive, unconscious impulses and the conscious mind's need to prevent these abhorrent unacceptable thoughts from entering awareness. He first used hypnosis, and later "free association" and other classical psychoanalytical techniques, to explore his theories.

Ironically, Freud originally intended classical psychoanalysis to be primarily an investigative tool rather than a form of treatment. His colorful case histories—"The Rat Man," "The Wolf Man," "Little Hans," "Anna O," etc.—were published to support his evolving theories as much as to promote psychoanalysis as a treatment method. Many current psychiatrists believe that these patients, whom Freud felt exhibited hysteria and other types of neuroses, would today clearly be identified as revealing borderline personalities.

Post-Freud Psychoanalytic Writers

Psychoanalysts who followed Freud were the main contributors to the modern concept of the borderline syndrome.[1] In 1925, Wilhelm Reich's *The Impulsive Character* described attempts to apply psychoanalysis to certain unusual characterological disorders that he encountered in his clinic. He found that the "impulsive character" was often immersed in two sharply contradictory feeling states at the same time, but was able to maintain the states without apparent discomfort via the splitting mechanism—a concept that has become central to all subsequent theories on the borderline syndrome, particularly Kernberg's (described below).

In the late 1920s and early 1930s, the followers of the British psychoanalyst Melanie Klein investigated the cases of many patients who seemed just beyond the reach of psychoanalysis, and today might be considered borderline patients. The Kleinians focused on psychological dynamics as opposed to biological-constitutional factors.

The term *borderline* was first coined by Adolph Stern in 1938 to describe a group of patients who did not seem to fit into the primary diagnostic classifications of neuroses and psychoses.[2] They were, Stern felt, on the "border." These individuals were obviously more ill than neurotic patients—in fact, "too ill for classical psychoanalysis"—yet they did not, like psychotic patients, continually misinterpret the real world. Though, like patients with neuroses, they displayed a wide range of anxiety symptoms, neurotic patients usually had a more solid, consistent sense of identity and used more mature coping mechanisms.

Throughout the 1940s and 1950s, other psychoanalysts began to recognize a population of patients who did not fit existing pathological descriptions. Some patients appeared to be neurotic or mildly symptomatic, but when they engaged in traditional psychotherapy, especially psychoanalysis, they "unraveled." Similarly, hospitalization would also exacerbate symptoms and increase the patient's infantile behavior and dependency on the therapist and hospital.

Other patients would appear to be severely psychotic, often diagnosed schizophrenic, only to make a sudden and unexpected recovery within a very short time. (Such dramatic improvement is inconsistent with the usual course of schizophrenia.) Still other patients exhibited symptoms suggestive of depression, but their radical swings in mood did not fit the usual profile of manic-depressive or depressive disorders.

Psychological testing also confirmed the presence of a new, unique classification. Certain patients performed normally on structured psychological tests (such as IQ tests), but on unstructured projective tests requiring narrative personalized responses (such as the Rorschach inkblot test), their responses were much more akin to those of psychotic patients, who displayed thinking and fantasizing on a more regressed, more childlike level.

During this postwar period, psychoanalysts fastened onto different aspects of the syndrome, seeking to develop a succinct delineation. In many ways the situation was like the old tale of the blind men who stood around an elephant and touched its various anatomical parts, trying to identify them. Each man described a different animal, of course, depending on which part he touched. Similarly, researchers were able to touch and identify different aspects of the borderline syndrome but could not quite see the whole organism. Many researchers (Zilboorg, Hoch and Polatin, Bychowski, and others)[3,4,5] and DSM-II (1968)[6] rallied around the schizophrenia-like aspects of the disorder, using such terms as "ambulatory schizophrenia," "pre-schizophrenia," "pseudoneurotic schizophrenia," and "latent schizophrenia" to describe the illness. Others concentrated on these patients' lack of a consistent core sense of identity. In 1942, Helene Deutsch described a group of patients who overcame an intrinsic sense of emptiness by a chameleon-like altering of their internal and external emotional experiences to fit the people and situations they were involved with at the moment. She termed this tendency of adopting the qualities of others as a means of gaining or retaining their love the "as-if personality."[7]

In 1953, Robert Knight revitalized the term *borderline* in his consideration of "borderline states."[8] He recognized that even though certain patients presented markedly different symptoms and were categorized with different diagnoses, they were expressing a common pathology.

After Knight's work was published, the term *borderline* became more recognized, and the possibility of using Stern's general borderline concept as a diagnosis became more acceptable. In 1968, Roy Grinker and his colleagues defined four subtypes of the borderline patient: (1) a severely afflicted group who bordered on the psychotic;

(2) a "core borderline" cluster with turbulent interpersonal relationships, intense feeling states, and loneliness; (3) an "as-if" group easily influenced by others and lacking in stable identity; and (4) a mildly impaired set with poor self-confidence and bordering on the neurotic end of the spectrum.[9]

Yet even with all this extensive pioneering research, the diagnosis of borderline personality, among working clinicians, was still drenched in ambiguity. It was considered a "wastebasket diagnosis" by many, a place to dump those patients who were not well understood, who resisted therapy, or who simply did not get better; the situation remained that way well into the 1970s.

As borderline personality became more rigorously defined and distinguishable from other syndromes, attempts were made to change the ambiguous and somewhat stigmatizing name. At one point, "unstable personality" was briefly considered during the development of DSM-III in the late 1970s. However, borderline character pathology was considered to be more stable in its instability, and that label did not better describe the syndrome and therefore did not endure. In 2020, the Royal College of Psychiatrists in England published a position paper ("Services for People Diagnosable with Personality Disorder"), questioning if even the phrase *personality disorder* is disparaging. Nevertheless, no other names have been prominently proposed as a replacement for borderline personality disorder.

In the 1960s and 1970s, two major schools of thought evolved to delineate a consistent set of criteria for defining the borderline syndrome. Like some other disciplines in the natural and social sciences, psychiatry was split ideologically into two primary camps—one more concept oriented, the other more influenced by descriptive, observable behavior that could be more easily retested and studied under laboratory conditions.

The empirical school, led by John G. Gunderson of Harvard and favored by many researchers, developed a structured, more behavioral definition, one based on reportable criteria and thus more accessible to research and study. This definition is the most widely accepted and in 1980 was adopted by DSM-III and perpetuated in DSM-IV and DSM-5 (see chapter 2).

The other more concept-oriented school, led by Otto Kernberg of Cornell and favored by many psychoanalysts, proposes a more psychostructural approach that describes the syndrome based on intrapsychic functioning and defense mechanisms rather than overt behaviors.

Kernberg's Borderline Personality Organization (BPO)

In 1967, Otto Kernberg introduced his concept of Borderline Personality Organization (BPO), a broader concept than the current DSM-5's Borderline Personality Disorder (BPD). Kernberg's conceptualization places BPO midway between neurotic and psychotic personality organization.[10,11] A patient with BPO, as defined by Kernberg, is less impaired than a psychotic patient, whose perceptions of reality are severely contorted, making normal functioning impossible. On the other hand, the individual with BPO is more disabled than a person with neurotic personality organization, who experiences anxiety as a result of emotional conflicts. The neurotic patient's perception of identity and system of defense mechanisms are usually more adaptive than those in BPO.

BPO encompasses BPD and other characterological disorders, such as paranoid, schizoid, antisocial, histrionic, and narcissistic personality disorders. In addition, it includes obsessive-compulsive and chronic anxiety disorders, hypochondriasis, phobias, sexual perversions, and dissociative reactions (such as dissociative identity disorder—also known as multiple personality disorder). In Kernberg's system, patients currently diagnosed with BPD would constitute only about 10 to 25 percent of patients classified BPO. A patient diagnosed with BPD is conceived as occupying a somewhat lower functioning, higher severity level within the overall BPO diagnosis.

Though Kernberg's system was not officially adopted by the American Psychiatric Association's DSM, his work has had (and continues to have) significant influence as a theoretical model for both clinicians and researchers. Transference-focused psychotherapy (TFP) is based on Kernberg's formulations (see chapter 8). In general, Kernberg's schema emphasizes the inferred internal mechanisms discussed below.

Variable Sense of Reality

Like those with neurotic symptoms, borderline patients retain contact with reality most of the time; however, under stress, the borderline patient can regress to a brief psychotic state. Marjorie, a twenty-nine-year-old married woman, sought therapy for increasing depression and marital disharmony. An intelligent, articulate woman, Marjorie communicated calmly throughout her initial eight sessions. She eagerly assented to a joint interview with her husband, but during the session she turned uncharacteristically loud and belligerent. Dropping her facade of self-control, she began to berate her husband for alleged infidelities. She accused her therapist of taking her husband's side ("You men always stick together!") and accused both of engaging in a conspiracy against her. The sudden transformation from a relaxed, mildly depressed woman to a raging paranoid one is quite characteristic of the kind of rapidly shifting borders of reality observed in the borderline individual.

Nonspecific Weaknesses in Functioning

Borderline patients have great difficulty tolerating frustration and coping with anxiety. In Kernberg's framework, impulsive behavior is an attempt to diffuse this tension. These individuals also impose defective sublimation tools; that is, they are unable to channel frustrations and discomforts in socially adaptive ways. Though they may exhibit empathy, warmth, and guilt, these expressions are often rote, more manipulative gestures for display purposes only, rather than true manifestations of feeling. Indeed, the borderline patient may act as if he has totally forgotten a dramatic effusion that occurred only moments before, much like a child who suddenly emerges from a temper tantrum all smiles and laughter.

Primitive Thinking

Borderline individuals are capable of performing well in a structured work or professional environment, but below the surface linger grave self-doubts, suspicions, and fears. These internal thought processes may be surprisingly unsophisticated and primal, camouflaged by a stable facade of learned and rehearsed platitudes. Any circumstance that pierces the protective structure shielding her may unleash a flood of chaotic passions concealed within. The example of Marjorie (above) illustrates this point.

Projective psychological tests also reveal the primitive thought processes in BPO. These tests—such as the Rorschach and Thematic Apperception Test (TAT)—elicit associations to ambiguous stimuli, such as inkblots or pictures, around which the patient creates a story. Borderline interpretations typically resemble those of schizophrenic and other psychotic patients. Unlike the coherent, organized responses usually observed among a population with neurotic symptoms, those from borderline patients often involve bizarre, primitive images—for example, the borderline individual might see vicious animals cannibalizing one another, where the neurotic person sees a butterfly.

Primitive Defense Mechanisms

The coping mechanism of splitting (see chapter 2) preserves the borderline perception of a world of extremes—a view in which people and objects are either good or bad, friendly or hostile, loved or hated—in order to escape the anxiety of ambiguity and uncertainty.

In Kernberg's conceptualization, splitting often leads to magical thinking: superstitions, phobias, obsessions, and compulsions are used as talismans to ward off unconscious fears. Splitting also results in derivative defense mechanisms:

- *Primitive idealization*—insistently placing a person or object in the "all-good" category, so as to avoid the anxiety accompanying the recognition of faults in that person.

- *Devaluation*—an unrelenting negative view of a person or object; the opposite of idealization. Using this mechanism, the borderline person avoids the guilt of his rage—the "all-bad" person fully deserves it.

- *Omnipotence*—a feeling of unlimited power in which one feels incapable of failure or sometimes even of death. (Omnipotence is also a common feature of the narcissistic personality.)

- *Projection*—disavowing features unacceptable to the self and attributing them to others.

- *Projective identification*—a more complex form of projection in which the projector continues an ongoing manipulative involvement with another person, who is the object of the projection. The other person "wears" these unacceptable characteristics for the projector, who works to ensure their continued expression.

For example, Mark, a young, married man who is diagnosed with BPD, finds his own sadistic and angry impulses unacceptable and projects them onto his wife, Sally. Sally is then perceived by Mark (in his black-and-white fashion) to be a "totally angry woman." All of her actions are interpreted as sadistic. He unconsciously pushes her buttons to extract angry responses, thus confirming his projections. ("I'm not angry. You're the one who's angry!") In this way, Mark fears yet simultaneously controls his perception of Sally.

Pathological Concept of Self

Identity diffusion is Kernberg's conception of the borderline lack of a stable core sense of identity. Borderline identity is the consistency of Jell-O—it can be molded into any configuration that contains it, but it slips through the hands when you try to pick it up. This lack of substance leads directly to the identity disturbances outlined in criterion 3 of DSM-5's description of BPD (see chapter 2).

Pathological Concept of Others

As identity diffusion describes the lack of a stable concept of self, *object constancy* refers to the lack of a stable concept of others. Just as his own self-esteem depends on current circumstances, the borderline individual bases his attitude toward another person on the most recent encounter, rather than on a more stable and enduring perception grounded in a consistent, connected series of experiences.

Often he is unable to hold on to the memory of a person or object when he, she, or it is not present. Like a child who becomes attached to a transitional object that represents a soothing mother figure (such as Linus's attachment to his blanket in the *Peanuts* cartoons), he uses objects, such as pictures and clothing, to simulate the presence of another person. For example, when a person with borderline characteristics is separated from home for even a brief period, he typically takes many personal objects as soothing reminders of familiar surroundings. Teddy bears and other stuffed animals accompany him to bed, and snapshots of family are carefully placed around the room. If he is left home while his wife is away, he often stares longingly at her picture and her closet, and smells her pillow, seeking the comfort of familiarity.

For many borderline individuals, "out of sight, out of mind" is an excruciatingly real truism. Panic sets in when he is separated from a loved one because the separation feels permanent. Because memory cannot be adequately utilized to retain an image, he forgets what the object of his concern looks like, sounds like, feels like. To escape the panicky sensation of abandonment and loneliness, the borderline sufferer tries to cling desperately—calling, writing, using any means to maintain contact.

Over the last century, advancement in our conceptualization of the borderline syndrome has resulted in improvements in our understanding and treatment of these patients. As we move along into this century, we can expect further advances in our understanding of neurobiological, genetic, and environmental influences on the humanity we all share.

RESOURCES

Printed Materials

OVERVIEWS

"Borderline Personality Disorder." *Journal of the California Alliance for the Mentally Ill* 8, no. 1, 1997. Comments from experts, families, and persons with BPD.

Bokian, N. R., V. Porr, and N. E. Villagran. *New Hope for People with Borderline Personality Disorder.* Roseville, CA: Prima Publishing, 2002. A readable book for the layperson, emphasizing better prognosis.

Friedel, R. O. *Borderline Personality Disorder Demystified: An Essential Guide for Understanding and Living with BPD,* rev. ed. Boston: De Capo Press, 2018. A readable guide for families.

Gunderson, J. G. *Borderline Personality Disorder: A Clinical Guide,* 2nd ed. Washington, DC: American Psychiatric Publishing, 2008. Directed primarily for practitioners; includes a comprehensive list of resources.

Gunderson, J. G., and P. D. Hoffman. *Understanding and Treating Borderline Personality Disorder: A Guide for Professionals and Families.* Washington, DC: American Psychiatric Publishing, 2005. A readable review for clinicians and families.

Kreisman, J. J., and H. Straus. *Sometimes I Act Crazy: Living with Borderline Personality Disorder.* Hoboken, NJ: Wiley, 2004. Detailed review of

BPD symptoms, many from the patient's perspective, and recommendations for coping; directed toward families.

FAMILY AND PERSONAL ACCOUNTS

Aguirre, B. A. *Borderline Personality Disorder in Adolescents: A Complete Guide to Understanding and Coping When Your Adolescent Has BPD.* Beverly, MA: Fair Winds Press, 2007. Dealing with the adolescent borderline.

Gunderson, J. G., and P. D. Hoffman. *Beyond Borderline: True Stories of Recovery from Borderline Personality Disorder.* Oakland, CA: New Harbinger Publications, 2016. Personal stories of BPD.

Kreger, R. *The Essential Family Guide to Borderline Personality Disorder.* Center City, MN: Hazelden, 2008. Follow-up to *Stop Walking on Eggshells* with suggestions for the family.

Kreger, R., and P. T. Mason. *Stop Walking on Eggshells: Taking Your Life Back When Someone You Care About Has Borderline Personality Disorder,* 2nd ed. Oakland, CA: New Harbinger Publications, 2010. An instructive manual.

Kreisman, J. J. *Talking to a Loved One with Borderline Personality Disorder: Communication Skills to Manage Intense Emotions, Set Boundaries & Reduce Conflict.* Oakland, CA: New Harbinger Publications, 2018. Practical communication techniques.

Manning, S. Y. *Loving Someone with Borderline Personality Disorder.* New York: Guilford Press, 2011. Dealing with a BPD loved one.

Moskovitz, R. *Lost in the Mirror: An Inside Look at Borderline Personality Disorder,* 2nd ed. Dallas: Taylor Publications, 2001. Intimate descriptions of borderline pain.

Reiland, R. *Get Me Out of Here: My Recovery from Borderline Personality Disorder.* Center City, MN: Hazelden Publishing, 2004. A personal account.

Roth, K., and F. B. Friedman. *Surviving a Borderline Parent: How to Heal Your Childhood Wounds and Build Trust, Boundaries, and Self-Esteem.* Oakland, CA: New Harbinger Publications, 2003. For the children of borderline parents.

Walker, A. *Siren's Dance: My Marriage to a Borderline: A Case Study.* Emmaus, PA: Rodale, 2003. A spouse's experience.

Websites

BORDERLINE PERSONALITY DISORDER DEMYSTIFIED
www.bpddemystified.com
This is a general site animated by Robert O. Friedel, MD, a leading psychiatrist and author of *Borderline Personality Disorder Demystified*.

BORDERLINE PERSONALITY DISORDER RESOURCE CENTER
bpdresourcecenter@nyp.org
888-694-2273
Provides educational materials and treatment resources.

BPD CENTRAL
www.bpdcentral.com
One of the oldest sites, with many suggested books and articles.

BPD RECOVERY
www.bpdrecovery.com
A site for individuals recovering from BPD, emphasizing cognitive behavioral treatment.

FACING THE FACTS
www.bpdfamily.com
One of the largest sites providing information and support for families.

MAYO CLINIC INFORMATION
mayoclinic.com/health/borderline-personality-disorder/DS00442
General information and answers to questions.

NATIONAL EDUCATION ALLIANCE FOR BORDERLINE PERSONALITY DISORDER (NEA-BPD)
www.borderlinepersonalitydisorder.com
Support and education for patients, relatives, and professionals.

NATIONAL INSTITUTE OF MENTAL HEALTH SUMMARY
www.nimh.nih.gov/health/publications/borderline-personality-disorder
-fact-sheet/index.shtml
General information.

PERSONALITY DISORDERS AWARENESS NETWORK (PDAN)

www.pdan.org

PDAN works to increase public awareness about the impact of BPD on children, relationships, and society.

TREATMENT AND RESEARCH ADVANCEMENTS ASSOCIATION FOR PERSONALITY DISORDER (TARA4BPD)

www.tara4bpd.org

National nonprofit organization advocates for individuals with BPD and their families, sponsors workshops and seminars, operates a national resource and referral center, and articulates BPD issues to congressional legislators.

Treatment Centers

McLEAN HOSPITAL

115 Mill Street
Belmont, MA 02478
877-372-3068

NEW YORK-PRESBYTERIAN WESTCHESTER BEHAVIORAL HEALTH CENTER

21 Bloomingdale Road
White Plains, NY 10605
888-694-5700
914-682-9100

AUSTEN RIGGS CENTER

25 Main Street
Stockbridge, MA 01262
austenriggs.org/borderline-personality-disorder-treatment
800-51-RIGGS

SILVER HILL HOSPITAL

208 Valley Road
New Canaan, CT 06840
866-542-4455
www.SilverHillHospital.org

NOTES

1. THE WORLD OF BORDERLINE PERSONALITY DISORDER

1. Bridget F. Grant, S. Patricia Chou, Rise B. Goldstein, et al., "Prevalence Correlates, Disability, and Comorbidity of DSM-IV Borderline Personality Disorder: Results from the Wave 2 National Epidemiologic Survey on Alcohol and Related Conditions," *Journal of Clinical Psychiatry* 69 (2008): 533–44.

2. Rachel L. Tomko, Timothy J. Trull, Phillip K. Wood, et al., "Characteristics of Borderline Personality Disorder in a Community Sample: Comorbidity, Treatment Utilization, and General Functioning," *Journal of Personality Disorders* 28 (2014): 734–50.

3. Klaus Lieb, Mary C. Zanarini, Christian Schmahl, et al., "Borderline Personality Disorder," *Lancet* 364 (2004): 453–61.

4. Mark Zimmerman, Louis Rothschild, and Iwona Chelminski, "The Prevalence of DSM-IV Personality Disorders in Psychiatric Outpatients," *American Journal of Psychiatry* 162 (2005): 1911–18.

5. Donna S. Bender, Andrew E. Skodol, Maria E. Pagano, et al., "Prospective Assessment of Treatment Use by Patients with Personality Disorders," *Psychiatric Services* 57 (2006): 254–57.

6. Marvin Swartz, Dan Blazer, Linda George, et al., "Estimating the Prevalence of Borderline Personality Disorder in the Community," *Journal of Personality Disorders* 4 (1990): 257–72.

7. James J. Hudziak, Todd J. Boffeli, Jerold J. Kreisman, et al., "Clinical

Study of the Relation of Borderline Personality Disorder to Briquet's Syndrome (Hysteria), Somatization Disorder, Antisocial Personality Disorder, and Substance Abuse Disorders," *American Journal of Psychiatry* 153 (1996): 1598–606.

8. Mary C. Zanarini, Frances R. Frankenburg, John Hennen, et al., "Axis I Comorbidity in Patients with Borderline Personality Disorder: 6-Year Follow-Up and Prediction of Time to Remission," *American Journal of Psychiatry* 161 (2004): 2108–114.

9. Renée El-Gabalawy, Laurence Y. Katz, and Jitender Sareen, "Comorbidity and Associated Severity of Borderline Personality Disorder and Physical Health Conditions in a Nationally Representative Sample," *Psychosomatic Medicine* 72 (2010): 641–47.

10. Lachlan A. McWilliams and Kristen S. Higgins, "Associations Between Pain Conditions and Borderline Personality Disorder Symptoms: Findings from the National Comorbidity Survey Replication," *Clinical Journal of Pain* 29 (2013): 527–32.

11. Frances R. Frankenburg and Mary C. Zanarini, "The Association Between Borderline Personality Disorder and Chronic Medical Illnesses, Poor Health-Related Lifestyle Choices, and Costly Forms of Health Care Utilization," *Journal of Clinical Psychiatry* 65 (2004): 1660–65.

12. Frances R. Frankenburg and Mary C. Zanarini, "Personality Disorders and Medical Comorbidity," *Current Opinion in Psychiatry* 19 (2006): 428–31.

13. Cheng-Che Shen, Li-Yu Hu, and Ya-Han Hu, "Comorbidity Study of Borderline Personality Disorder: Applying Association Rule Mining to the Taiwan National Health Insurance Research Database," *BMC Medical Informatics and Decision Making* 17 (2017): 8.

14. Taylor Barber, Whitney Ringwald, Aidan Wright, et al., "Borderline Personality Disorder Traits Associate with Midlife Cardiometabolic Risk," *Personality Disorders: Theory, Research, and Treatment* 11 (2020): 151–56.

15. Mehmet Dokucu and Robert Cloninger, "Personality Disorders and Physical Comorbidities: A Complex Relationship," *Current Opinion in Psychiatry* 32 (2019): 435–41.

16. Craig Johnson, David Tobin, and Amy Enright, "Prevalence and Clinical Characteristics of Borderline Patients in an Eating-Disordered Population," *Journal of Clinical Psychiatry* 50 (1989): 9–15.

17. Joel Paris and Hallie Zweig-Frank, "A 27-Year Follow-Up of Patients with Borderline Personality Disorder," *Comprehensive Psychiatry* 42 (2001): 482–84.

18. Alexander McGirr, Joel Paris, Alain Lesage, et al., "Risk Factors for Suicide Completion in Borderline Personality Disorder: A Case-Control Study of Cluster B Comorbidity and Impulsive Aggression," *Journal of Clinical Psychiatry* 68 (2007): 721–29.

19. Thomas Widiger and Paul T. Costa Jr., "Personality and Personality Disorders," *Journal of Abnormal Psychology* 103 (1994): 78–91.

20. John M. Oldham, "Guideline Watch: Practice Guideline for the Treatment of Patients with Borderline Personality Disorder," *Focus* 3 (2005): 396–400.

21. Robert L. Spitzer, Michael B. First, Jonathan Shedler, et al., "Clinical Utility of Five Dimensional Systems for Personality Diagnosis," *Journal of Nervous and Mental Disease* 196 (2008): 356–74.

22. American Psychiatric Association, *Diagnostic and Statistical Manual of Mental Disorders*, 5th ed., Text Revision (Washington, DC: American Psychiatric Association, 2013): 663.

23. Lisa Laporte and Herta Guttman, "Traumatic Childhood Experiences as Risk Factors for Borderline and Other Personality Disorders," *Journal of Personality Disorders* 10 (1996): 247–59.

24. Mary C. Zanarini, Lynne Yong, Frances R. Frankenburg, et al., "Severity of Reported Childhood Sexual Abuse and Its Relationship to Severity of Borderline Psychopathology and Psychosocial Impairment Among Borderline Inpatients," *Journal of Nervous and Mental Disease* 190 (2002): 381–87.

25. Elizabeth Lippard and Charles Nemeroff, "The Devastating Clinical Consequences of Child Abuse and Neglect: Increased Disease Vulnerability and Poor Treatment Response in Mood Disorders," *American Journal of Psychiatry* 177 (2020): 20–36.

26. Kyle Esteves, Christopher Jones, Mark Wade, et al., "Adverse Childhood Experiences: Implications for Offspring Telomere Length and Psychopathology," *American Journal of Psychiatry* 177 (2020): 47–57.

27. Ayline Maier, Caroline Gieling, Luca Heinen-Ludwig, et al., "Association of Childhood Maltreatment with Interpersonal Distance and Social Touch Preferences in Adulthood," *American Journal of Psychiatry* 177 (2020): 37–46.

28. Carolyn Z. Conklin and Drew Westen, "Borderline Personality Disorder in Clinical Practice," *American Journal of Psychiatry* 162 (2005): 867–75.

29. Thomas H. McGlashan, "The Chestnut Lodge Follow-Up Study III: Long-Term Outcome of Borderline Personalities," *Archives of General Psychiatry* 43 (1986): 20–30.

30. L. Hastrup, P. Jennum, R. Ibsen, et al., "Societal Costs of Borderline Personality Disorders: A Matched-Controlled Nationwide Study of Patients and Spouses," *Acta Psychiatrica Scandinavica* 140 (2019): 458–67.

31. Louis Sass, "The Borderline Personality," *New York Times Magazine*, August 22, 1982, 102.

32. Mary C. Zanarini, Frances R. Frankenburg, John Hennen, et al., "Prediction of the 10-Year Course of Borderline Personality Disorder," *American Journal of Psychiatry* 163 (2006): 827–32.

33. Mary C. Zanarini, Frances R. Frankenburg, D. Bradford Reich, et al., "Time to Attainment of Recovery from Borderline Personality Disorder and Stability of Recovery: A 10-Year Prospective Follow-Up Study," *American Journal of Psychiatry* 168 (2010): 663–67.

34. Mary C. Zanarini, Frances R. Frankenburg, D. Bradford Reich, et al., "Attainment and Stability of Sustained Remission and Recovery Among Patients with Borderline Personality Disorder and Axis II Comparison Subjects: A 16-Year Prospective Follow-Up Study," *American Journal of Psychiatry* 169 (2012): 476–83.

35. Mary C. Zanarini, Frances R. Frankenburg, D. Bradford Reich, et al., "Fluidity of the Subsyndromal Phenomenology of Borderline Personality Disorder Over 16 Years of Prospective Follow-Up," *American Journal of Psychiatry* 173 (2016): 688–94.

36. J. Christopher Perry, Elisabeth Banon, and Floriana Ianni, "Effectiveness of Psychotherapy for Personality Disorders," *American Journal of Psychiatry* 156 (1999): 1312–21.

2. CHAOS AND EMPTINESS

1. Stefano Pallanti, "Personality Disorders: Myths and Neuroscience," *CNS Spectrums* 2 (1997): 53–63.

2. Jerold J. Kreisman and Hal Straus, *Sometimes I Act Crazy: Living with Borderline Personality Disorder* (Hoboken, NJ: Wiley, 2004): 13.

3. K. Schroeder, H. L. Fisher, I. Schafer, et al., "Psychotic Symptoms in

Patients with Borderline Personality Disorder: Prevalence and Clinical Management," *Current Opinion Psychiatry* 26 (2013): 113–19.

4. Heather Schultz and Victor Hong, "Psychosis in Borderline Personality Disorder: How Assessment and Treatment Differs from a Psychotic Disorder," *Current Psychiatry* 16 (2017): 25–29.

5. Jess G. Fiedorowicz and Donald W. Black, "Borderline, Bipolar, or Both?" *Current Psychiatry* 9 (2010): 21–32.

6. Mark Zimmerman, Caroline Balling, Kristy Dalrymple, et al., "Screening for Borderline Personality Disorder in Psychiatric Outpatients with Major Depressive Disorder and Bipolar Disorder," *Journal of Clinical Psychiatry* 80 (2019): 18m12257.

7. Adam Bayes and Gordon Parker, "Differentiating Borderline Personality Disorder (BPD) from Bipolar Disorder: Diagnostic Efficiency of DSM BPD Criteria," *Acta Psychiatrica Scandinavica* 141 (2020): 142–48.

8. M. Zimmerman and T. Morgan, "The Relationship Between Borderline Personality Disorder and Bipolar Disorder," *Dialogues in Clinical Neuroscience* 15 (2013): 79–93.

9. Mark Zimmerman, "Borderpolar: Patients with Borderline Personality Disorder and Bipolar Disorder," Lecture at Psych Congress, October 4, 2019.

10. Henrik Anckarsater, Ola Stahlberg, Tomas Larson, et al., "The Impact of ADHD and Autism Spectrum Disorders on Temperament, Character, and Personality Development," *American Journal of Psychiatry* 163 (2006): 1239–44.

11. Ralf Kuja-Halkola, Kristina Lind Juto, Charlotte Skoglund, et al., "Do Borderline Personality Disorder and Attention-Deficit/Hyperactivity Disorder Co-Aggregate in Families? A Population-Based Study of 2 Million Swedes," *Molecular Psychiatry* (2021): 341–49.

12. Carlin J. Miller, Janine D. Flory, Scott R. Miller, et al., "Childhood Attention-Deficit/Hyperactivity Disorder and the Emergence of Personality Disorders in Adolescence: A Prospective Follow-Up Study," *Journal of Clinical Psychiatry* 69 (2008): 1477–84.

13. Alexandra Philipsen, Mathias F. Limberger, Klaus Lieb, et al., "Attention-Deficit Hyperactivity Disorder as a Potentially Aggravating Factor in Borderline Personality Disorder," *British Journal of Psychiatry* 192 (2008): 118–23.

14. Andrea Fossati, Liliana Novella, Deborah Donati, et al., "History of

Childhood Attention Deficit/Hyperactivity Disorder Symptoms and Borderline Personality Disorder: A Controlled Study," *Comprehensive Psychiatry* 43 (2002): 369–77.

15. Pavel Golubchik, Jonathan Sever, Gil Zalsman, et al., "Methylphenidate in the Treatment of Female Adolescents with Co-occurrence of Attention Deficit/Hyperactivity Disorder and Borderline Personality Disorder: A Preliminary Open-Label Trial," *International Clinical Psychopharmacology* 23 (2008): 228–31.

16. C. Schmahl, M. Meinzer, A. Zeuch, et al., "Pain Sensitivity Is Reduced in Borderline Personality Disorder, but Not in Posttraumatic Stress Disorder and Bulimia Nervosa," *World Journal of Biological Psychiatry* 11 (2010): 364–71.

17. Randy A. Sansone and Lori A. Sansone, "Chronic Pain Syndromes and Borderline Personality," *Innovations in Clinical Neuroscience* 9 (2012): 10–14.

18. Matthias Vogel, Lydia Frenzel, Christian Riediger, et al., "The Pain Paradox of Borderline Personality and Total Knee Arthroplasty (TKA): Recruiting Borderline Personality Organization to Predict the One-Year Postoperative Outcome," *Journal of Pain Research* 13 (2020): 49–55.

19. Randy A. Sansone and Lori A Sansone, "Borderline Personality and the Pain Paradox," *Psychiatry* 4 (2007): 40–46.

20. James J. Hudziak, Todd J. Boffeli, Jerold J. Kreisman, et al., "Clinical Study of the Relation of Borderline Personality Disorder to Briquet's Syndrome (Hysteria), Somatization Disorder, Antisocial Personality Disorder, and Substance Abuse Disorders," *American Journal of Psychiatry* 153 (1996): 1598–606.

21. Vedat Sar, Gamze Akyuz, Nesim Kugu, et al., "Axis I Dissociative Disorder Comorbidity in Borderline Personality Disorder and Reports of Childhood Trauma," *Journal of Clinical Psychiatry* 67 (2006): 1583–90.

22. Richard P. Horevitz and Bennett G. Braun, "Are Multiple Personalities Borderline?" *Psychiatric Clinics of North America* 7 (1984): 69–87.

23. Julia A. Golier, Rachel Yehuda, Linda M. Bierer, et al., "The Relationship of Borderline Personality Disorder to Posttraumatic Stress Disorder and Traumatic Events," *American Journal of Psychiatry* 160 (2003): 2018–24.

24. Melanie S. Harned, Shireen L. Rizvi, and Marsha M. Linehan, "Impact

of Co-Occurring Posttraumatic Stress Disorder on Suicidal Women with Borderline Personality Disorder," *American Journal of Psychiatry* 167 (2010): 1210–17.

25. Jack Tsai, Ilan Harpaz-Rotem, Corey E. Pilver, et al., "Latent Class Analysis of Personality Disorders in Adults with Posttraumatic Stress Disorder: Results from the National Epidemiologic Survey on Alcohol and Related Conditions," *Journal of Clinical Psychiatry* 75 (2014): 276–84.

26. Andrew E. Skodol, John G. Gunderson, Thomas H. McGlashan, et al., "Functional Impairment in Patients with Schizotypal, Borderline, Avoidant, or Obsessive-Compulsive Personality Disorder," *American Journal of Psychiatry* 159 (2002): 276–83.

27. T. J. Trull, D. J. Sher, C. Minks-Brown, et al., "Borderline Personality Disorder and Substance Use Disorders: A Review and Integration," *Clinical Psychological Review* 20 (2000): 235–53.

28. Mary C. Zanarini, Frances R. Frankenburg, John Hennen, et al., "Axis I Comorbidity in Patients with Borderline Personality Disorder: 6-Year Follow-Up and Prediction of Time to Remission," *American Journal of Psychiatry* 161 (2004): 2108–14.

29. Randy A. Sansone and Lori A. Sansone, "Substance Use Disorders and Borderline Personality: Common Bedfellows," *Innovations in Clinical Neuroscience* 8 (2011): 10–13.

30. Drew Westen and Jennifer Harnden-Fischer, "Personality Profiles in Eating Disorders: Rethinking the Distinction Between Axis I and Axis II," *American Journal of Psychiatry* 158 (2001): 547–62.

31. Alexia E. Miller, Sarah E. Racine, E. David Klonsky, "Symptoms of Anorexia Nervosa and Bulimia Nervosa Have Differential Relationships to Borderline Personality Disorder Symptoms," *Eating Disorders* (July 15, 2019): 1–14 doi: 10.1080/10640266.2019.1642034.

32. Randy A. Sansone and Lori A. Sansone, "Personality Pathology and Its Influence on Eating Disorders," *Innovations in Clinical Neuroscience* 3 (2011): 14–18.

33. Regina C. Casper, Elke D. Eckert, Katherine A. Halmi, et al., "Bulimia: Its Incidence and Clinical Importance in Patients with Anorexia Nervosa," *Archives of General Psychiatry* 37 (1980): 1030–35.

34. Shirley Yen, Jessica Peters, Shivani Nishar, et al., "Association of Borderline Personality Disorder Criteria with Suicide Attempts," *JAMA Psychiatry* 78 (2021): 187–94.

35. Sidra Goldman-Mellor, Mark Olfson, Cristina Lidon-Moyano, et al., "Association of Suicide and Other Mortality with Emergency Department Presentation," *JAMA Network Open* 2 (2019); doi: 10.1001/jamanetworkopen.2019.17571.

36. Beth S. Brodsky, Kevin M. Malone, Steven P. Ellis, et al., "Characteristics of Borderline Personality Disorder Associated with Suicidal Behavior," *American Journal of Psychiatry* 154 (1997): 1715–19.

37. Paul H. Soloff, Kevin G. Lynch, Thomas M. Kelly, et al., "Characteristics of Suicide Attempts of Patients with Major Depressive Episode and Borderline Personality Disorder: A Comparative Study," *American Journal of Psychiatry* 157 (2000): 601–8.

38. Alexander McGirr, Joel Paris, Alain Lesage, et al., "Risk Factors for Suicide Completion in Borderline Personality Disorder: A Case-Control Study of Cluster B Comorbidity and Impulsive Aggression," *Journal of Clinical Psychiatry* 68 (2007): 721–29.

39. Christina M. Temes, Frances R. Frankenburg, Garrett M. Fitzmaurice, et al., "Deaths by Suicide and Other Causes Among Patients with Borderline Personality Disorder and Personality-Disordered Comparison Subjects Over 24 Years of Prospective Follow-Up," *Journal of Clinical Psychiatry* 80 (2019): 30–36.

40. D. E. Rodante, L. N. Grendas, S. Puppo, et al., "Predictors of Short- and Long-Term Recurrence of Suicidal Behavior in Borderline Personality Disorder," *Acta Psychiatrica Scandinavica* 140 (2019): 158–68.

41. American Psychiatric Association, DSM-5 (2013): 663–66.

42. Christian G. Schmahl, Bernet M. Elzinga, Eric Vermetten, et al., "Neural Correlates of Memories of Abandonment in Women with and Without Borderline Personality Disorder," *Biological Psychiatry* 54 (2003): 142–51.

43. Norman Rosten, *Marilyn: An Untold Story* (New York: New American Library, 1967), 112.

44. Natalie Dinsdale and Bernard Crespi, "The Borderline Empathy Paradox: Evidence and Conceptual Models for Empathic Enhancements in Borderline Personality Disorder," *Journal of Personality Disorders* 27 (2013): 172–95.

45. Gregor Domes, Nicole Ower, Bernadette von Dawans, et al., "Effects of Intranasal Oxytocin Administration on Empathy and Approach Motivation in Women with Borderline Personality Disorder: A Randomized

Controlled Trial," *Translational Psychiatry* Open Access 9 (2019); doi: 10.1038/s41398-019-0658-4.

46. Norman Mailer, *Marilyn: A Biography* (New York: Grosset & Dunlap, 1973), 86.

47. Mailer, *Marilyn*, 108.

48. Robert Wolf, Phillip Thomann, Fabio Sambataro, et al., "Orbitofrontal Cortex and Impulsivity in Borderline Personality Disorder: An MRI Study of Baseline Brain Perfusion," *European Archives of Psychiatry and Clinical Neuroscience* 262 (2012): 677–85.

49. Barbara Stanley, Marc J. Gameroff, Venezia Michalsen, et al., "Are Suicide Attempters Who Self-Mutilate a Unique Population?" *American Journal of Psychiatry* 158 (2001): 427–32.

50. John G. Gunderson and Lois W. Choi-Kain, "Working with Patients Who Self-Injure," *JAMA Psychiatry* 76 (2019): 976–77.

51. Randy A. Sansone, George A. Gaither, and Douglas A. Songer, "Self-Harm Behaviors Across the Life Cycle: A Pilot Study of Inpatients with Borderline Personality," *Comprehensive Psychiatry* 43 (2002): 215–18.

52. P. Moran, C. Coffey, H. Romaniuk, et al., "The Natural History of Self-Harm from Adolescence to Young Adulthood: A Population-Based Cohort Study," *Lancet* 379 (2012): 236–43.

53. Paul H. Soloff, Kevin G. Lynch, and Thomas M. Kelly, "Childhood Abuse as a Risk Factor for Suicidal Behavior in Borderline Personality Disorder," *Journal of Personality Disorders* 16 (2002): 201–14.

54. Nikolaus Kleindienst, Martin Bohus, Petra Ludascher, et al., "Motives for Nonsuicidal Self-Injury Among Women with Borderline Personality Disorder," *Journal of Nervous and Mental Disease* 196 (2008): 230–36.

55. Rosemarie Kleutsch, Christian Schmahl, Inga Niedtfeld, et al., "Alterations in Default Mode Network Connectivity During Pain Processing in Borderline Personality Disorder," *Archives of General Psychiatry* 69 (2012): 993–1002.

56. Thomas H. McGlashan, Carlos M. Grilo, Charles A. Sanislow, et al., "Two-Year Prevalence and Stability of Individual DSM-IV Criteria for Schizotypal, Borderline, Avoidant, and Obsessive-Compulsive Personality Disorders: Toward a Hybrid Model of Axis II Disorders," *American Journal of Psychiatry* 162 (2005): 883–89.

3. ROOTS OF THE BORDERLINE SYNDROME

1. Randy A. Sansone and Lori A. Sansone, "The Families of Borderline Patients: The Psychological Environment Revisited," *Psychiatry* 6 (2009): 19–24.

2. A. Amed, N. Ramoz, P. Thomas, et al., "Genetics of Borderline Personality Disorder: Systematic Review and Proposal of an Integrative Model," *Neuroscience & Biobehavioral Reviews* 40 (2014): 6–19.

3. Charlotte Skoglund, Annika Tiger, Christian Rück, et al., "Familial Risk and Heritability of Diagnosed Borderline Personality Disorder: A Register Study of the Swedish Population," *Molecular Psychiatry*, published online June 3, 2019: 1–10; doi.org/10.1038/s41380-019-0442-0.

4. John G. Gunderson, Mary C. Zanarini, Lois W. Choi-Kain, et al., "Family Study of Borderline Personality Disorder and Its Sectors of Psychopathology," *Archives of General Psychiatry* 68 (2011): 753–62.

5. Ted Reichborn-Kjennerud, Eivind Ystrom, Michael C. Neale, et al., "Structure of Genetic and Environmental Risk Factors for Symptoms of DSM-IV Borderline Personality Disorder," *JAMA Psychiatry* 70 (2013): 1206–14.

6. M. A. Distel, J. J. Hottenga, T. J. Trull, et al., "Chromosome 9: Linkage for Borderline Personality Disorder Features," *Psychiatric Genetics* 18 (2008): 302–7.

7. Joanne Ryan, Isabelle Chaudieu, Marie-Laure Ancelin, et al., "Biological Underpinnings of Trauma and Post-Traumatic Stress Disorder: Focusing on Genetics and Epigenetics," *Epigenomics* 8 (2016): 1553–69.

8. Jerold J. Kreisman and Hal Straus, *Sometimes I Act Crazy: Living with Borderline Personality Disorder* (Hoboken, NJ: Wiley, 2004), 13–15.

9. Katja Bertsch, Matthias Gamer, Brigitte Schmidt, et al., "Oxytocin and Reduction of Social Threat Hypersensitivity in Women with Borderline Personality Disorder," *American Journal of Psychiatry* 170 (2013): 1169–77.

10. Sabine Herpertz and Katja Bertsch, "A New Perspective on the Pathophysiology of Borderline Personality Disorder: A Model of the Role of Oxytocin," *American Journal of Psychiatry* 172 (2015): 840–51.

11. Natalie Thomas, Caroline Gurvich, and Jayashri Kulkarni, "Borderline Personality Disorder, Trauma, and the Hypothalamus-Pituitary-Adrenal Axis," *Neuropsychiatric Disease and Treatment* 15 (2019): 2601–12.

12. Barbara Stanley and Larry J. Liever, "The Interpersonal Dimension of Borderline Personality Disorder: Toward a Neuropeptide Model," *American Journal of Psychiatry* 167 (2010): 24–39.

13. Alan R. Prossin, Tiffany M. Love, Robert A. Koeppe, et al., "Dysregulation of Regional Endogenous Opioid Function in Borderline Personality Disorder," *American Journal of Psychiatry* 167 (2010): 925–33.

14. Eric Lis, Brian Greenfield, Melissa Henry, et al., "Neuroimaging and Genetics of Borderline Personality Disorder: A Review," *Journal of Psychiatry and Neuroscience* 32 (2007): 162–73.

15. Dan J. Stein, "Borderline Personality Disorder: Toward Integration," *CNS Spectrums* 14 (2009): 352–56.

16. Ning Yuan, Yu Chen, Yan Xia, et al., "Inflammation-Related Biomarkers in Major Psychiatric Disorders: A Cross-Disorder Assessment of Reproducibility and Specificity in 43 Meta-Analyses," *Translational Psychiatry* 9 (2019): 1–13.

17. Paul A. Andrulonis, Bernard C. Glueck, Charles F. Stroebel, et al., "Organic Brain Dysfunction and the Borderline Syndrome," *Psychiatric Clinics of North America* 4 (1980): 47–66.

18. Margaret Mahler, Fred Pine, and Anni Bergman, *The Psychological Birth of the Human Infant* (New York: Basic Books, 1975).

19. A Letter from T. E. Lawrence to Charlotte Shaw (August 18, 1927), as quoted by John E. Mack, *A Prince of Our Disorder: The Life of T. E. Lawrence* (Boston: Little, Brown, 1976), 31.

20. Sally B. Smith, *Diana in Search of Herself* (New York: Random House, 1999), 38.

21. Jenna Kirtley, John Chiocchi, Jon Cole, et al., "Stigma, Emotion Appraisal, and the Family Environment as Predictors of Carer Burden for Relatives of Individuals Who Meet the Diagnostic Criteria of Borderline Personality Disorder," *Journal of Personality Disorders* 33 (2019): 497–514.

22. Andrea Fossati and Antonella Somma, "Improving Family Functioning to (Hopefully) *Improve* Treatment Efficacy of Borderline Personality Disorder: An Opportunity Not to Dismiss," *Psychopathology* 57 (2018): 149–59.

23. Norman Mailer, *Marilyn: A Biography* (New York: Grosset & Dunlap, 1973): 86.

24. *The Mail on Sunday* (June 1, 1986), as quoted in Sally B. Smith, *Diana in Search of Herself*, 10.

25. Andrew Morton, *Diana: Her True Story—In Her Own Words* (New York: Simon & Schuster, 1997), 33–34.

26. John G. Gunderson, John Kerr, and Diane Woods Englund, "The Families of Borderlines: A Comparative Study," *Archives of General Psychiatry* 37 (1980): 27–33.

27. Hallie Frank and Joel Paris, "Recollections of Family Experience in Borderline Patients," *Archives of General Psychiatry* 38 (1981): 1031–34.

28. Ronald B. Feldman and Herta A. Gunman, "Families of Borderline Patients: Literal-Minded Parents, Borderline Parents, and Parental Protectiveness," *American Journal of Psychiatry* 141 (1984): 1392–96.

4. THE BORDERLINE SOCIETY

1. Christopher Lasch, *The Culture of Narcissism* (New York: Norton, 1979), 34.

2. Louis Sass, "The Borderline Personality," *New York Times Magazine* (August 22, 1982), 13.

3. Peter L. Giovacchini, *Psychoanalysis of Character Disorders* (New York: Jason Aronson, 1975).

4. Christopher Lasch (1978): 5.

5. David S. Greenwald, *No Reason to Talk About It* (New York: Norton, 1987).

6. Paul A. Andrulonis, personal communication, 1987.

7. Patrick E. Jamieson and Dan Romer, "Unrealistic Fatalism in U.S. Youth Ages 14 to 22: Prevalence and Characteristics," *Journal of Adolescent Health* 42 (2008): 154–60.

8. World Health Organization, Global Health Estimates, "Adolescent Heath Epidemiology," 2016.

9. Oren Miron, Kun Hsing Yu, Rachel Wilf-Miron, et al., "Suicide Rates Among Adolescents and Young Adults in the United States, 2000–2017," *JAMA* 321 (2019): 2362–64.

10. Nikki Graf, "A Majority of U.S. Teens Fear a Shooting Could Happen at Their School, and Most Parents Share Their Concern," Pew Research Center, April 18, 2018.

11. "Number, Time, and Duration of Marriages and Divorces," Washington, DC: U.S. Census Bureau, 2005: 7–10; Philip N. Cohen, "The Coming Divorce Decline," *Socius* 5 (2019): 1–6; https://doi.org/10.1177/2378023119873497.

12. Philip N. Cohen, "The Coming Divorce Decline," *Socius* 5 (2019): 1–6; https://doi.org/10.1177/2378023119873497.

13. Christopher Lasch, *The Culture of Narcissism*, 30.

14. Pew Research Center, Fact Sheet, May 14, 2019, https://www.pewforum.org/fact-sheet/changing-attitudes-on-gay-marriage.

15. Robert P. Jones and Daniel Cox, "How Race and Religion Shape Millennial Attitudes on Sexuality and Reproductive Health," Findings from the 2015 Millennials, Sexuality, and Reproductive Survey, Public Research Institute, 2015.

16. Jason Fields, "Children's Living Arrangements and Characteristics: March 2002," Current Population Reports, P20-547, U.S. Census Bureau, 2003.

17. U.S. Census Bureau Report, "American Families and Living Arrangements," November 17, 2016.

18. Stephanie Kramer, "U.S. Has Highest Rate of Children Living in Single-Parent Households," Pew Research Center, December 12, 2019.

19. Jason Fields, U.S. Census Bureau, 2003.

20. Edward F. Zigler, "A Solution to the Nation's Child Care Crisis," paper presented at the National Health Policy Forum, Washington, DC (1987), 1.

21. U.S. Department of Health and Human Services Administration for Children and Families, *Child Maltreatment 2003* (Washington, DC: U.S. Government Printing Office, 2003), Summary of Key Findings, 4–34.

22. David Brooks, "The Nuclear Family Was a Mistake," *The Atlantic* (March 2020).

23. U.S. Department of Health and Human Services Administration for Children, Youth, and Families, *Child Maltreatment 2007* (Washington, DC: U.S. Government Printing Office, 2009), 24.

24. Judith L. Herman, *Father-Daughter Incest* (Cambridge, MA: Harvard University Press, 1981).

25. National Clearinghouse on Child Abuse and Neglect Information, Long-Term Consequences of Child Abuse and Neglect, Washington, DC, 2005.

26. Susan Jacoby, "Emotional Child Abuse: The Invisible Plague," *Glamour* (October 1984); Edna J. Hunter, quoted in *USA Today* (August 1985): 11.

27. W. Hugh Missildine, *Your Inner Child of the Past* (New York: Simon & Schuster, 1963).

28. Judith Wallerstein and J. B. Kelly, "The Effect of Parental Divorce:

Experiences of the Preschool Child," *Journal of the American Academy of Child Psychiatry* 14 (1975): 600–16.

29. Ibid.

30. M. Hetherington, "Children and Divorce," in *Parent-Child Interaction: Theory, Research, and Prospect,* ed. R. Henderson, *Psychiatric Opinion* 11 (1982): 6–15.

31. David A. Brent, Joshua A. Perper, Grace Moritz, et al., "Post-Traumatic Stress Disorders in Peers of Adolescent Suicide Victims: Predisposing Factors and Phenomenology," *Journal of the American Academy of Child and Adolescent Psychiatry* 34 (1995): 209–15.

32. Chaim F. Shatan, "Through the Membrane of Reality: Impacted Grief and Perceptual Dissonance in Vietnam Combat Veterans," *Psychiatric Opinion* 11 (1974): 6–15.

33. Chaim F. Shatan, "The Tattered Ego of Survivors," *Psychiatric Annals* 12 (1982): 1031–38.

34. "Concern Mounts Over Rising Troop Suicides," CNN.com, February 3, 2008; www.cnn.com/2008/US/02/01/military.suicides (accessed August 18, 2009).

35. Chaim F. Shatan, "War Babies," *American Journal of Orthopsychiatry* 45 (1975): 289.

36. "Faith in Flux: Changes in Religious Affiliation in the U.S.," Pew Forum on Religion and Public Life, April 27, 2009, http://pewforum.org/Faith -in-Flux.aspx (accessed July 7, 2010).

37. Amanda Lenhart and Mary Madden, "Social Networking Websites and Teens," Pew Internet and American Life Project, January 7, 2007, www .pewinternet.org/Reports/2007/Social-Networking-Websites-and -Teens.aspx (accessed September 2, 2009).

38. Monica Anderson and Jinjing Jiang, "Teens, Social Media, and Technology," Pew Research Center, https://www.pewresearch.org/internet/2018 /05/31/teens-social-media-technology-2018.

39. Robin Hamman, "Blogging4business: Social Networking and Brands," Cybersoc.com, April 4, 2007, www.cybersoc.com/2007/04/blogging 4busine/(accessed September 14, 2009). Paper delivered April 4, 2007, summarizing Microsoft findings.

40. Jean M. Twenge and W. Keith Campbell, *The Narcissism Epidemic: Living in the Age of Entitlement* (New York: Free Press, 2009), 1–4.

41. Amanda Lenhart, "Teens and Mobile Phones over the Past Five Years," Pew Research Center, 2009.

42. "Mass Shooting Tracker," *Mass Shooting Tracker*. Archived from the original on January 14, 2018.

43. Michael S. Schmidt, "F.B.I. Confirms a Sharp Rise in Mass Shootings Since 2000," *New York Times*, September 24, 2014; "Mass Shootings in America 2009–2020," Everytownresearch.org (accessed April 25, 2020).

44. "Healthcare, Mass Shootings, 2020 Presidential Election Causing Americans Significant Stress," American Psychological Association, Stress in America Survey, 2019.

45. Substance Abuse and Mental Health Services Administration (SAMHSA), *Key Substance Use and Mental Health Indicators in the U.S.: Results from the 2018 National Survey on Drug Use and Health* (Rockville, MD: Center for Behavioral Health Statistics and Quality, 2019).

46. Larry Alton, "We're Underestimating the Role of Social Media in Mass Shootings, and It's Time to Change," thenextweb.com (accessed May 6, 2020).

47. Jonathan Wareham, "Should Social Media Platforms Be Regulated?" *Forbes*, February 10, 2020.

48. Nili Solomonov and Jacques P. Barber, "Conducting Psychotherapy in the Trump Era: Therapists' Perspectives on Political Self-Disclosure, the Therapeutic Alliance, and Politics in the Therapy Room," *Journal of Clinical Psychology* 75 (2019): 1508–18.

49. Sarah R. Lowe and Sandro Galea, "The Mental Health Consequences of Mass Shootings," *Trauma, Violence, and Abuse* 18 (2017): 62–82.

50. Sarah R. Lowe and Sandro Galea, 2017, 79–82.

51. Statements on MSNBC *All In with Chris Hayes*, March 12, 2020, and MSNBC News, March 14, 2020.

52. Megan A. Moreno, "Cyberbullying," *JAMA Pediatrics* 168 (2014): 500.

53. Mitch van Geel, Paul Vedder, and Jenny Tanilon, "Relationship Between Peer Victimization, Cyberbullying, and Suicide in Children and Adolescents: A Meta-analysis," *JAMA Pediatrics* 168 (2014): 435–42.

54. "Identity Theft by Households, 2005–2010," U.S. Department of Justice, Bureau of Justice Statistics, 2011, NCJ 236245; "Victims of Identity Theft, 2016," Bureau of Justice Statistics, 2019, NCJ 251147.

55. GlobalWebIndex (2015), "The Demographics of Tinder Users" (accessed April 27, 2020).

56. "Crimes Linked to Tinder and Grindr Increase Seven-Fold," *Daily Telegraph* (UK), March 16, 2016; Alyssa Murphy, "Dating Dangerously: Risks Lurking Within Mobile Dating Apps," *Catholic University Journal of Law and Technology* 26 (2018).

57. J. Strubel and T. A. Petrie, "Love Me Tinder: Body Image and Psychosocial Functioning Among Men and Women," *Body Image* 21 (2017): 34–38.

6. FAMILY AND FRIENDS: HOW TO COPE

1. C. Porter, J. Palmier-Claus, A. Branitsky, et al., "Childhood Adversity and Borderline Personality Disorder: A Meta-analysis," *Acta Psychiatrica Scandinavica* 141 (2020): 6–20.

2. Jasmin Wertz, Avshalom Caspi, Antony Ambler, et al., "Borderline Symptoms at Age 12 Signal Risk for Poor Outcomes During the Transition to Adulthood: Findings from a Genetically Sensitive Longitudinal Cohort Study," *Journal of the American Academy of Child and Adolescent Psychiatry* 59 (2020): 1165–77.e2.

3. Andrew M. Chanen, Martina Jovev, and Henry J. Jackson, "Adaptive Functioning and Psychiatric Symptoms in Adolescents with Borderline Personality Disorder," *Journal of Clinical Psychiatry* 68 (2007): 297–306.

4. David A. Brent, Joshua A. Perper, Charles E. Goldstein, et al., "Risk Factors for Adolescent Suicide: A Comparison of Adolescent Suicide Victims with Suicidal Inpatients," *Archives of General Psychiatry* 45 (1988): 581–88.

5. Alexander McGirr, Joel Paris, Alain Lesage, et al., "Risk Factors for Suicide Completion in Borderline Personality Disorder: A Case-Control Study of Cluster B Comorbidity and Impulsive Aggression," *Journal of Clinical Psychiatry* 68 (2007): 721–29.

6. Trees Juurlink, Margreet Ten Have, Femke Lamers, et al., "Borderline Personality Symptoms and Work Performance: A Population-Based Survey," *BMC Psychiatry* 18 (2018): 202.

7. Jerold J. Kreisman and Hal Straus, *Sometimes I Act Crazy: Living with Borderline Personality Disorder* (Hoboken, NJ: Wiley, 2004).

8. Jerold J. Kreisman, *Talking to a Loved One with Borderline Personality*

Disorder: Communication Skills to Manage Intense Emotions, Set Boundaries & Reduce Conflict (Oakland, CA: New Harbinger, 2018).

9. Barbara Stanley, Marc Gameroff, Venezia Michalsen, et al., "Are Suicide Attempters Who Self-Mutilate a Unique Population?" *American Journal of Psychiatry* 158 (2001): 427–32.

10. Randy Sansone, George Gaither, and Douglas Songer, "Self-Harm Behaviors Across the Life Cycle: A Pilot Study of Inpatients with Borderline Personality Disorder," *Comprehensive Psychiatry* 43 (2002): 215–18.

11. Leo Sher, Sarah Rutter, Antonia New, et al., "Gender Differences and Similarities in Aggression, Suicidal Behavior, and Psychiatric Comorbidity in Borderline Personality Disorder," *Acta Psychiatrica Scandinavica* 139 (Suppl.) (2019): 145–53.

12. Galit Geulayov, Deborah Casey, Liz Bale, et al., "Suicide Following Presentation to Hospital for Non-fatal Self-Harm in the Multicentre Study of Self-Harm: A Long-Term Follow-up Study," *The Lancet Psychiatry* 6 (2019): 1021–30.

13. Anna Szücs, Katalin Szanto, Aidan Wright, et al., "Personality of Late- and Early-Onset Elderly Suicide Attempters," *International Journal of Geriatric Psychiatry* 35 (2020): 384–95.

14. Hannah Gordon, Selina Nath, Kylee Trevillion, et al., "Self-Harm Ideation, and Mother-Infant Interactions: A Prospective Cohort Study," *Journal of Clinical Psychiatry* 80 (2019): 37–44.

15. J. J. Muehlenkamp, L. Claes, L. Havertape, et al., "International Prevalence of Adolescent Non-Suicidal Self-Injury and Deliberate Self-Harm," *Child and Adolescent Psychiatry and Mental Health* 6 (2012): article no. 10; doi: 10.1186/1753-2000-6-10.

16. Bryan Denny, Jin Fan, Samuel Fels, et al., "Sensitization of the Neural Salience Network to Repeated Emotional Stimuli Following Initial Habituation in Patients with Borderline Personality Disorder," *American Journal of Psychiatry* 175 (2018): 657–64.

7. SEEKING, FINDING, AND ENGAGING IN THERAPY

1. American Psychiatric Association, "Practice Guideline for the Treatment of Patients with Borderline Personality Disorder," *American Journal of Psychiatry* 158 (2001, October Suppl.): 4.

2. Paul Links, Ravi Shah, and Rahel Eynan, "Psychotherapy for Border-

line Personality Disorder: Progress and Remaining Challenges," *Current Psychiatry Reports* 19 (2017): 16.

3. Otto Kernberg, *Borderline Conditions and Pathological Narcissism* (New York: Jason Aronson, 1975).

4. James F. Masterson, *Psychotherapy of the Borderline Adult* (New York: Brunner/Mazel, 1976).

5. Norman D. Macaskill, "Therapeutic Factors in Group Therapy with Borderline Patients," *International Journal of Group Psychotherapy* 32 (1982): 61–73.

6. Wendy Froberg and Brent D. Slife, "Overcoming Obstacles to the Implementation of Yalom's Model of Inpatient Group Psychotherapy," *International Journal of Group Psychotherapy* 37 (1987): 371–88.

7. Leonard Horwitz, "Indications for Group Therapy with Borderline and Narcissistic Patients," *Bulletin of the Menninger Clinic* 1 (1987): 248–60.

8. Judith K. Kreisman and Jerold J. Kreisman, "Marital and Family Treatment of Borderline Personality Disorder," in *Family Treatment of Personality Disorders: Advances in Clinical Practice*, ed. Malcolm M. MacFarlane (New York: Haworth Clinical Practice Press, 2004): 117–48.

9. Bina Nir, "Transgenerational Transmission of Holocaust Trauma and Its Expressions in Literature," *Genealogy* 2 (2018): 49; https://doi.org/10.3390/genealogy2040049.

10. Maria Ridolfi, Roberta Rossi, Giorgia Occhialini, et al., "A Clinical Trial of a Psychoeducation Group Intervention for Patients with Borderline Personality Disorder," *Journal of Clinical Psychiatry* 81 (2020): 41–46.

11. Thomas A. Widiger and Allen J. Frances, "Epidemiology and Diagnosis, and Comorbidity of Borderline Personality Disorder," in *American Psychiatric Press Review of Psychiatry*, ed. Allen Tasman, Robert E. Hales, and Allen J. Frances, vol. 8 (Washington, DC: American Psychiatric Publishing, 1989): 8–24.

8. SPECIFIC PSYCHOTHERAPEUTIC APPROACHES

1. Anna Bartak, Djora I. Soeteman, Roes Verheul, et al., "Strengthening the Status of Psychotherapy for Personality Disorders: An Integrated Perspective on Effects and Costs," *Canadian Journal of Psychiatry* 52 (2007): 803–9.

2. John G. Gunderson, *Borderline Personality Disorder: A Clinical Guide,*

2nd ed. (Washington, DC: American Psychiatric Publishing, 2008): 242–43.

3. Cameo F. Borntrager, Bruce F. Chorpita, Charmaine Higa-McMillan, et al., "Provider Attitudes Toward Evidence-Based Practices: Are the Concerns with the Evidence or with the Manuals?" *Psychiatric Services* 60 (2009): 677–81.

4. Aaron T. Beck, Arthur Freeman, and Denise D. Davis, *Cognitive Therapy of Personality Disorders*, 2nd ed. (New York: Guilford, 2004).

5. Marsha M. Linehan, *Cognitive-Behavioral Treatment of Borderline Personality Disorder* (New York: Guilford, 1993).

6. Marsha M. Linehan, *DBT Skills Training Handouts and Worksheets*, 2nd ed. (New York: Guilford, 2014).

7. Nancee Blum, Bruce Pfohl, Don St. John, et al., "STEPPS: A Cognitive-Behavioral Systems-Based Group Treatment for Outpatients with Borderline Personality Disorder—A Preliminary Report," *Comprehensive Psychiatry* 43 (2002): 301–10.

8. Donald Black and Nancee Blum, *Systems Training for Emotional Predictability and Problem Solving for Borderline Personality Disorder: Implementing STEPPS Around the Globe*, 1st ed. (New York: Oxford University Press, 2017).

9. Jeffrey E. Young, Janet S. Klosko, and Marjorie E. Weishaar, *Schema Therapy: A Practitioner's Guide* (New York: Guilford, 2003).

10. Otto F. Kernberg, Michael A. Selzer, Harold W. Koeningsberg, et al., *Psychodynamic Psychotherapy of Borderline Patients* (New York: Basic Books, 1989).

11. Frank E. Yeomans, John F. Clarkin, and Otto F. Kernberg, *A Primer for Transference-Focused Psychotherapy for the Borderline Patient* (Lanham, MD: Jason Aronson, 2002).

12. Peter Fonagy, "Thinking About Thinking: Some Clinical and Theoretical Considerations in the Treatment of a Borderline Patient," *International Journal of Psychoanalysis* 72, pt. 4 (1991): 639–56.

13. Anthony Bateman and Peter Fonagy, "Mentalization-Based Treatment," *Journal for Mental Health Professionals* 33 (2013): 595–613.

14. Anthony Bateman and Peter Fonagy, *Mentalization-Based Treatment for Borderline Personality Disorder: A Practical Guide* (Oxford, UK: Oxford University Press, 2006).

15. Anthony Bateman and Peter Fonagy, "8-Year Follow-Up of Patients Treated for Borderline Personality Disorder: Mentalization-Based Treatment Versus Treatment as Usual," *American Journal of Psychiatry* 165 (2008): 631–38.

16. Maaike Smits, Dine Feenstra, Hester Eeren, et al., "Day Hospital versus Intensive Out-Patient Mentalisation-Based Treatment for Borderline Personality Disorder: Multicentre Randomised Clinical Trial," *British Journal of Psychiatry* 216 (2020): 79–84.

17. John Gunderson, *Handbook of Good Psychiatric Management for Borderline Personality Disorder* (Washington, D.C.: American Psychiatric Publishing, 2014).

18. Robert J. Gregory and Anna L. Remen, "A Manual-Based Psychodynamic Therapy for Treatment-Resistant Borderline Personality Disorder," *Psychotherapy: Theory, Research, Practice, Training* 45 (2008): 15–27.

19. Eric M. Plakun, "Making the Alliance and Taking the Transference in Work with Suicidal Borderline Patients," *Journal of Psychotherapy Practice and Research* 10 (2001): 269–76.

20. Allan Abbass, Albert Sheldon, John Gyra, et al., "Intensive Short-Term Dynamic Psychotherapy for DSM-IV Personality Disorders: A Randomized Controlled Trial," *Journal of Nervous and Mental Disease* 196 (2008): 211–16.

21. Antonio Menchaca, Orietta Perez, and Astrid Peralta, "Intermittent-Continuous Eclectic Therapy: A Group Approach for Borderline Personality Disorder," *Journal of Psychiatric Practice* 13 (2007): 281–84.

22. John F. Clarkin, Kenneth N. Levy, Mark F. Lenzenweger, et al., "Evaluating Three Treatments for Borderline Personality Disorder: A Multiwave Study," *American Journal of Psychiatry* 164 (2007): 922–28.

23. Josephine Giesen-Bloo, Richard van Dyck, Philip Spinhoven, et al., "Outpatient Psychotherapy for Borderline Personality Disorder: Randomized Trial of Schema-Focused Therapy vs. Transference-Focused Psychotherapy," *Archives of General Psychiatry* 63 (2006): 649–58.

24. Antoinette D. I. van Asselt and Carmen D. Dirksen, "Outpatient Psychotherapy for Borderline Personality Disorder: Cost-Effectiveness of Schema-Focused Therapy vs. Transference-Focused Psychotherapy," *British Journal of Psychiatry* 192 (2008): 450–57.

25. Shelley McMain, Tim Guimond, David Steiner, et al., "Dialectical Behavior Therapy Compared with General Psychiatric Management for Border-

line Personality Disorder: Clinical Outcomes and Functioning Over a 2-Year Follow-Up," *American Journal of Psychiatry* 169 (2012): 650–61.

26. Robert J. Gregory and S. Sachdeva, "Naturalistic Outcomes of Evidence-Based Therapies for Borderline Personality Disorder at a Medical University Clinic," *American Journal of Psychotherapy* 70 (2016): 167–84.

9. MEDICATIONS: THE SCIENCE AND THE PROMISE

1. Ted Reichborn-Kjennerud, "Genetics of Personality Disorders," *Psychiatric Clinics of North America* 31 (2008): 421–40.

2. Randy A. Sansone and Lori A. Sansone, "The Families of Borderline Patients: The Psychological Environment Revisited," *Psychiatry* 6 (2009): 19–24.

3. Bernadette Grosjean and Guochuan E. Tsai, "NMDA Neurotransmission as a Critical Mediator of Borderline Personality Disorder," *Journal of Psychiatry and Neuroscience* 32 (2007): 103–15.

4. Antonia S. New, Marianne Goodman, Joseph Triebwasser, et al., "Recent Advances in the Biological Study of Personality Disorders," *Psychiatric Clinics of North America* 31 (2008): 441–61.

5. Bonnie Jean Steinberg, Robert L. Trestman, and Larry J. Siever, "The Cholinergic and Noradrenergic Neurotransmitter Systems and Affective Instability in Borderline Personality Disorder," in *Biological and Neurobehavioral Studies of Borderline Personality Disorder* (Washington, DC: American Psychiatric Publishing, 2005): 41–62.

6. Katja Bertsch, Ilinca Schmidinger, Inga D. Neumann, et al., "Reduced Plasma Oxytocin Levels in Female Patients with Borderline Personality Disorder," *Hormones and Behavior* 63 (2013): 424–29.

7. Mary C. Zanarini, Catherine R. Kimble, and Amy A. Williams, "Neurological Dysfunction in Borderline Patients and Axis II Control Subjects," in *Biological and Neurobehavioral Studies of Borderline Personality Disorder* (Washington, DC: American Psychiatric Publishing, 2005): 159–75.

8. José Manuel De la Fuente, Julio Bobes, Coro Vizuete, et al., "Neurologic Soft Signs in Borderline Personality Disorder," *Journal of Clinical Psychiatry* 67 (2006): 541–46.

9. Eric Lis, Brian Greenfield, Melissa Henry, et al., "Neuroimaging and Genetics of Borderline Personality Disorder: A Review," *Journal of Psychiatry and Neuroscience* 32 (2007): 162–73.

10. Niall McGowan, Guy Goodwin, Amy Bilderbeck, et al., "Actigraphic

Patterns, Impulsivity and Mood Instability in Bipolar Disorder, Borderline Personality Disorder and Healthy Controls," *Acta Psychiatrica Scandinavica* 141 (2020): 374–84.

11. American Psychiatric Association, "Practice Guideline for the Treatment of Patients with Borderline Personality Disorder," *American Journal of Psychiatry* 158 (2001, October Suppl.).

12. Mary C. Zanarini and Frances R. Frankenburg, "Omega-3 Fatty Acid Treatment of Women with Borderline Personality Disorder: A Double-Blind Placebo-Controlled Pilot Study," *American Journal of Psychiatry* 160 (2003): 167–69.

13. Christopher Pittenger, John H. Krystal, and Vladimir Coric, "Initial Evidence of the Beneficial Effects of Glutamate-Modulating Agents in the Treatment of Self-Injurious Behavior Associated with Borderline Personality Disorder" (Letter to the Editor), *Journal of Clinical Psychiatry* 66 (2005): 1492–93.

14. Kyle Lapidus, Laili Soleimani, and James Murrough, "Novel Glutamatergic Drugs for the Treatment of Mood Disorders," *Neuropsychiatric Disease and Treatment* 9 (2013): 1101–12.

15. Ulrike Feske, Benoit Mulsant, Paul Pilkonis, et al., "Clinical Outcome of ECT in Patients with Major Depression and Comorbid Borderline Personality Disorder," *American Journal of Psychiatry* 161 (2004): 2073–80.

16. Kfir Feffer, Sarah K. Peters, Kamaldeep Bhui, et al., "Successful Dorsomedial Prefrontal rTMS for Major Depression in Borderline Personality Disorder: Three Cases," *Brain Stimulation* 10 (2017): 716–17.

17. American Psychiatric Association, *Diagnostic and Statistical Manual of Mental Disorders, Revised*, 3rd ed. (DSM-III-R) (Washington, DC: American Psychiatric Association, 1987): 16.

18. Michael H. Stone, *The Fate of Borderline Patients: Successful Outcome and Psychiatric Practice* (New York: Guilford, 1990).

19. Wiebke Bleidorn, Patrick Hill, Mitza Back, et al., "The Policy Relevance of Personality Traits," *American Psychologist* 74 (2019): 1056–67.

20. Mary C. Zanarini, Frances R. Frankenburg, John Hennen, et al., "The McLean Study of Adult Development (MSAD): Overview and Implications of the First Six Years of Prospective Follow-Up," *Journal of Personality Disorders* 19 (2005): 505–23.

21. Andrew E. Skodol, John G. Gunderson, M. Tracie Shea, et al., "The Collaborative Longitudinal Personality Disorders Study: Overview and Implications," *Journal of Personality Disorders* 19 (2005): 487–504.

22. John G. Gunderson, Robert L. Stout, Thomas H. McGlashan, et al., "Ten-Year Course of Borderline Personality Disorder: Psychopathology and Function from the Collaborative Longitudinal Personality Disorders Study," *Archives of General Psychiatry* 68 (2011): 827–37.

10. UNDERSTANDING AND HEALING

1. Andrew Morton, *Diana: Her New Life* (Philadelphia: Trans-Atlantic Publications, 1995), 155.

APPENDIX A. ALTERNATIVE MODELS FOR DIAGNOSING BPD

1. *Diagnostic and Statistical Manual of Mental Disorders*, 5th ed. (DSM-5) (Washington, DC: American Psychiatric Association, 2013), 645.

2. Lee Anna Clark, Bruce Cuthbert, Roberto Lewis-Fernandez, et al., "Three Approaches to Understanding and Classifying Mental Disorder: ICD-11, DSM-5, and the National Institute of Mental Health's Research Domain Criteria (RDoC)," *Psychological Science in the Public Interest* 18 (2017): 72–145.

3. *Diagnostic and Statistical Manual of Mental Disorders*, 5th ed. (DSM-5), 663–66.

4. *International Classification of Diseases,* 10th rev. (ICD-10) (Geneva: World Health Organization, 1992).

5. *International Classification of Diseases,* Proposed 11th rev. (ICD-11) (Geneva: World Health Organization), 2019.

6. Joel Yager and Robert E. Feinstein, "Potential Applications of the National Institute of Mental Health's Research Domain Criteria (RDoC) to Clinical Psychiatric Practice: How RDoC Might Be Used in Assessment, Diagnostic Processes, Case Formulation, Treatment Planning, and Clinical Notes," *Journal of Clinical Psychiatry* 78 (2017): 423–32.

7. K. Bertsch, Section Editor, "The NIMH Research Domain Criteria (RDoC) Initiative and Its Implications for Research on Personality Disorder," *Current Psychiatry Reports* 21 (2019).

APPENDIX B. EVOLUTION OF THE BORDERLINE SYNDROME

1. Michael H. Stone, "The Borderline Syndrome: Evolution of the Term, Genetic Aspects, and Prognosis," *American Journal of Psychotherapy* 31 (1977): 345–65.

2. Adolph Stern, "Psychoanalytic Investigation of and Therapy in the Border Line Group of Neuroses," *Psychoanalytic Quarterly* 7 (1938): 467–89.

3. Gregory Zilboorg, "Ambulatory Schizophrenia," *Psychiatry* 4 (1941): 149–55.

4. Paul Hoch and Philip Polatin, "Pseudoneurotic Forms of Schizophrenia," *Psychiatric Quarterly* 23 (1949): 248–76.

5. Gustav Bychowski, "The Problem of Latent Psychosis," *Journal of the American Psychoanalytic Association* 4 (1953): 484–503.

6. *Diagnostic and Statistical Manual of Mental Disorders*, 2nd ed. (DSM-II) (Washington, DC: American Psychiatric Association, 1968).

7. Helene Deutsch, "Some Forms of Emotional Disturbance and the Relationship to Schizophrenia," *Psychoanalytic Quarterly* 11 (1942): 301–21.

8. Robert P. Knight, "Borderline States," *Bulletin of the Menninger Clinic* 17 (1953): 1–12.

9. Roy R. Grinker, Beatrice Werble, and Robert C. Drye, *The Borderline Syndrome* (New York: Basic Books, 1968).

10. Otto Kernberg, "Borderline Personality Organization," *Journal of the American Psychoanalytic Association* 15 (1967): 641–85.

11. Otto Kernberg, *Borderline Conditions and Pathological Narcissism* (New York: Jason Aronson, 1975).

INDEX

Aaron (cult follower seeking
  direction), 45
abandonment
  fear of, 38–39, 161–62, 276–77
  rapprochement phase of separation-
    individuation, 68–70, 72, 83–84
Abby (overlapping illnesses), 147–48
abuse
  and blame, 152
  child, 13, 75, 96–98, 152–53
  during separation and divorce,
    99–100
  effect on offspring's
    chromosomes, 13
  emotional, 97–98, 152–53
  neglect, 97–98
  physical, 97, 152
  sexual, 97, 152
adolescence, 72–74, 108–9, 153–55
adulthood, 155–57
affective disorders, 29–30
aging
  with BPD, 17–18
  BPD throughout the life cycle,
    153–57
  dealing with an older BPD
    parent, 157
  and suicide attempts, 168

Albee, Edward, 202
alcoholism, 34
Alicia and Adam (effect of changes on
  a relationship), 256–57
Alliance-Based Therapy
  (ABT), 222
Allison and Michael (refocusing
  anger), 173
alternative DSM-5 model for
  personality disorders (AMPD),
  261–63
Amin and Michelle (participants in a
  destructive relationship), 41
Anderson family (chaotic household
  with BPD), 57–62, 66
anger
  focusing on, 167
  intense rage, 53–54, 173
  toward mental health professionals,
    53–54
  unpredictable outbursts, 146–47,
    172–73
  in the workplace, 16
Ann and Liam (masochism and
  sadism in a relationship), 90
Annette (victimization),
  126–28
anorexia nervosa, 34–35, 44–45

antidepressants
  monoamine oxidase inhibitors
    (MAOIs), 232–33
  selective serotonin reuptake
    inhibitors (SSRIs), 232–33
  serotonin-norepinephrine reuptake
    inhibitors (SNRIs), 232
  tricyclic antidepressants (TCAs),
    232–33
antipsychotics (neuroleptics), 233–34
antisocial personality disorder, 33–34
anxiolytics (antianxiety agents), 234
art therapy, 202–3
as-if personality, 270–71
attention deficit hyperactivity disorder
    (ADHD), 30–31
Audrey (extreme mood shifts), 51
autism spectrum disorder (ASD), 36

Barlow, Lisa (cultural and family
    effects on BPD), 77–80, 89–90,
    97–98
Beck, Aaron, 213
bibliotherapy, 202
bipolar disorder, 29–30
blame and child abuse, 152
Borderline Personality Disorder (BPD)
  by age group, 17–18, 153–57
  and associated personality
    disorders, 33–34
  and attention deficit hyperactivity
    disorder (ADHD), 30–31
  and autism spectrum disorder
    (ASD), 36
  categorical criteria for diagnosis,
    10–11, 259–60
  celebrities and fictional characters
    with, 19–20, 133–34
  chameleon aspect of, 138, 270

  compared to affective disorders,
    29–30
  compared to schizophrenia and
    psychosis, 29
  and compulsive behaviors, 35–36
  connection to other medical
    diseases, 6, 8
  countertransference, 187–88
  diagnostic criteria, 37–55, 161–74,
    184, 259–60
  difficulties diagnosing and defining,
    5–6, 82–83, 146–47, 269–72
  dimensional approach to diagnosis,
    9–10, 260
  and dissociative disorders, 32
  and eating disorders, 34–35
  environmental effects on the
    development of, 63, 66, 75–76
  evolution of, 267–77
  genetic component, 62–66, 76,
    228–29
  geographic and cultural factors,
    18–19
  helping someone with, 148–50
  and hospitalization, 203–8
  increasing frequency of diagnosis,
    82–83
  interaction of symptoms, 56, 147–48
  and pain tolerance, 31
  pathology of, 21–22
  and post-traumatic stress disorder
    (PTSD), 32–33
  and premature death, 37
  recovery from, 155, 238–39
  relationship to other disorders,
    27–29, 147, 269–72
  research and treatment advances,
    20–21, 210–12, 223–26, 264–65
  and socioeconomic factors, 18
  and somatization disorder, 31–32

statements to avoid when dealing
with, 174–75
statistics of, 4–5, 7–8, 21
and substance abuse, 34, 154
subtypes of, 270–71
and suicide, 8, 12, 37
transference, 185–87
treatment of, 73–74, 147, 183–84,
208–9, 210–12, 230–31
Borderline Personality Organization
(BPO)
defined, 272
primitive thinking, 274
splitting as a defense mechanism,
274–75
weaknesses in functioning, 273–74
boundaries, setting, 162
the brain
brain injury or disease, 65, 230
changes in brain metabolism and
structure of, 65, 230
the limbic system, 213
neurotransmitters, 64, 228–29, 235
perceiving pain, 51, 65
reactions to negative stimuli, 169
bulimia, 34–35
bullying. *See* cyberbullying

Campbell, W. Keith, 104
Carlos (self-destructive behavior), 49
Carrie (patient with BPD), 23–26, 42,
53–54
case studies using SET-UP
communication strategies
Annette (victimization), 126–28
Christie and Martin (difficulties
with identity), 138–41
Gloria and Alex (contradictory
statements), 119–22
Kevin and Mr. and Mrs. Hopkins
(follow-through), 134–37
Marnie and Robin (stress-induced
delusions), 141–43
Neil (accepting bad feelings),
123–25
Pat and Jake (object constancy),
130–33
Rich (emptiness), 129–30
Cat's Cradle (Vonnegut), 103
celebrities and fictional characters
with BPD, 19–20, 133–34
The Centaur (Updike), 39
change
effect of societal change on people,
85–86
fear of, 246–47
frequent and drastic, 45
learning to "limp," 251
making adjustments during
marriage and pregnancy,
92–93
making adjustments to maintain a
balanced relationship, 256–57
modifying one's personality traits,
249–50
practicing, 250
self-assessment, 247–50
character, 26
child abuse. *See* abuse
child development
children's need for physical
intimacy during parents' divorce,
99–100
effects of evolving family structures
on children, 95–96
inconsistencies in child-rearing,
150–51
object relations theory, 67–71
the parent-child relationship, 66

child development (*cont.*)
   separation-individuation period,
      68–71, 72
   viewing childhood experiences as
      an adult, 252–53
Christie and Martin (difficulties with
      identity), 138–41
Clarke, Mary, 74
cognitive behavioral approaches
   cognitive behavioral therapy (CBT),
      184–85, 213
   dialectical behavioral therapy (DBT),
      20, 70, 213–15, 221, 223–24, 260
   focus on current thinking processes,
      185, 212
   schema-focused therapy (SFT),
      216–17, 222, 224
   systems training for emotional
      predictability and problem
      solving (STEPPS), 215
communication
   statements to avoid when dealing
      with BPD patients, 174–75
   between therapy sessions, 181
   using the SET-UP principles, 143
compulsive behaviors, 35–36
conflicts
   adolescent, 72–74
   childhood, 71–72
   trauma, 74–75
consistency
   during child-rearing, 150–51
   to cope with mood changes, 171
conversion therapy, 183
cortisol, 64
costs
   cost-effectiveness of schema-focused
      therapy (SFT) and transference-
      focused psychotherapy (TFP), 224
   of hospital care, 205

reimbursement rates for
      psychotherapy, 225
   societal costs of BPD, 18
countertransference, 187–88
Covid-19 pandemic, 68, 92, 107–8
cults, 36, 45
cultural changes, effect of on BPD,
      81–82
The Culture of Narcissism (Lasch),
      81, 104
curing BPD, 155, 238–39
cyberbullying, 108–9

Debbie (family therapy), 199–200
depression, 29
Deutsch, Helene, 270
Diagnostic and Statistical Model of
      Mental Disorders (DSM)
   DSM-I, 8
   DSM-II, 8
   DSM-III, 6, 8, 238
   DSM-5, 6, 10–11, 26, 168,
      259–63, 264
   alternative DSM-5 model for
      personality disorders (AMPD),
      261–63
   categorical paradigms, 8–9, 259–60
   diagnostic criteria of BPD, 37–55,
      161–74, 184, 259–60
   dimensional approach to diagnosis,
      9–10, 260
   ICD-11 model of personality
      disorders, 263–64
   Research Domain Criteria (RDoC),
      264–65
dialectical behavioral therapy (DBT),
      20, 70, 213–15, 221, 223–24, 260
Diana, Princess of Wales, 71, 74–75,
      162, 255

differentiation phase of child
 development, 68
dissociative disorders, 32
dissociative identity disorder (DID), 32
divorce, 82, 89, 99–101, 151, 155
drug abuse, 34, 154
Dynamic Deconstructive
 Psychotherapy (DDP), 222

eating disorders
 anorexia nervosa, 34–35, 44–45
 bulimia, 34–35
Elaine (group therapy), 197–98, 201
Elizabeth (process of healing BPD),
 240–47, 251, 252–55, 257
emotions
 emotional hemophilia, 11–13
 emotional overreactivity, 213–14
 while dealing with a BPD patient,
 160–61
empathy, 40
Empathy statements (SET-UP
 system of communication), 115,
 116–17
emptiness, 52, 128–30, 171–72
engulfment, 39
environment
 influences on the development of
 BPD, 63
 object relations theory, 67–71
 the parent-child relationship, 66
 removing weapons and harmful
 objects from the, 169
ethical issues. *See* countertransference
expressive therapies, 201–3
extremes
 abrupt mood changes, 51, 169–71
 difficulties evaluating a
 situation, 253

in parenting behavior, 66
political polarization, 105–6

family
 characteristic features of BPD
 childhoods, 150–51, 252–53
 evolving family structures, 94–96
 father absence, 99–101, 150
 the "faux family" of social media,
 103–4
 link between family trauma and
 BPD, 74–75
 relationships with extended,
 82, 102
 treatment of the entire, 73–74, 199
family therapy, 198–201
Fatal Attraction (film), 133–34
fathers. *See* men
fear
 of abandonment, 38–39, 161–62,
 276–77
 of a catastrophic event, 87–88
 of change, 246–47
follow-through, 134–37
Fonagy, Peter, 218–19
Freud, Sigmund, 19, 80, 267–68
function levels of BPD patients,
 155–56

gender
 and BPD, 17
 roles, 80–81, 91–93
 same-sex marriage, 93
 sexual orientation, 94
 transsexualism, 94
generic drugs, 236–37
genetics, 62–66, 76, 228–29
geographical mobility, 102

geographic and cultural factors, 18–19, 102

Giovacchini, Peter L., 87

Gloria and Alex (contradictory statements), 119–22

glutamate, 235

good psychiatric management (GPM), 220–21, 222, 224

Greene, Graham, 252

Gregory, Robert, 222

Grindr, 110

Grinker, Roy, 270–71

group therapy, 195–97

Gunderson, John G., 211, 220–21, 271–72

Hewitt, James, 71

Hillel, 250

histrionic personality disorder, 34

Hitler, Adolf, 19–20

homeopathic and herbal remedies for BPD, 234–35

hormones
    cortisol, 64
    neurotransmitters, 64, 229
    oxytocin, 64, 229

hospitalization
    acute, 205–6
    of BPD patients, 203–5
    care standards, 207–8
    long-term, 206–8
    partial, 208

humor, 175

hypermobility, 102

hypnosis, 182

ICD-11 model of personality disorders, 263–64

identity
    actors' search for, 74
    chameleon aspect of a person with BPD, 138, 164
    establishing a separate sense of, 253–55
    gender identity, 94
    identity diffusion, 217–18, 276
    inauthenticity ("faking it"), 44
    instability of, 42–43, 164–65
    lacking a clear sense of, 12–13
    making drastic life changes, 45
    seeking acceptance and structure through cults, 45
    and self-esteem, 43

identity theft, 109

The Impulsive Character (Reich), 268–69

impulsivity
    coping with, 165–67
    as a criterion of BPD, 46–47

indecision, 253

inflammation, 65

Intensive Short-Term Dynamic Psychotherapy (ISTDP), 222–23

Intermittent-Continuous Eclectic Therapy (ICE), 223

International Classification of Diseases, World Health Organization. See ICD-11 model of personality disorder

intimacy. See relationships, romantic

Jack (BPD patient with dependency on others), 149–50

Jennifer (patient with BPD), 1–4, 15, 48–49, 206–7

jobs. See the workplace

Joyce (self-destructive use of alcohol), 47

Judy (comparing different therapies), 221–22

Julie (challenges in treatment of BPD), 176–80

Justin (extreme mood shifts), 51

Kernberg, Otto, 217, 272–76

ketamine, 235

Kevin and Mr. and Mrs. Hopkins (follow-through), 134–37

Klein, Melanie, 269

Knight, Robert, 270

Larry and Phyllis (coping with self-destructive behavior), 166–67

Lasch, Christopher, 81, 87, 104

Lawrence, T. E., 69–70

Lennon, John, 97

LGBTQ+ issues
 conversion therapy, 183
 Grindr, 110
 same-sex marriage, 93
 sexual orientation, 94
 transsexualism, 94

Lindsay and Nelson (coping with an unhealthy relationship), 163

Linehan, Marsha, 20, 213

Lisa (destabilized family life). *See* Barlow, Lisa

Lois (dealing with an older BPD parent), 157

loneliness, 107

Lorenzo (transient delusions), 54–55

loyalties, group, 85

Mahler, Margaret, 67–71

Mailer, Norman, 43–44, 74

manipulation
 manifestations of, 40
 self-harm as, 50

Marilyn: An Untold Story (Rosten), 39

Marilyn (Mailer), 43–44

Marjorie (rapidly shifting sense of reality), 273

Mark and Sally (projective identification), 275

Marnie and Robin (stress-induced delusions), 141–43

marriage
 making adjustments during, 92–93
 same-sex, 93

masochism, 90

mass shootings, 104–6

"The 'Me' Decade and the Third Great Awakening" (article), 104

medication. *See* pharmacotherapy

Melanie (adolescent in family with borderline interactions), 73

Memento (film), 46

men
 father absence, 99–101, 150
 the working father, 91–92

mental health
 increases in mental illness diagnoses, 105
 as a journey, 255–56
 long-term effects of mass shootings, 106–7

mentalization, 218–19

mentalization-based therapy (MBT), 218–20, 222

Meredith and Ben (coping with rapid mood changes), 169–70

Method acting for establishing an identity, 43–44

Michelle and Amin (participants in a destructive relationship), 41
Missildine, Hugh, 98
Monroe, Marilyn, 19–20, 39, 43–44, 74
mood changes
abrupt and extreme, 51, 169–71
brain reactions to negative stimuli, 169
emotional hemophilia, 11–13
mood stabilizers, 233
mothers. *See* women
multiple personality disorder, 32
Murthy, Vivek, 107
music therapy, 202

narcissism, 104
The Narcissism Epidemic (Twenge and Campbell), 104
narcissistic personality disorder, 33
nature *vs.* nurture debate, 62–63, 75–76, 228–29
neglect, 97–98, 152
Neil (accepting bad feelings), 123–25
neuroendocrinology, 229
neuroleptics (antipsychotics), 233–34
neurotransmitters, 64, 228–29, 235
Nicole (expressive therapy program), 202–3
non-suicidal self-injury (NSSI), 168–69
Nora (using a paradox approach), 165
no-win dilemmas, 164, 170–71

object constancy
childhood conflicts, 71–72
phase of child development, 70–71
in relationships, 40–41, 130–33, 276–77

transitional objects, 70–71, 162
object relations theory, 67–68
omega-3 fatty acid preparations, 234–35
opiate antagonists, 234
oxytocin, 64, 229

pain
the brain's perception of, 51, 65
the pain paradox, 31
self-mutilation, 48, 50–51
paranoid delusions, 54, 141, 173–74
parenting
common BPD roles and family issues, 66, 150–51
consistent mothering, 151
effects of evolving family structures on children, 95–96
extreme behavior, 66
father absence, 99–101, 150
permissive child-rearing practices, 101–2
re-parenting, 216–17
separation-individuation period of child development, 68–71, 72
shifting gender roles, 91–93
stepparenting, 155
Pat and Jake (object constancy), 130–33
perfectionism, 44–45
personality
making changes to one's, 249–50
as a series of intersecting trait lines, 248–50, 261–62
personality disorders
antisocial personality disorder, 33–34
and Borderline Personality Disorder (BPD), 33–34

diagnosing, 9, 259–65
Emotionally Unstable Personality
  Disorder, 263
histrionic personality disorder, 34
narcissistic personality disorder, 33
symptoms of, 27
traits, 26–27
treatment of, 27
pharmacotherapy
  antidepressants, 232–33
  anxiolytics, 234
  customization of drugs to
    individual patients, 230–31
  generic drugs, 236–37
  homeopathic and herbal remedies,
    234–35
  ketamine, 235
  mood stabilizers, 233
  neuroleptics (antipsychotics), 233–34
  off-label use, 236
  opiate antagonists, 234
  for personality disorders, 27, 227
  by symptom cluster, 235
physical activity, 172
politics
  extreme polarization, 105–6
  tribal politics, 106
post-traumatic stress disorder (PTSD),
  32–33
The Power and the Glory (Greene), 252
practicing phase, 68
pregnancy
  making adjustments during, 92–93
  self-harming fantasies during, 168
premature death, 37
psychoanalysis, 268–69
psychodrama, 202
psychodynamic treatments
  focus on the past and the
    present, 217

good psychiatric management
  (GPM), 220–21, 222, 224
mentalization-based therapy
  (MBT), 218–20, 222
transference-focused psychotherapy
  (TFP), 217–18, 222, 223–24
psycho-educational group (PEG)
  programs, 203
psychosis
  in schizophrenia, 29
  transient psychosis in stressful
    situations, 54–55, 173–74
psychotherapy
  commonalities among different
    strategies, 211–12
  exploratory therapy, 194
  for personality disorders, 27
  as the primary treatment for BPD,
    181, 210–12
  process of, 184–85
  reimbursement rates of, 225
  standardization of, 211
  supportive therapy, 194–95

rage. *See* anger
Raniere, Keith, 45
rapprochement phase of child
  development, 68–70, 72, 83–84
Ray (frustrations of others with BPD),
  145–46
reactionary behavior, 72
recreation and relaxation, 159–60
Reich, Wilhelm, 268–69
relationships, romantic
  with a BPD patient, 13, 39–42,
    162–63
  between BPD patients in group
    therapy, 197
  engulfment, 39

relationships, romantic (*cont.*)
  maintaining, 15–16, 255–56
  making adjustments to maintain a
    balanced relationship, 256–57
  manipulation, 40
  masochism, 90
  shingling, 90–91
research and treatment advances,
    20–21, 210–12, 223–26, 264–65
Research Domain Criteria (RDoC),
    264–65
Rich (emptiness), 129–30
Rosten, Norman, 39

Sam (difficulties seeking a romantic
    partner), 41–42
Sanchez, Jill, 54–55
Sass, Louis, 82
schema-focused therapy (SFT),
    216–17, 222, 224
schizophrenia, 29, 269, 270
school shootings, 104–5, 106–7
self-assessment, 247–50
self-destructive behavior, 46–47,
    64–65, 122, 165
self-esteem, 43
self-harm
  alternative activities, 169
  reasons for, 49–50, 64–65
  self-mutilation, 48, 50–51, 64–65,
    168–69
  as self-punishment, 36, 47–49
  taking seriously, 155
separation anxiety, 72
separation-individuation period of
    development
  differentiation phase, 68
  object constancy phase, 70–71
  practicing phase, 68

rapprochement phase, 68–70, 72,
    83–84
separations from parents during
    childhood, 151
SET-UP system of communication
  about, 112–14, 143–44
  as the basis for effective
    psychotherapy, 211
  case studies, 119–43
  goals of, 113–14
  to maintain a BPD relationship,
    160–61, 164
  Support, Empathy, Truth aspects of,
    114–18, 149
  Understanding and Perseverance
    aspects of, 118–19, 143–44
sexuality
  dating and hookup websites, 110
  promiscuity, 35–36
  relaxed sociosexual mores, 89–91
  sexual orientation, 94
  transsexualism, 94
social cues, 40
social factors
  changing family structures and
    interactions, 80–81
  cultural changes, 81–82
  polarization, 85–86
  social changes, 81, 84
  social rapprochement, 83–84
social interactions and social
    isolation, 107, 165, 172
social media
  cyberbullying, 108–9
  the "faux family," 103–4
  and physical interactions, 81–82
  warning signs of mass shootings
    and hate crimes, 105–6
socioeconomic factors, 18
solitude, 38–39

somatization disorder, 31–32
Sometimes I Act Crazy (Kreisman
    and Straus), 64
splitting
    as a defense mechanism, 14–15, 71,
      72, 217–18, 274–75
    perception of hospital staff
      members, 204
    when discussing politics, 106
    Wilhelm Reich's research on, 268–69
split treatment, 237–38
standardization of psychotherapy, 211
state disorders, 26
Stephanie (emotional abuse), 152–53
Stern, Adolph, 269
stress
    effect on BPD and other anxiety
      disorders, 229
    transient psychosis in stressful
      situations, 54–55
structure in American society, 81,
    83–86
substance abuse, 34, 154
suicide
    and BPD patients, 8, 12, 37, 167–69
    cluster suicides, 45–46
    risks of, 8, 88, 167–68
    suicidal threats, 47–48, 149, 167–68
    and teenagers, 154–55
Support statements (SET-UP system of
    communication), 115, 116
systems training for emotional
    predictability and problem
    solving (STEPPS), 215

technology
    cell phones, 104–5
    cyberbullying, 108–9
    dating and hookup websites, 110

the "faux family," 103–4
and physical interactions, 81–82
and the pursuit of precision, 86
teenagers, 153–55
temperament, 26
Terry (use of predicting to quash
    impulsivity), 167
testing, psychological, 269–70, 274
therapists
    author's experiences, 176–80
    choosing a therapist, 189–91
    countertransference, 187–88, 189
    difficulties treating BPD patients,
      180–81
    finding the right therapist, 193, 212
    relationship between patient and,
      182, 188–89, 192–93
therapy
    art therapy, 202–3
    bibliotherapy, 202
    comparing cognitive behavioral
      approaches with psychodynamic
      treatments, 221–22
    conversion therapy, 183
    duration of, 183–84
    excessive communication between
      sessions, 181
    expressive therapies, 201–3
    family therapy, 198–201
    getting a second opinion, 191–92
    goals of, 182–83, 190
    group therapy, 195–97
    initial assessment period and
      treatment plan, 190–91
    music therapy, 202
    psychodrama, 202
Tillich, Paul, 38
time
    devaluation of the past, 87
    fear of the future, 87–88

time (*cont.*)
  life since 2010, 104–10
  stalling before replying, 170–71
therapy focused on current thinking
    processes vs. looking at the past,
    212–21
Tinder, 110
Tolstoy, Leo, 44, 52
Tough Love groups, 122
trait disorders, 26–27
transference, 185–87
transference-focused psychotherapy
    (TFP), 217–18, 222, 223–24, 260
transitional objects, 70–71,
    162, 276
trauma
  of child abuse, 152–53
  link between BPD and, 74–75
treatment
  approaches to avoid, 181–82
  of BPD and an additional mental
    illness, 147
  customization of drugs to
    individual patients, 230–31
  of the entire family, 73–74
  evaluating the various options,
    223–25
  off-label use of pharmaceuticals, 236
  physical (non-pharmaceutical)
    treatments, 237
  recommendations, 181
  rewards of, 208–9
  split treatment, 237–38
  by symptom cluster, 235
tribal politics, 106
trust, 254–55
Truth statements (SET-UP system
    of communication), 115–16,
    117–18
Twenge, Jean M., 104

2010 and beyond
  Covid-19 pandemic, 68, 92, 107–8
  intense societal changes, 104–5
  mass shootings, 106–7
  politics, 105–6
  technology and social media, 108–10
twin studies of BPD, 228

the unconscious mind, 267–68
Updike, John, 39

van Gogh, Vincent, 53
victimization, 125–26, 128
violence and avoiding physical
    conflict, 133, 173
Vonnegut, Kurt, 44, 103

Who's Afraid of Virginia Woolf?
    (Albee), 202
Wolfe, Tom, 104
women
  with BPD, 17
  consistent mothering, 151
  evolution of traditional roles, 91–93
  mothers of BPD patients, 150
  the working mother, 91–92
the workplace
  dealing with BPD coworkers or
    managers, 159
  employee assistance programs
    (EAPs), 158
  hiring a BPD employee, 158–59
  managing BPD in, 16

Young, Jeffrey, 216
young adulthood, 155

ABOUT THE AUTHORS

Jerold J. Kreisman, MD, is a distinguished clinical psychiatrist, researcher, and educator who has lectured widely in this country and abroad. In addition to articles, book chapters, and a blog ("I Hate You, Don't Leave Me") for *Psychology Today*, he has authored *Sometimes I Act Crazy: Living with Borderline Personality Disorder*, with Hal Straus, and *Talking to a Loved One with Borderline Personality Disorder*. Dr. Kreisman is a Distinguished Life Fellow of the American Psychiatric Association.

Hal Straus is the author or coauthor of seven books on psychology, health, and sports topics. He has published numerous articles in national magazines, including *American Health, Men's Health, Ladies' Home Journal,* and *Redbook*. He recently retired from his position as director of publications at the American Academy of Ophthalmology.